# Thistle Soup

# PETER KERR

SUMMERSDALE

Summersdale Publishers Ltd
46 West Street
Chichester
West Sussex
PO19 1RP
UK

www.summersdale.com

Printed and bound in Great Britain.

ISBN 1 84024 265 5

Book illustrated by Peter Kerr.
Illustrations copyright Peter Kerr © 2002

Front cover illustration by Melanie Barnes.

A true Scot, Peter Kerr was born in Lossiemouth, Morayshire, and since his early childhood has spent most of his life in East Lothian. He is author of the bestselling Mallorca travelogues *Snowball Oranges* and WHSmith Travel Book Award shortlisted *Mañana, Mañana*. *Thistle Soup* is his third book.

# CONTENTS

To catch dame Fortune's golden smile,
Assiduous wait upon her;
And gather gear by every wile
That's justified by honour;
Not for to hide it in a hedge,
Nor for a train-attendant;
But for the glorious privilege
Of being independent.

From 'Epistle To A Young Friend' – May 1786
Robert Burns, 1759–96

## CHAPTER ONE

## LEANING AGAINST THE WIND

'No enough purchase o' the feet, that's the problem,' said Jimmy Walker, the County Council roadman responsible for maintaining the stretch of road running past the entrance to my grandparents' farm near the market town of Haddington, about seventeen miles east of Scotland's capital city. A summer shower had moistened the grass growing on the banked verge – long weedy grass, which Jimmy was busy cutting down with his scythe. And, despite Jimmy's habitual assertion that his *tackety buits* gave him a *gran' grip o' the grun'*, the slippery underfoot conditions on this occasion had clearly showed scant respect for the ranks of hobnails glinting from the upturned soles of his boots while he floundered on his back in the bottom of the ditch.

'Thoo's no bad skaithed, is thoo, Cheemy?' inquired my grandfather, reaching down on one knee to offer the old roadman a hand which, to me, looked like a number nine shovel with fingers.

Whether or not Jimmy had fully understood my

grandfather's expression of concern, delivered in the lilting dialect of his native Orkney, I don't know, but he chuckled good-naturedly to himself as he clambered out of the ditch.

'Christ, ma erse is fair soakit!' he observed in the local East Lothian vernacular, then plucked the drenched dungaree cloth from the cleft of his backside. 'Need tae get the buits intae the cobbler's fur a new set o' tackets.'

My grandfather was laughing now too. 'Ya-a-as, she's a bugger when thoo hasno' enough purchase o' the feet, right enough, boy.' He produced a paper five-pack of Woodbine cigarettes from his waistcoat pocket, passing one of the infamous little 'coffin nails' to Jimmy, then cupping a thumbnail-ignited match between his huge hands while they both lit up.

'Aye, nothin' like kindlin' up a fag tae put a heat in ye when the water's runnin' oot the erse o' yer breeks,' Jimmy opined stoically. 'Ken what Ah mean, Tam?' Rheumy-eyed, he did his best to stifle a splutter as the stinging tobacco reek assaulted his lungs. 'Rare wee fags, the Woodbines, eh?'

Marvelling at the mysterious pleasure that both men were deriving from drawing deeply on their cigarettes, then cleverly exhaling the thick white smoke through flaring nostrils, I silently wished that I could join in the ritual. But, being not quite four years old, I'd have to wait a while yet. About a couple of months, as I remember.

My grandfather patted Jimmy's back. 'We'll leave thee tae get on with the work then, Cheemy. I'm away tae check the kye up the hill field.' Then he turned to me. 'Come now, peedie boy – we'll get Fanny tae give us a lift tae see the cattle beasts.'

'Peedie' is the Orkney word for 'small', so it followed that my grandfather should call me 'peedie boy'. He'd always done so, and I was used to it. The youngest of a line of three living Peters, I was also used to being called – originally to avoid confusion when we were all together – Wee Pete, Pedro, Young Pate (Pate is Scots for Pete), Paitrick, Pat and even Paderooski (pronounced as spelt). In fact, it was reaching the stage when I would automatically answer to just about any name beginning with the letter 'P'.

Fanny was a young Clydesdale mare, a gentle giant of an animal with the richest of bay coats, a narrow white blaze bisecting her face, and a kindly expression of eye that gave the clue to her disposition. She was my grandfather's pride and joy. He had brought her down from Orkney along with the nucleus of his herd of Ayrshire milking cows just a few years earlier. My father remembers seeing him standing on the pier at Edinburgh's port, long overcoat blowing in the wind, battered trilby pulled firmly down to his ears, while he supervised the unloading of a small tramp steamer that had been chartered to transport all his worldly possessions south from his native islands across well over two hundred miles of sea. Implements and crates were all marked in stencilled letters: *CARGO OF THOMAS MUIR – STROMNESS TO LEITH.*

He would only have been in his mid-fifties, I suppose, but seeming ancient in my three-year-old's eyes. Though not a particularly big man, he was as strong as an ox, like most who had spent all of their lives since boyhood working with heavy horses. His favourite footwear, no matter what the weather, was a pair of old wellington boots, the tops turned down, and bought deliberately two sizes too big to accommodate a generous lining of straw.

'Keeps the feet nice and dry on sweatin' hot days, and nice and cosy when it's cowld,' was his way of looking at it.

And his flat-cap 'bunnet' was another feature of his everyday apparel. I even recall him wearing it in bed when he was down with the flu one time, and I don't remember ever seeing him without it on his head until many years later when he was hospitalised after being kicked in the face by one of his beloved horses. And he did have a face to match his personality; a strong-featured face, with a glint of humour in his eyes, but with a set to his jaw that told you he wouldn't suffer fools gladly. He was a typical Orcadian, in fact; ruggedly durable in a way that reflects the climate of those windswept northerly isles, and with an underlying 'don't meddle with me' look of honesty about him. He carried the pride of his Norse heritage quietly but unreservedly.

So, what had caused him to leave the large farm of Backaskaill on the island of Sanday to move lock, stock and barrel to this little farm, scarcely big enough to be viable, in a part of the country that he had never even visited before? To follow his family is the simple answer to that. His three daughters, my mother included, had had to leave Sanday when they reached the age of ten or eleven to attend the secondary school at Kirkwall on the Mainland island of Orkney, staying in lodgings and only returning home by steamer for school holidays three times a year. It must have been a traumatic wrench for young girls who had been brought up in the security of a farming family in a fine big house and with six hundred acres to roam over – including the wide, deserted expanse of the silver-sanded Backaskaill Bay. They would go to the parish school on horseback or by pony and gig every day, never thinking that such carefree times would ever end. But going away to secondary school was something which island youngsters like them just had to cope with eventually, and it would turn out to be an experience which no doubt helped develop their independence of character for later in life. They would never return to live on Sanday, for each one, on leaving school at the age of seventeen, would move south to Edinburgh or London to continue their respective education.

Then came the turn of the youngest child, Jim, my grandparents' only son and the apple of his mother's eye. What would life have been like on that fairly remote island for two middle-aged folk suddenly deprived of the last of their family? Not the sort of life that appealed to them, apparently. Backaskaill was sold and they moved to a smaller farm known as 'Broonstoon' near the town of Stromness on Mainland Orkney. From Stromness Jim could make the daily fifteen-mile journey back and forth to school in Kirkwall. And so ended the family's generations-old association with the island of Sanday and the end of their tenure of a large farm that had been bought by the sweat and determination of James Muir, my great-grandfather. He, I believe, began adult life as a crofter, scraping a living on a little Sanday croft – or smallholding – called 'Lealand'.

I never knew my great-grandparents, as both had died many years before I was born. But I do have old sepia photographs of them – life-size head-and-shoulder studio portraits showing them stiffly posed in their Victorian Sunday best, their faces hand-tinted by the photographer, as was the fashion in those bygone days. James has a full beard, as was also in vogue back then, but you can see enough of his features to tell that he probably had a kindly nature. Yet he also has that no-nonsense look inherited by his son, although it's my great-grandmother, an elegantly good-looking woman, who has the same steely tenacity as

13

my grandfather's burning in her eyes. It isn't hard to recognise in her facial expression the doggedness that would have been necessary to support and encourage her husband while attempting, against considerable odds, to improve his relatively modest station in life. She would have been the wind beneath his wings, I'm sure.

So, they augmented the subsistence livelihood gleaned from the croft by opening a small general store in a shed by the roadside; a farm shop a century or more before such agricultural diversification became the norm. And while his wife minded the store, my great-grandfather would travel the byways between the farms of Sanday with a horse-drawn van, selling the same produce as in the shop. Everything from milk to string and knitting needles, from potatoes to pots and pans, and even jams, bread and cheeses made by his wife in her 'spare time'. It must have been a hard life for them, particularly when bringing up a family of four young children as well. But they prospered, and by the time my grandfather left school at the age of twelve, his parents were already well established as the proprietors of the square mile of fertile land that constitutes Backaskaill Farm.

Even then, no business opportunity was neglected in order to mollify what we must presume was an extremely supportive bank manager. The sandy grass links that skirt the shoreline of Backaskaill Bay were riddled with rabbit warrens – a handy source of both food for the family and much needed extra income. Fishing, too, became part of a dramatically changed way of life from that which they had known at Lealand. Overlooking the sea as the farm did, it made good sense to harvest that as well. And yet no one in the family could swim, as is often the case with people who live by the shore and take to such treacherous seas in little boats. Another legacy of this family's seafaring Viking roots, perhaps.

Orkney, like its neighbouring archipelago of Shetland to the north, only became part of Scotland in what has been described as 'an unredeemed pawning operation' between the Scottish and Scandinavian crowns six hundred years ago. The Norsemen had ruled these islands for six centuries before that. And the fiercely independent Orcadians and Shetlanders have never been slow to recall this fact publicly whenever they feel they are being treated less than fairly by the British government. James III of Scotland 'lent' 58,000 florins to hard-up King Christian I of Denmark, Norway and Sweden as part of an arrangement which involved Christian's daughter Margaret becoming betrothed to James and the islands being 'mortgaged' to Scotland in lieu of a dowry; and those florins were never repaid. But, as the islanders warn the 'ferry-lowpers' who rule their islands from the south, that's not to say that the money can't or won't be repaid yet – and by the islanders themselves! The temptation to do so when the riches of North Sea oil were discovered in their territorial waters must have been great.

According to my mother, the family flourished at Backaskaill and enjoyed a hard-working but idyllic lifestyle – everyone mucking in (the girls as well) to do what had to be done to run a large farm in one of the most exposed, but tranquil and unspoiled settings anywhere in the British Isles.

'The wind could be a nuisance, though,' she told me. 'But living on a low-lying island so far north on the edge of the Atlantic Ocean, you soon get used to it. In fact, when the westerly gales howl in from Canada in winter, you can actually lean against the wind in Orkney – if you have the knack, that is. Otherwise you could end up landing on your bahookie in Norway!'

On moving to Broonstoon on the Mainland of Orkney, my grandparents found themselves in a very different farming environment from the one they'd enjoyed on Sanday. Broonstoon was a small dairy place, the farmers of which had traditionally provided milk for the population of Stromness. Which is precisely what my grandfather did – driving a horse and cart round the town delivering milk every day. He did all the work with the assistance of my grandmother, an educated woman, an ex-schoolteacher and accomplished musician, who, although a native of the Orkney island of Westray and well used to farm work, would have little expected in her middle years to be rising at five in the morning to hand-milk a herd of dairy cows every day. But she did so without complaint, and was destined to do likewise for many more years to come.

The blow came when their son Jim announced one day that he had no real interest in a farming future, and instead wanted to become an accountant. Naturally, this would involve leaving Orkney, just as his sisters had done before him. So, ultimately he moved to Edinburgh to commence an apprenticeship with an accountancy firm in the city. And my grandparents found themselves alone once more, the last of their offspring having flown the nest – for good, it seemed certain. They asked my mother to look for a farming foothold for them near Edinburgh. It was 1938 and the world was heading for another war – not the best of times, it could be said with some justification, to be upping sticks with a view to starting a new farming venture in a totally unfamiliar part of the country. But that's precisely what they did, my mother having secured the tenancy of the fifty-acre Cuddy Neuk holding for them. Being an astute businessman, it may well have been my grandfather's hope to use the place merely as a stepping stone to a larger farm, once he'd found his feet within the East Lothian agricultural community, that is.

Then the war broke out and the county started to fill up with thousands of armed forces, all of whom would have to be fed; a commercial opportunity that my grandfather was quick to recognise. Farming was classified by the government as a Reserved occupation, freeing the participants from the requirement of being conscripted for military service. Jim was asked by his parents to resign his post with the accountancy firm and come to work with them at Cuddy Neuk. They were going to need all the help they could muster. It was a move that saved young Jim from being called up, it can't be denied, but it was also to prove the end of his budding career as an accountant and the start of a farming life in which his heart never truly belonged. But, to his eternal credit, when the fateful decision had to be made, he put family interests before his own.

'Steady there, Fanny lass,' my grandfather crooned to the young mare as he buckled the bridle onto that massive head of hers. Still murmuring soothing words, he backed her out of her stall and led her towards the stable door, her great shod feet clumping over the cobbles with a hollow metallic clatter. I watched the emergence of this magnificent giant from a safe position behind the horse trough outside in the yard.

It was then that Nellie the Border collie, as much a pet as a working dog (seldom a successful combination of occupations in that most intelligently-feisty of breeds!), decided to indulge her daredevil habit of nipping at the heels of animals big enough to kick her into orbit. Stallion, mare, bull or cow, it made no difference to Nellie – she had to make her presence felt whenever her master was handling these, to her, creatures of a lower order than either human or collie. The 'I'm in charge' trait of her breed was always in the forefront of Nellie's hyperactive mind, ever ready to be triggered into suicidal action at even the most questionable of opportune moments.

Fanny knew Nellie well enough. They had grown up together at Broonstoon in Orkney and had even travelled down to Leith bunked together for company in the hold of the boat. Even now, Nellie spent her sleeping hours curled up in a straw-strewn corner of Fanny's stall. They were chums. But, on this occasion, a slightly skittish streak in Fanny's canny nature sparked a reaction to Nellie tugging at the long, silky feathers of her hind fetlocks. Whinnying in fright, she made a bolt for the stable door, rearing as she entered the yard, my grandfather holding on for dear life to her bridle while simultaneously hurling abuse and flailing welly-clad feet at his 'bliddy eejit' of a dog.

Then the strangest of things happened. He took a rag from his pocket and held it under Fanny's muzzle for but the briefest of seconds. That seemed to steady her. Then he raised his lips to her face and said something. Only one word, I think, but said in such hushed tones behind a cupped hand that I couldn't really hear. As if by magic, Fanny's panic was dispelled and she stood absolutely still while my grandfather threw a sack over her back and lifted me up to sit astride the base of her powerful, curved neck. He stood on the horse trough to climb onto her back behind me, sitting sideways in the favoured way of horsemen of that era. Then, with a gentle clicking of his tongue and a flick of the rope reins, he coaxed the great animal into motion. 'Tschk, tschk! Gid-*up*, lass!'

A narrow dirt lane, known in these parts simply as 'the old road', runs at the foot of a long banking along the lower boundary of Cuddy Neuk, and gives access to all the fields. Bordered by the ubiquitous East Lothian hawthorn hedges, and dotted on either side by wind-bent trees, the old road stretches straight as a furrow for three-quarters of a mile to the entrance of the farthest field on the farm. It's said that it was originally a Roman way, then a coach road, linking up a bit farther west with the road from Edinburgh, and to the east with the ancient route to London which once ran along the spine of the Garleton Hills. Certainly, on this particular summer morning, with only the sound of birdsong competing with the steady thump of Fanny's hooves as we ambled along, it would have been easy to imagine a mail coach drawn by a team of horses lurching its dusty way towards us through the heat haze that shimmered over the surface of the road ahead. I didn't realise it then, of course, but I was sampling a way and pace of country life that would all too soon disappear forever.

'Had on tight, peedie boy,' my grandfather said when we finally made it to the farthest field gate. 'Had on tight tae Fanny's mane now.'

At that, he tugged on the left rein and dug the heels of his wellington boots into Fanny's flanks. '*Hie*, lass! *Hup* there!'

With a snort of compliance and a toss of her proud head, Fanny duly wheeled left and, putting on a spurt of speed, clambered sure-footed up the bank and through the gateway. Despite gripping the coarse hair of her mane with grimly-clenched fists, I think the sudden change in Fanny's gait and the consequent pecking motion of her head would have thrown me from her swaying withers (a fearsomely long way to the ground for a little sprog like me) had my grandfather not anticipated the likelihood and grabbed me firmly by the scruff of the neck.

'Thoo's safe enough, boy,' he laughed on hearing my involuntary squeak of panic. 'I'll look oot for thee – never fret.' He gave Fanny another dig in the ribs. 'Hup there, lass! *Hup* there!'

We entered a field of ripening oats, Fanny climbing the narrow headland between hedge and gold-green crop, making for the hill field that rose in rocky knowes up ahead. Because its craggy contours made cultivation difficult, the long-established turf which covered the hill field had escaped, thus far, the effects of the wartime government's subsidised 'Plough-up Policy', which encouraged farmers to turn over such old grassland in order to increase the nation's food-growing capacity. Its twelve acres provided the only permanent grazing on Cuddy Neuk, its elevated position making the hill field a healthy summer pasture for the farm's younger cattle – bullock stirks that would later be housed for fattening, and Ayrshire heifers which would one day join the milking herd as replacements for the older cows.

A gentle breeze drifted in from the west as we climbed higher, a whisper of warm air sighing through the tall oats, setting them swaying in waves which spread over the field like a meandering tide. The breeze also carried on its breath the first hint of the approaching harvest – a whiff of that soothing smell of dusty, ripe grain and sun-warmed straw that would soon pervade the surrounding countryside. In a week or two, men with scythes would open 'roads' for clattering reaper binders to enter the fields and cut the first cereal crops, early varieties of barley destined for the malting floors of Scotland's world-famous whisky distilleries.

But there was another smell too – a strangely out of place smell of spice, which I noticed fleetingly as my grandfather lifted me down from Fanny's back on reaching the gate to the hill field. It was a smell which I didn't recognise then, but one which lingered in my memory, the way such seemingly insignificant things from childhood do. Only many years later, when more exotic ingredients had started to be stocked in kitchen cupboards, did I realise that the aroma which had drifted from my grandfather's waistcoat pocket was that of cumin. And into that same pocket he had folded the little piece of cloth which he'd earlier held to Fanny's nose to calm her. All I got from him on asking about this in his twilight years was a wry smile and a returned question: 'What's cumin, peedie boy?'

He was a *little* more forthcoming about what he had whispered to Fanny on that same distant occasion, however. The Horseman's Word, he called it. A secret word given to ploughboys during their initiation into an almost masonic brotherhood of men who shared the waking hours of their lives with the workhorses on Scottish farms in those far off days. A magical word which would subdue the most fractious of horses and bring the animal under the horseman's complete control. Why, merely whispering the Word to a horse would make it do anything you wanted. And even before I could ask him what the incantation was, he referred me to the oath that all farm lads had to take on being given the secret during a midnight ritual which involved – in addition to a copious intake of whisky –

shaking hands with the Devil. They had to swear 'neither to dite, write nor recite' the Word to anyone outside the brotherhood, or …

*'May my flesh be torn to pieces with a wild horse, and my heart be cut through with a horseman's knife, and my bones buried in the sands of the seashore where the tide ebbs and flows …'*

Tying Fanny's reins to the gatepost, we tramped up the steep grassy slope to the topmost point in the hill field, the breeze freshening as we went, my grandfather muttering that he wondered where the 'bliddy hell' the kye were. He needn't have worried. The cattle saw us before we saw them, and came thundering towards us in a curiosity-fuelled race, a high-spirited stampede of about twenty bucking and bellowing young animals. I took up a prudent position behind my grandfather. He, in turn, waited until they were almost upon us, then flapped his arms up and down like a bird and barked swear words at them. If the Horseman's Word meant nothing to cattle beasts, Orkney-accented oaths clearly did. The little herd came to a slithering halt just a couple of feet away from us, big innocent eyes looking expectantly at my grandfather as if waiting for a sermon to be delivered. While he counted them and strolled about checking their condition, one brave young bullock, his natural inquisitiveness getting the better of him, ventured forward and tried to sniff my grandfather's counting finger with flaring, snotty nostrils. For his impertinence he was rewarded with a sharp slap on the nose from a shovel-sized hand. He and his gang, having quickly tired of appraising two dull humans, then turned tail and hurtled as one down the hill to speak to Fanny.

Standing as we were on top of a rocky hillock, my grandfather turned me round to face westwards 'just for a peedie minute, to see what weather's likely'. I've stood on that same spot countless times since then – always, when in summer, with a lark singing in the clear air high above – and I've never once failed to be just as entranced as I was on that first occasion. As a small boy, it seemed to me that you could see the whole world from there. The wide East Lothian plain, justifiably known as the Garden of Scotland, stretching under an infinite sky all the way to the soft purple summits of the Lammermuir Hills in the south; to the north, the faint blue outline of Highland peaks, mysterious miles away over a wide sweep of sea; in the west, the rise of the Pentland Hills behind Edinburgh, the city itself seeming no more than a huddle of grey matchboxes from this distance; below and beyond us in every direction, lush farmland undulating away among clumps of woodland, the farmsteads linked by ribbons of road and track that wind between eccentric boundaries – ancient demarcation lines of properties etched more by nature than by the design of man. Field after fertile field, small by today's standards and still sheltered by hedgerows or drystone walls, most now long dispensed with in the name of efficiency, gave the landscape the timeless look of a randomly patchworked quilt back then.

'Look thee there!' my grandfather said, gesturing westwards. 'A storm comin', see? That's the thing I like aboot this spot, boy. It'll never be Orkney, but thoo can see the weather comin' for all that – just like back on Sanday.'

The wind seemed to rise as he spoke. A huge mass of cloud was billowing up in the western sky, casting shadowy shapes which were already scudding towards us over the land.

'He's goin' to be an ill one, peedie boy!' my grandfather grinned, scarcely able to hide his glee. 'Ya-a-as, just like back on Sanday.' He laughed out loud in a sort of benignly manic way. 'Thoo'll be able to lean against the wind in a minute, sure as there's sharn on a pig-hoose shovel!'

The notion of leaning against the wind had been on my mind since my mother's passing mention of it a while before. Now, the prospect of actually being able to practise the art at any moment was already filling me with a mix of excitement and alarm. We were standing at the edge of a rocky bluff, the land falling away steeply before us, then levelling into a grassy glen where a spring rose into a watering hole for the cattle. It was no more than a twenty-foot drop to that little mud-fringed pool, but the prospect of landing head first in it if the wind-leaning trick failed wasn't one that I relished just then. Knees quaking as the ever more blustery wind began to buffet us, I took a judicious step back from the edge.

The sky turned leaden above us, obliterating the warm rays of the sun and changing a peaceful, pastoral scene into a murky and threatening world in which, being hardly four years old, I suddenly didn't want to be. Squally rain began to lash at us, stinging my face like little liquid bullets as it swept in horizontally from the west. I could hear the wind now. Its sound was all around me – not the gentle whisper that had rustled through the oat field just a few minutes earlier, but an angry howl. To my imaginative and frightened young ears, it was like the roar of a dragon.

Struggling to keep my feet, I looked to my grandfather, still by my side, one hand in his pocket, the other holding down his flat-cap bunnet. To my utter confusion, he was thoroughly enjoying himself, totally in his element, laughing loudly into the teeth of the wind as if daring it to do its worst. He was back on Sanday, revelling in the wild weather of his island home, scorning the wrath of the storm gods like a hero from some ancient Nordic fable. I grabbed hold of his trouser leg for support.

And then I noticed it. The attitude of his body had changed. The change was almost imperceptible, but it *had* changed, nonetheless. Feet apart, heels firmly braced against a low step of rock, his whole body was inclined slightly forward, defying gravity. He was leaning against the wind. Truly leaning against the wind! I was transfixed.

He glanced down at me, his eyes sparkling with the thrill of the experience, his face creased into an almost child-like grin of delight. The fairground grin of a kid at the start of a big dipper ride.

'What fun, peedie boy!' he yelled at me above the howl of the wind. 'Ya-a-as, what bliddy fun, eh?'

Suddenly gripped by the foolhardiness of innocence, I allowed my fear to desert me. Anything an old man like that could do, I could surely do as well. I began to release my hold on his trouser leg – finger by cautious finger. Then, staggering a little to keep my balance, I adopted the required position of the feet, thrust my hands into my trouser pockets, took a deep breath, and crossed the Rubicon. There wasn't even time to experience a modicum of the desired feeling of gravity-defiance, because a split second later I was flat on my face in a large cow pat, the green dung diluted into a porridge-like consistency by the pelting rain.

Once more I felt the clutch of strong fingers at the scruff of my neck. Once more I felt the embarrassment of inadequacy in the company of this revered grandparent – a man who could light matches with his thumbnail, could blow smoke out of his nose, could calm a startled horse with a word, could command respect from cattle by swearing at them, and, most mysterious of all, could really lean against the wind.

'Thoo'll have to practise hard afore thoo can do yon trick, peedie boy,' he laughed, hauling me unceremoniously to my feet. 'Or maybe thoo just needs to be born in Orkney.'

I looked up at him sheepishly, then looked down at my muck-covered clothes.

'Weel, weel, now, never fret,' he said, patting my head, then offering me a huge finger to take hold of. 'We'll get thee hame tae the hoose and scrape thee intae the midden.'

We laughed about my misadventure all the way home along the old road on Fanny's back. The storm had passed and the sun was shining brightly again, Grandfather's damp clothes smelling vaguely of cumin and Woodbines, mine reeking unmistakably of cow shit. It's funny how such silly wee occasions as that stick in your mind. Half a lifetime later, I would stand alone on that same knowe at the top of the hill field, looking out over that same precious view, and reliving those cherished childhood moments. The wind would be blowing on that day too, though my mind would be filled with thoughts less easy than returning to the Cuddy Neuk steading on horseback, my grandfather's comforting presence behind me, the sound of his laughter in my ears.

## CHAPTER TWO

## GAS MASKS, TWO ROMEOS AND A GHOST

Every day, the roar of Hurricanes and the distinctive Merlin drone of Spitfires and Mosquitos filled the skies. And as dusk fell, the throbbing engines of Bleinheims and Beaufighters flying out towards the North Sea hummed a sombre but reassuring lullaby to bedtime children. The sound of those Allied aircraft was something that local families had become accustomed to – an all-too-familiar sound which told them that, for the moment at least, all was well.

And then the sirens would wail their chill warning. To the staccato thud of ack-ack guns, searchlight beams would pierce and criss-cross the night sky, while little groups of villagers scurried for shelter through the blacked-out streets, and mothers lifted sleeping babes from their cots to hold them close and pray that the foreboding thrum of approaching air-raiders would pass overhead with bombs unreleased.

This was wartime, the early 1940s, and the hitherto sleepy agricultural county of East Lothian had become host to many thousands of service men and women – not just British, but Canadians, Poles, Australians and New Zealanders, some Americans too – air forces mainly, though with a considerable presence of ground troops as well. The topography of the county, its proximity to the sea and strategically important targets higher up the Firth of Forth had made it an ideal location for the establishment of large military airfields. At the outset of war, the wide plain that spreads inland from the coast to the gentle slopes of the Garleton Hills provided the crucial geographic conditions for the siting of those long runways which might be needed to accommodate even the heaviest of bombers. And the rich surrounding farmland would be the breadbasket from which to feed the massive influx of service personnel required to man and defend those vital bases.

I suppose my first memories of those days date from when I was less than three years old – memories punctuated by the sights and sounds and the daily routine of a countryside at war. The aeroplanes, people in uniform, the claustrophobic confusion of getting used to putting on a Mickey Mouse gas mask 'for my own good'. Dried eggs, cans of 'National' powdered milk, being made to swallow spoonfuls of horrible cod-liver oil – also 'for my own good'. Buses fuelled by gas contained in 'bubbles' bulging from their roofs or hauled behind on little trailers affectionately called 'chestnut roasters'. Cars' headlamps masked by shades, louvered downwards to deflect their telltale light from any night-visiting Heinkels or Junkers that happened to be passing overhead on their way for another attempt at blitzing the Forth Bridge, perhaps.

And few childhood cravings for sweets. Not because we didn't like them, but simply because the stringency of food rationing dictated that children of that era didn't miss what they'd never, or hardly ever, had. Even commonplace imported fruits that are taken for granted today were nothing but strange names to us 'utility babies' – titles of popular songs like 'Yes! We Have No Bananas' merely stating an inescapable fact of life for most folk in wartime Britain.

We – that's my parents, my sister Minnie and I – lived in the little coastal town of Gullane at the time. Known to golfers throughout the world for its wonderful links courses, the most famous of which is Muirfield, Gullane is a haven of quiet affluence in a beautiful-but-workaday agricultural landscape. My father, a native of the county, was serving in the RAF and had managed to wangle a posting to a hush-hush radar station near the neighbouring village of Dirleton, on the pretext that he was needed to help out on my maternal grandparents' farm during any spare time he might have between hush-hush radarring duties. A cushy number, by all accounts, but a credit to his wangling-in-wartime prowess, nonetheless. His mastery of flannel (bullshit baffles brains in the armed forces, remember) had first helped transport him from a soulless training camp for rookie airmen at Padgate, two hundred miles away near the English city of Manchester. A posting back north to 'nearer home' would be just the ticket, as his Commanding Officer had smiled when signing the travel warrant.

Either the CO had a grasp of geography ill-befitting a flying ace of his rank, or he had a distinctly perverted sense of humour. On the other hand, maybe he simply had a bullshit-resistant brain. Whatever, my father soon found himself on guard duty with a pike for a weapon (rifles were in notably short supply in Britain during the early months of war!) on a windswept airfield near the little fishing town of Lossiemouth on the Moray Firth coast. Undoubtedly north, Scotland certainly, but just about as far from 'home' as Manchester. Not, I hasten to add, that my father disliked Lossiemouth. Far from it. In fact, he enjoyed aspects of it sufficiently for me to have been conceived and born there. But it still wasn't 'home'.

That was when his 'needed on the family farm' ploy was first employed, and, bullshit shields lowered, his then Commanding Officer fell for it. This selfless desire to do his bit for the war effort on two fronts was to be encouraged, the CO judged. My father would be given a posting to a base in East Lothian at the first opportunity. Somewhere handy for the farm.

A wizard wheeze, in RAF parlance, for a townie ex-civil servant whose hay and hoe credentials were sketchy, to say the least. But he was to be heading 'home' at last. My grandfather arranged the rental of a little house in Gullane for us, and my mother, Minnie and I were dispatched south to await my father's imminent transfer from Lossiemouth.

'Shite!' was the first word he uttered when my mother opened the door to him a couple of months later.

'Charmed, I'm sure,' she replied. 'Lovely to see *you* again too.'

'Bloody CO!' he grumped, dumping his kitbag in the hall.

'He fixed you up with a posting to East Lothian just as you asked, didn't he? So why gripe? Enjoying yourself too much with all those flirty WAAFs in Lossiemouth since we left, no doubt. Bit of a comedown having to behave like a married man again, is it?'

'Shite!'

My sister and I listened from the sanctuary of the kitchen

while our parents' touching reunion rite built up steam. We'd heard similar 'conversations' between them often enough before, so we weren't unduly worried. They adored each other. All mummies and daddies did. We knew that. Ours just had a funny way of showing it, that was all.

'And don't use that foul language in front of the children. You're not in the sergeants' mess now, you know – surrounded by your man-eating packs of Air Force floozies. Bunch of loose-knickered tarts, the lot of them!'

'Shite!'

These 'conversations' did have a way of being a bit one-sided, I'd already noticed. Still, I was on the receiving end of a master class on the pronunciation of the 'shite' word – an essential upwards gradient on the learning curve for a two-year-old. Now there was 'loose-knickered' to add to my infantile vocabulary. Fascinating. And there was that other word too ...

'What's floozies?' I whispered to my sister.

'Sh-h-h-h-h!' she hissed, frowning. 'You'll find out when you're big!'

That's rich, I thought, coming from someone not much more than a year older than me. Still, a year's a lot when you only have two to your name, so I duly clammed up and tuned in once more to the ongoing parental 'conversation' out in the hall.

'And you stink of drink! Just like you, isn't it? You haven't seen your wife and children for two whole months and you have to go boozing before you come home! Typical!'

'I only had one pint at –'

'One pint, my foot! Your breath smells like – like –'

'A brewery horse's fart?'

Before my mother could muster a suitable retort, my father got the last word in – for once ...

'I'm away to the pub!'

The really attractive thing about the location of the little house in Gullane, as far as my father was concerned at any rate, wasn't just that it was only a few miles from my grandparents' farm, but that it was directly across the street from Bisset's Hotel, and the entrance to the bar at that! Bisset's public bar – now, as then, a favourite watering hole for much of the male population of the village. Not so much, it has to be said, for the distinctly well-heeled males who inhabit the grand houses on Gullane Hill, *some* of whom, in the affected fashion of Edinburgh's Morningside-dwellers, pronounce Gullane as Gillen, but rather for the down-to-earth local 'worthies', who speak without 'a bool in the mooth' and pronounce Gullane the way they maintain it *should* be pronounced.

'Can they no read?' I've often heard it asked. 'How the hell can it be Gillen when it's spelt *Gull*in? It's like callin' somebody a fickin' kint!'

That's the sort of no-nonsense, take-me-as-you-find-me male clientele that Bisset's bar attracts today – and was patronised by back then as well.

'Male chauvinist pig!' my mother muttered to the front door which my father had just slammed shut behind him.

'What's a shove nest?' I whispered to Minnie.

She looked at me in that condescending way that know-it-all, four-year-old big sisters do, then scoffed, 'A breed of pig, silly.'

So much to learn, I pondered, sighing. 'How long will I be two and a half?' I asked my mother as she entered the kitchen, a note of desperation in my voice.

'Not much longer now, pet,' she smiled, patting my head in that long-suffering way that harrassed mums of tirelessly inquisitive toddlers somehow manage to do. 'Just have patience, hmm?'

'And, Mummy, he doesn't even know what flooses and shove nests is,' Minnie blurted out, patting me on the head too, while shaking *her* head in that spot-the-loony way that big sisters reserve for their younger siblings.

Mother giggled, (why, I didn't know), winked at my sister and bent down to tidy the ribbon-bow in her hair. 'Aha,' she smiled, 'but we can't expect a wee boy like him to be as clever as a big girl like *you*, can we?'

'No,' my sister said – triumphantly.

'Shite!' I said to myself – fluently.

'Come and have your tea,' our mother said – maternally.

Our father, on coming home from the pub a little later, looked a lot more relaxed than he had previously sounded.

'Steamboats,' my sister whispered to me, nodding sagely towards Dad, who smiled a contented smile and came over to the table to give us both a big, beer-scented cuddle. I remember wondering why grown-up men liked drinking stuff which, to my innocent olfactories, smelled worryingly like cow pee. Something else to learn.

'Where's the boat, Daddy?' I asked, prompting a loud 'tut' and a look of incredulity from my sister.

'Came by train, Paderooski,' my father replied. 'And bus. Mind you, I'd've been about as quick coming by sea, I can tell you.'

Totally confused now, I sunk resignedly into my two-and-a-half year-old's quagmire of unworldly-wise ignorance and concentrated on trying to cut up my scrambled eggs on toast as efficiently as my sister. But it was good to have our father back home, no matter how he had travelled. That much I did know. And I could see that my mother felt the same way, a knowing little smile lighting her face as she presented him with his plate of scrambled eggs.

'Feeling a bit less grumpy now?'

'Aye, well, sorry about that. But honest, you've no idea how much I needed that drink over at Bisset's just now.' He fanned a yawn with his hand. 'God, what a night and day it's been.'

He went on to tell how the nocturnal train journey from Inverness to Edinburgh, a notoriously slow, stop-at-every-telegraph-pole ordeal at the best of times back then, had taken over twelve hours instead of the usual four or so. A goods train derailment somewhere in the middle of a bleak Highland nowhere the apparent cause. And his train had been packed to bursting with military personnel of all varieties, either going on leave, returning from leave or, mainly, en route to new postings. Typically, all the seats had been taken by the time he'd run from the ever-late Lossie bus and clambered aboard at Inverness station. So, he'd been obliged to spend the entire sleepless trip on a draughty corridor floor, crammed uncomfortably together in blackout darkness with countless other shivering, disgruntled souls. Human sardines in uniform, cursing the war, the Army, the Air Force, the Navy and, most of all just then, the bloody useless railway system. On top of that, they'd all run out of fags hours before the nightmare journey's end. Pure, pain-in-the-butt purgatory – literally!

To crown it all, the local train that would have taken him from Edinburgh to his new posting at Drem Airfield, just a couple of miles from Gullane, was cancelled. No reason was given to those hapless passengers waiting on the windy platform at Waverley Station, of course, and no apology offered by the disinterested female voice honking the announcement over the Tannoy. There was a war on, after all, and you had to accept such little inconveniences.

Tired, grubby, cold, skint, hungry and generally pissed right off, Dad headed straight for the London and North-Eastern Railways bar and a much-deserved pint of beer. Refreshed (modestly, as befitted his station), he'd then embarked upon the final twenty miles of his journey to Drem, by bus – or rather by three buses, changing at Musselburgh and Haddington being the order of the day. Three tortoise-paced, slat-seated, arse-grooving, gas-propelled hours later he was knocking on his new Commanding Officer's door, his foundering spirits buoyed up by the knowledge that, at *last*, he had managed to pull off that elusive posting back 'home'. A smug little smile played mischievously beneath his neatly trimmed, Douglas Fairbanks Jr moustache while he stood to attention and saluted his new leader, a well-fed man sitting at his desk engrossed in a pile of WWII paper.

'Dismissed, Kerr!' the much-braided one grunted, a cynical smirk elevating one side of the pukka, officer-issue growth on *his* top lip, making him look, my father had mused, like a bull walrus with wind. 'You'll find this to be self-explanatory,' the walrus added, casting my father but the briefest of glances as he handed him one particular piece of WWII paperwork.

Dad, in turn, handed it to my mother over his scrambled eggs. 'And that,' he said, jabbing an irritated finger at the offending document, 'is why, after rounding off that hellish trip by hoofing it all the way from the 'drome to here – kitbag and all – I was feeling just a *wee* bit peeved.' He watched Mother scanning the typewritten sheet. 'See what I mean?'

'They've posted you *again*? *Already*?'

'That's right. Cock-up, the Drem boss-wallah said. Not

required here, old boy …' He leaned over and pointed to one word on the paper, '… but there.'

'*Turn*house!'

My mother's startled expression had me instantly disturbed.

'What's a turn, Daddy?' I urged.

'In this instance, it's something that should be spelt S-H-I-T,' my father muttered distractedly, no doubt contemplating with dismay the long daily journey that now faced him in order to reach his new posting.

Puzzled, I looked at my sister for enlightenment, eliciting a haughty toss of the head, which I was too naive to twig was only a cover-up for her equal puzzlement.

'You wouldn't understand, even if I told you,' she pooh-poohed. 'And look! You've got scrambled eggs all over your trousers!' Grabbing this timely opportunity to divert attention from the alien world of spelling, she proceeded to shovel the bits of egg from my lap with a large spoon – and none too gently at that.

'Careful you don't hurt him,' said my mother, looking up momentarily from the piece of paper.

Too late.

For the very first time, I experienced that unique boy-soprano-making pain in the privates that would become an all-too-familiar sensation many years later when playing rugby at school. Grip and leverage are the basic requirements for that vital push forward in a rugby scrum. And if you played in the front row, as I usually did, you soon learned that your so-called scrum chums behind you aren't too fussy about what they grab in order to achieve that essential purchase of the feet – as Jimmy Walker would have put it.

But, as a two-and-a-half year-old, I was still unaccustomed to such sporting sophistications. All I knew was that the ache in the spoon-walloped area took a while to go away, adding discomfort to confusion.

'What's them for?' I asked my mother while she helped me into the bath at bedtime.

'What are what for, pet?'

'Them,' I said, pointing at my still-smarting appendages, then giving them a soothing rub.

'Oh, you'll find out soon enough.' My mother smiled in that patient way of hers, patted my head again, then poured a bowlful of lukewarm water over it. 'And leave them alone. It's not good for you.'

None the wiser, I mulled over the mystery for a few moments, then asked the question that my mother must have known would crop up sooner or later – why didn't my sister have dangly bits like me?

'Because she doesn't need them.'

'Why?'

'Just because. Now, close your eyes and I'll wash your hair with these nice soapy bubbles. Hmm? There's a good boy.'

I fell asleep that night trying to cope with the frustrating reality that there were far more questions than answers in life. And I suspected that being a mere two-and-a-half year-old really wasn't helping matters in my particular case.

So much to learn indeed, and so little time. If my mother was to be believed (and who else would I believe?), I'd soon be four, like my sister. But, unlike my sister, I still didn't really know what a shove nest was, far less the necessity of being lumbered with a set of apparently useless groin-danglers. I longed to make it to the age of five when, surely, knowledge of all such subtleties of life would be mine.

We didn't see much of our father for a while after that evening. He left the house hours before we kids woke in the morning – standing with his gas mask bag over his shoulder in the dark road waiting for the first of a series of gas-buses that would transport him the twenty-five tedious miles to Turnhouse Airfield on the far side of Edinburgh. At the other end of the day, we'd be tucked up in bed and sound asleep long before he finally made his blacked-out way home. But at least he *was* 'home'. Not exactly in the cushy way he'd envisaged, unfortunately, but it could have been worse. He could have been strapped into a Lancaster bomber flying across the Channel every night, with flack and machine gun bullets doing their best to create another kind of blackout for him – a permanent one.

And he always had the refuge of Bisset's bar to retreat to for a spot of well-earned relaxation occasionally. Bisset's was more than just a 'local' for my father, as I was to find out years later when I could understand such things. It was a place of inspiration, a fount of local yarns related by pawky old characters over nips of whisky and half pints of beer round a roaring fire on long winter nights. It was a muse for thoughts that were destined to feature in a collection of poems that my father would then write in the style of his beloved Rabbie Burns, and which I still have to this day in a little home-made book, covered in RAF brown paper and typed (perhaps by a WAAF floozie?) on cheap RAF typing paper on a wobbly RAF typewriter. Each verse contains one ordinary young man's observations of lives being lived by ordinary folk in one of perhaps a thousand like villages throughout the land in those traumatic days.

But Bisset's clientele wasn't restricted to couthie old locals back then. The international armed forces personnel in the area hadn't been slow to appreciate the atmosphere of the most popular boozer in the village either. And the Poles were in the forefront – male fashion plates, all (in the opinion of the less sartorially urbane) dandies who wore 'scent', had perplexingly impeccable manners, gold teeth and a way with the ladies that had the native males muttering curses of resentment into their pint glasses …

'Pansified scunners!'

Unable to compete with the exotic allure, style and general Slavonic panache – or *bealin' patter* as it was locally known – of these charming wartime 'guests' in their country, the Gullane chaps had to resort to the only weapon available to them – a wicked sense of humour. Or, for humour, read cruelty … if you like.

'D'ye shag here often, hen?' one young Polish officer (some say they all seemed to be officers!) was heard to enquire gallantly of a fair Gullane maiden when asking her to dance at the village hop one Saturday evening. He'd just completed a crash course in 'ethnic' chat up lines from the regulars in Bisset's public bar. She did as he'd unwittingly enquired, as it happens – *very* often – and the young officer was delightedly surprised when his dazzling foxtrot footwork was swiftly hijacked by the maiden as she swept him out of the back door of the village hall.

'Geeza length o' yer garlic sausage, darlin'!' she panted passionately, pinning him against the gents' lavatory wall.

Food rationing, don't forget, *was* the order of the day.

But how less romantic the outcome could have been.

Take the occasion when, for instance, on the long daily bus journey to Turnhouse Airfield, my father witnessed a much less happy ending to a suspiciously similar scenario. An immaculately uniformed Polish major boarded the bus at the gates of one of the local mansion houses that had been requisitioned to billet the hundreds of his countrymen stationed in the area. After swiftly surveying the interior of the bus for 'talent', and smiling boldly at any that caught his eye, he took the only empty seat, which just happened to be by the door. Despite the officer's game attempts to exchange pleasantries in a language of which he clearly had little knowledge, the old man seated next to him merely scowled and developed a sudden interest in the passing scenery. But the Polish major was made of sterner stuff than to be put off by such parochial reserve.

A little later in the journey, the bus came to the coal-mining town of Tranent, a place with a reputation for having a distinctly pugnacious element within its worthy population of hard-working folk. The proud people of Tranent aren't known as 'The Belters' for nothing, as our hapless young Polish officer was about to find out. His talent-spotting eyes lighted on the solitary figure of an extremely attractive young lady waiting at the bus stop up ahead. He sat to attention, dusted off his lapels and medal ribbons, adjusted his cuffs and got up.

'*Mademoiselle,*' he purred to the stunningly pretty girl, helping her on board.

She blushed coyly as he gently lifted her hand. Then, raising a lip to reveal a tantalising flash of gold, he motioned her towards his vacated seat. A stiff little bow, a sharp click of his booted heels, then the fatal words: 'Plees, Quasimodo, dump yer fat arse doon there.'

The girl's right uppercut was delivered with deadly accuracy and with a force at odds with her petite stature.

'Aye, ring ma bell, son!' she muttered as she stepped over the felled fop to take his seat. 'And dinnae take the hump, eh. Nothin' personal, like.'

He got off at the next stop – perhaps to look for a dentist.

But such spiky little episodes were all predictable parts of life's tapestry in a country area suddenly inundated with strangers. Gradually, as is the way of things, mistrust and animosity waned, then friendships and even romances blossomed. Admittedly, most were just passing relationships that ended with the war, but some, particularly in the case of the Poles, who had no free homeland to return to at the end of hostilities, resulted in marriage and, therefore, total and permanent integration into the local population. And a valuable addition to the community those young Polish men proved to be, too – their enterprising natures and healthy appetite for work resulting in the setting up and development of many businesses which would contribute considerably to the local economy over the years.

After a few months of enduring the daily Gullane-to-Turnhouse trek, my father's wangling touch magically returned, and he managed to sweet-talk his current Commanding Officer into posting him to the new hush-hush radar station at Dirleton, just a short bike ride along the road from where we lived. And that's when my fond attachment to the place that was eventually to become such a major influence on my life really began.

On days off, or during occasional longer periods of leave, my father would set out, always with the family in tow, to lend a much-needed hand to my grandparents at Cuddy

Neuk Farm. We'd take a bus from Gullane as far as was possible, then walk the final mile or so up the brae from Ballencrieff crossroads, where the bus turned off westwards towards Edinburgh. And the view to the south which pans out ahead as you progress up the winding Haddington road, even all these years later and no matter how far away I've lived, is one that I still regard as being synonymous with 'home'.

'What are they doing?' I asked, one placid autumn morning just after we'd left the bus.

'*They're congregating for me and my gal*,' sang my mother, repeating the first line of a popular song of the time.

'What's conga-gatin'?'

I suppose I'd have been about four years old by then, but still with a lot more to learn than I'd hoped I would on reaching that mature age.

'That's what all those birds are doing,' my father explained. 'Swirling about up there like that – flocking together – congregating.'

'Why are they congo-ratin'?'

'That's what birds do, silly,' my sister pointed out with a sniff of superiority. 'Teacher told us about it yesterday. They get together, fly into trees, jump up and down and lay eggs. Then all the baby birds break the eggs and grow feathers.' She shook her head and tutted a reproachful tut. 'And all because of conker-gratin'.'

Our parents chuckled quietly, exchanging grown-up glances that were beyond me. Now that my sister had started school, I reckoned I was falling even further behind in the general knowledge stakes. Oh well, shite, I thought – I'd just watch the birds conker-gratin' or whatever and ask more questions later … when I could be bothered.

These particular birds appeared to be a fairly equal mix of seagulls and rooks, large flocks of them wheeling and gliding effortlessly above a field on Byres Farm, which, as I've noticed many times since then, they always favour for such get-togethers. But I still don't know why they do it. Unlike swallows and other migrating birds, these aren't making communal plans for a big trip to Africa. The gulls would ultimately be heading no further than a couple of miles down to Aberlady Bay. And the crows? Probably only a few hundred yards to the woods on Byres Hill.

I've even looked at old maps to see if there's some clue as to why the birds choose that particular spot for their apparently purposeless meetings. But nothing. Just vague evidence of a fetchingly named Clinky Mill and a nearby hamlet with the curiously un-Scottish name of Caldera. Not a trace of either remains now, and I've found no one who knows what caused their disappearance, or even when it happened. Could the birds be the ghosts of past Clinky Millers and forgotten generations of Caldera-dwellers come back to watch over the site of their former homes? Only the birds will ever know.

No such fanciful thoughts entered my juvenile head on that crisp autumn morning, however. Why the birds behaved like that was just one more 'why?' to add to a growing list, and I think I must have been fairly resigned to the situation by then. I'd have been happy enough just to be wandering up the road to visit my grandparents again. It was all part of a cosy and secure family feeling that, despite the fact that there was a war on, I no doubt took for granted. It was just how things were. Not that we were particularly well off. Far from it. We wanted for none of the essentials of life, though, and we were together – two basic blessings that so many were without in war-torn Europe just then. But what does a kid of those tender years know about the realities of war anyway? For me, it just meant a lot of aeroplanes, sirens going off occasionally and all the other routine things related to a life that I accepted as normal. It all seemed fine to me.

There was still an early-morning nip in the air, and I remember my father taking my hand to keep me on the move.

'Walk a wee bit faster, Paderooski, and you'll be nice and warm. There's a good lad.'

I was too small to see over the whinstone walls and berry-spangled hawthorn hedges that border the fields on either side of the road, but I could hear and smell the evidence of autumn farm work being carried out all around. The shout of a ploughman urging on his pair of Clydesdale horses as they turned the first sod of the season; the damp smell of the new-furrowed earth; the screech of seagulls swooping down from their lofty congregations to devour worms exposed, and even mice unhoused, by the plough. Further on, there was the groan of a little tractor and the sweet whiff of its paraffin exhaust smoke as it toiled away at the same task. For this was a time of transition on the land – that pivotal period, lauded by some and lamented by others, when the tractor was gradually taking over from the stalwart and trusty 'Clydes' on most Scottish farms.

And there was another smell to savour on that bright October morning – a smell drifting on the limpid air from further away than the immediately surrounding fields, I guessed, but a typical and comforting country smell all the same. The smell of cattle dung. A smell less common now than then, when most farms kept a few milk cows or some fattening bullocks, whose 'courts' had to be mucked out and a midden made after the beasts were turned out to pasture in springtime. A healthy tang that blends well with the musty smell of the stubble fields on which the muck's being spread, and with the earthy freshness of the turned soil as it's being ploughed in. A wholesome smell, unlike the gagging stench of pig slurry or the sickly pong of poultry litter. For all that, the smell of cow dung is still a smell that improves with distance – something of which my failed attempt at leaning against the wind had already made me aware.

'It's Big Jim,' our mother said.

Minnie held her nose. 'Pooh! He stinks!'

It wasn't the smell she was referring to, Mother laughingly explained, pointing up ahead. 'No, it's Jim *spreading* the manure. See him now?'

Sure enough, there he was, working with a horse and cart in a field on the face of the hill about half a mile away. Jim, my mother's younger brother, was looked on by my sister and me as more *our* brother than an uncle, so easily did we get on with him. He would only have been in his very early twenties at the time, and a devotee of all the usual things that young men of that age are interested in – the opposite sex, the pub, going dancing, his car, another pub, and so on. And he worked long and hard on the farm into the bargain. Yet he always found time to have fun with us kids as well, even taking us to the pictures in Haddington whenever they were showing a film that he thought we'd like. Movies featuring the likes of Laurel and Hardy, Hopalong Cassidy, Lassie, Tarzan – family flicks like that. Occasionally, if he felt a bit flush, or if my sister and I weren't already sound asleep when the girl came round at the interval, he'd buy us choc-ices. But these were wartime choc-ices – blocks of creamless ice cream that had the texture and taste of saccharin-laced snow, and a meagre coating of dark 'chocolate' which could have passed for edible Bakelite. But we knew no better and relished the luxury. Sometimes, as a special treat, Jim would even take us all the way to Edinburgh, to a cartoon theatre that existed at the west end of Princes Street back then. How many single fellows of his age could be bothered with all the hassle of keeping two chattering, question-asking toddlers happy for two hours at the movies? But Big Jim did, took it all in his stride, *and* he made us laugh. He was our hero.

I looked ahead to where he was working – from that range just a matchstick man, alone with a toy horse in a wide expanse of land. Away to his left I could now see the little Cuddy Neuk farmhouse sitting on the brow of the hill by a bend in the road, and although it was something else I took for granted then, it was occupying a site which commands one of the most fabulous views in that part of Scotland. It encompasses some of the same features as can be seen from the top of the hill field, but from a different elevation and, if anything, from a more subtle angle.

Looking out westwards over rolling farmland from the front of the house, the entire Firth of Forth is laid out before you like a wide, mountainless fjord. On the far side, the hills of Fife step gently away into a seemingly limitless horizon. And before the river estuary narrows towards the famous Forth Railway Bridge some twenty-five miles upstream, the city of Edinburgh lies miniaturised in the lee of Castle Hill and the spectacular crags of Arthur's Seat.

To sit and gaze at the sun setting behind the distant summit of Ben Lomond, with cottonwool clouds painted every shade of mauve, gold and red, and scattering shards of glittering glass over the waters of the Firth, is a priceless visual experience which I would grow to treasure.

Byres Hill, at 590 feet the highest of the modest but ruggedly picturesque Garleton Hills, overlooks the farm and sports on its crest a tall round tower, known locally as simply 'the monument'. It was erected in 1824 'by his loyal tenants' in memory of the Earl of Hopetoun, the owner and laird of much of the rich surrounding farmland in those days. It's a landmark which can be seen from all over the county and far beyond. And the views from its 'cup-and-saucer' platform at the top are truly breathtaking – as is the climb up the 132 steps of its spiral staircase which has to be negotiated first!

As we started to trudge up the final steep rise towards the farm that morning, a wisp of mist still hung characteristically above Byres Hill, obscuring all of the monument except the topmost few feet, and making the cup-and-saucer appear as if miraculously suspended in space. And I innocently believed that they were, Big Jim having told me that, on such occasions, the main column of the monument had been carried off in the night by the eponymous resident of the adjacent Giant Hill, leaving the top of the tower hanging from sky hooks on invisible ropes. I've found out since that nobody else has ever heard of this myth, so I can only presume that it was an extension of one of many such Orcadian folk tales of fantastic creatures which Jim would have been brought up with, and of which I would hear much more from my grandparents as time went by. Strange beings and beasts of land and sea, whose stories were rooted deep in the Norse history of their native islands.

Jimmy Walker the roadman was cleaning out a drain at the side of the road by the farm gate. On seeing us approach, he grinned as he struggled to his feet and adopted his customary relaxing position – hands clasped over the handle of his shovel, one hobnail-booted foot raised to rest on the top of the shovel's blade.

'Aye, folks, no a bad day for the size o' the place, eh?'

My parents chuckled their reciprocated greetings.

Jimmy was one of those ruddy-faced characters who positively oozed country bonhomie. His round, cheery features beamed out from beneath the skip of his bunnet which, when getting ready for a *guid blether* with a passing acquaintance, he would push back from his face whilst simultaneously pulling the skip slightly to one side. Then a rolled-up fag would be lit as he studiously selected the topic of today's conversation.

'Cuddy Neuk, eh?' he said, nodding towards the farm buildings rising up from the high grass bank behind him. Did we know where the name of the farm came from, like?

No, they didn't, my parents replied in unison. My father crossed his legs and folded his arms in anticipation of the forthcoming dissertation. My mother leaned an elbow on his shoulder. Minnie and I yawned and clung to their legs for a rest.

'Well, ye surely ken what a cuddy is, d'ye no?' Jimmy half asked, half assumed.

'Aye, a horse,' my father confirmed.

'An' a neuk?'

'That's a nook, a corner,' my mother said.

'There ye are, then – Cuddy Neuk – Horse's Corner, if ye like.'

'Mummy,' my sister whispered, pulling her mother's skirt, 'why's that man got lumps of hair growing out of his nose?'

Ah well, that was to keep the midgies from flying up his 'snotterbox', Jimmy chortled. 'When Ah'm busy scythin' in the summertime, lass.'

Minnie went all bashful and hid behind her mother, peeping out after a moment to see if Jimmy was still looking at her.

He wasn't. 'See that wee dyke yonder?' he said, pointing towards the side of the road opposite the farm gate.

(NB: Contrary to what non-Scots might think, he wasn't alluding to a diminutive lesbian lurking in the ditch, but simply using the Scottish word for a wall.)

'Uh-huh?' my father replied expectantly.

'Well, there's a loupin-on stane in it.'

My father asked him why there would be a mounting-stone – a step to help you up into the saddle of your horse – built into a field wall away out here.

'Ye dinnae believe me, eh?' Jimmy was clearly a bit miffed. 'Come an' see then!'

He guided us over the road and pulled the grass back from the low wall, gesturing to us in a told-you-so sort of way. And there it was right enough – a neatly chiselled stone step protruding from its rough-cut neighbours about a couple of feet from the ground.

'I still don't understand why it should be there,' my father confessed.

Jimmy gave his head a little twitch, winked and pulled a self-satisfied smirk. 'Aha, but ye're no usin' yer peepers, son. Ye have tae be a roadman tae notice them things. See, take sights at this!'

At that, he lifted his jacket which had been draped over the wall, and exposed a length of smooth stone a couple of feet wide, as deep as the wall and positioned about waist-high.

'Windae sill, intit!'

My father shrugged. 'So there must have been a cottage here at one time, right?'

'Nah, nah, lad – no a cottage.' Jimmy gave my father a prod in the ribs and looked him square in the eye. 'Cuddy Neuk, see?' As if welcoming the look of confusion on my father's face, he then added triumphantly, 'No a cottage, son – a *pub*!'

'Well, well, imagine that,' my father laughed. He gave Jimmy's shoulder a slap. 'Pity it still wasn't here, eh?'

They both chuckled contentedly, savouring the notion for a few moments, before my mother interrupted their musings by asking: 'But why Cuddy Neuk? I'm still none the wiser.'

It would have been a carters' bar, Jimmy was delighted to explain – a resting place for man and horse halfway up the long drag from the coast at Aberlady to the top of Garleton Ridge, where the road begins its descent to Haddington.

'Aberlady, see? One time the port o' Haddington, like. Boats tradin' wi' the Low Countries. Grain an' tatties an' wool an' coal leavin' Aberlady – the boats arrivin' loaded wi' roof tiles for ballast.' That's was why so many old cottages in these parts happened to have red-pantiled roofs, Jimmy explained. 'Dutch-style. Of course, that was in the days afore Aberlady Bay got sanded up, like. Afore my time, mind. Oh aye – a *long* way afore my time.'

Just where Jimmy had gleaned this information about the one-time existence of a carters' tavern on the spot, I don't know. The gist of the story never left me, though, and when I was old enough to research the subject, I dredged through every local history book I could find and asked every historian and elderly resident who might have been able to corroborate Jimmy's claim. I drew a blank in every case. Old Jimmy, I concluded, had just been letting his over-fertile imagination run away with him. Then I happened upon an old map at a church hall jumble sale in Haddington one day. There, at the very point Jimmy Walker had led us to that morning, were the words 'Cuddy Neuk'. And that map had been printed a century and a half before the farm of the same name was created.

The discovery made the hairs rise on the back of my neck. By that time, old Jimmy had passed away, leaving me with a feeling of deep regret that such potentially rich sources of local history all over the land are so often allowed to take their folk knowledge to the grave with them. Jimmy was correct – you had to be a roadman to find out such things. The byway tales and yarns that the likes of Jimmy Walker must have picked up by word of mouth from even older worthies, who in turn had learned them at their mother's knee, would have been legion, but gone now forever. Today's roadmen don't get much feel, smell, sight or sound of such things, seated as they are in temperature-controlled, stereophonic comfort inside a glass cocoon atop a monster diesel-drinking tractor. A blast of Meat Loaf instead of the song of a blackbird or the welcome, unhurried chat of a passing ploughman or tramp. 'Conditioned' air electronically filtered and circulated to replace the sweet smell of scythe-cut grass and countless other seductive aromas of the countryside.

Purchase o' the feet – or lack of it – is no longer a problem.

'And then there's the ghostie,' Jimmy added, adopting a suitably creepy tone for the benefit of my sister and me, while winking surreptitiously at our parents. 'Ay-y-y-e … the Bogle o' Cuddy Neuk … *that's* his name!'

Right on cue, a strange, chillingly-grating noise descended from the skies high above. Jimmy let out a grizzly chortle.

It doesn't take much for a four-year-old to wet his pants, particularly when he hasn't had a wee-wee for the best part of half an hour – and that after a breakfast heavy on 'National' orange juice. Vitamin C was deemed good for kids even in those frugal times, I should add, and the government was doing its bit to make sure that the country's 'utility babies' got their share. By the time my mother pointed to the skein of wild geese flying over us, it was too late. I had already jettisoned my vital supply of Vitamin C for the day.

'Ah've heard tell he's the ghost o' an old innkeeper that died in this ditch here,' Jimmy continued darkly. 'Stottin' drunk, they say. Fell intae the ditch one night durin' a terrible storm. Drooned himsel', like.'

I listened awestruck, steam rising from my trousers in the sharp autumnal air. My sister did one of her most disparaging 'tuts', turned up her nose and retreated to the more acceptable ambience of her mother's lee side.

'Ye'll hear him – the Bogle o' Cuddy Neuk. Ye'll hear his moans and groans and the clinkin' o' his bottles as he thrashes aboot for dear life in yon ditch there.' Jimmy gave a little shudder, the pitch of his voice descending into a forboding drone. 'Oh aye, Ah've heard him masel', like. Oftwhiles … but only when the moon's shinin' bright. Fair frightenin', Ah'm tellin' ye.'

Realising that Jimmy's mischievous tale was becoming sufficiently gruesome to give my sister and me nightmares, our parents bade him their warm farewells and shepherded us back over the road towards the farm gate.

'And how d'ye ken if the moon's oot when ye're lyin' in yer bed at night?' Jimmy called after us, warming to his theme. He pointed up at the accumulating V-formations of geese flying inland from what is now a picturesque and peaceful nature reserve at Aberlady Bay, but was then just another heavily-mined stretch of the East Lothian coastline, strewn with huge concrete blocks intended to thwart the advance of invading tanks. The winter-visiting geese, Jimmy went on, flew inland every morning to graze the far fields on Cuddy Neuk, returning to the bay at nightfall. Except on cloudless moonlit nights, that is, when they would reverse their habit by flying in to graze during the hours of darkness. Why? Again, only the birds will ever know.

All I know is that it took a long time for me to banish the image of the ghostly innkeeper from my mind, especially when lying sleepless in bed on winter nights when the eerie gaggling of inland-flying geese pierced the curtained darkness of my room. But, as with most scary childhood imaginings, thoughts of the Bogle o' Cuddy Neuk did eventually fade from my mind ... until many years later, when the dreaded Bogle himself would manifest himself to me in the most unexpected and shocking of guises.

CHAPTER THREE

# THE HEN'S MARCH TO THE MIDDEN

The Cuddy Neuk farmhouse wasn't really a farm *house* at all, but really just a cottage, and not a particularly old one at that. For the little farm, like several others skirting the slopes of the Garleton Hills, had only been created in the late 1920s when, at the government's behest, two large farms were broken up into several smaller units, each with its own purpose-built house and steading. The exercise had all been part of the official promise of providing 'A Land Fit For Heroes' for surviving veterans of the First World War. Throughout the country, good farms of viable area, capable of supporting the farmer and his family, plus a staff of several men and *their* families, had been bought by the government and divided into individual holdings, ranging in size from four or five to a maximum of about fifty acres. The plan was then to rent these farmlets to 'heroes', giving each an opportunity to create his own little rural idyll, working away happily among his collection of hens, pigs or patches of soft fruit on the smaller units, or growing arable crops and rearing larger livestock on the holdings at the other end of the scale.

Paradise. Well, paradise in a vote-seeking politician's eye, perhaps, but in reality a scheme which attracted few 'heroes', but instead ended up as a magnet for go-ahead farm-workers keen to be their own men. Unfortunately, in many cases the tenants' ambition outweighed their ability to make a living on such inadequate acreages, particularly when starting off in woefully under-funded circumstances, as most were obliged to do. That said, many made a good go of things, but by the early forties, some of these eternally optimistic men had literally worked themselves to death trying to make ends meet. Even in the small Garleton community, there were too many premature widows. And when my grandparents first arrived at Cuddy Neuk, evidence of the previous occupier's desperate efforts to supplement his income was to be seen in the form of a large budgie-breeding cage occupying one entire wall of the living room.

Yes, it's all too easy to look back on those ostensibly simpler days when traditional farming methods still prevailed, and be lulled into thinking of the countryside as picture-book pretty and populated by carefree rustics tilling the soil in straw-chewing bliss. But in reality, farming, particularly on small farms, was an occupation in which the main ingredient was long hours of often back-breaking manual labour. But to those involved it was more than just a job or a business, it was (and still is) a way of life, an in-the-blood commitment to the land that precious few farming folk would swap for anything.

There was a dairy attached to one end of the Cuddy Neuk cottage, a small outhouse with a coal-fired boiler for sterilising milk buckets and churns, and with facilities for preparing liquid feed for the young calves. My grandmother (Granny Muir we called her) was doing precisely that when we arrived that October morning – carefully measuring and mixing the required quantity of dried 'milk' into buckets of warm water. Minnie and I always looked forward to calf-feeding times, not only because it was great fun to help bucket feed the young animals, some just a few days old, but also because it gave us the opportunity to raid the calf house larder, a rectangular tin bin, or *kist*, containing a dry mixture of maize flakes, rolled oats, protein pellets and, best of all, slivers of locust beans. These little chunks of sugary black carob pod were the best substitute for sweeties that we could find, except on the very rare occasions when the bin contained a few lumps of 'cow's chocolate'. It really was chocolate – milky-brown and deliciously sweet – but also containing a fair proportion of sawdust, fluff, hairs and other dubious matter from the factory floor from which it had been shovelled. Hence the reason for it being condemned for human consumption and designated instead as cattle feed. The presence of all those disgusting floor sweepings in the chocolate didn't bother us, though. To us, every unthinkably filthy morsel was pure Fruit and Nut. And, somehow, eating it never did us any harm. Only the cattle suffered, due to their share of the chocolate being substantially reduced by a pair of thieving, greedy kids with more sweet teeth than sense. But our view was that what the cattle didn't know wouldn't do them any harm. And neither it did.

Naturally, if Granny Muir had seen what we were up to, our little scam would have been brought to an abrupt end – but 'for our own good' only. Contrary to the generally perceived traits of her original profession, she didn't indulge in any schoolmarmish authoritarianism, didn't strike fear into an errant child with a killer look or a snapped reprimand. She didn't need to. Still as elegantly beautiful, albeit in a more mature way, as she appeared in her old graduation photograph from Edinburgh University, in which she looked as poised and demure as one of those young Edwardian ladies once featured in posters for Sunlight Soap, it took only a quiet word and a reproachful little smile for her to bring you back into line. She had the disposition of an angel, the patience of Job (she needed to, being married to our grandfather), yet, without complaint or a selfish thought, worked all the farm hours that God threw at her. The young Tom Muir must have had to be on his mettle to win the hand of Mary Pottinger when first she arrived on Sanday to teach at the little parish school. Competition from the other young blades on the island would have been fierce.

Fortunately for my sister and me, however, Granny Muir did have one weakness. Despite having fairly poor eyesight, she chose not always to wear her glasses when working about the farm, electing to save them for shopping trips to Haddington, or for when one of the regular delivery vans arrived in the yard. She liked to see what she was buying. I don't believe that this odd habit was the product of vanity, because she had no such vice, but was more due to an inherent sense of thriftiness. Glasses were an expensive item and should be looked after accordingly – that was possibly the thinking behind this little idiosyncrasy of hers. But whatever the reason, it meant that us kids could gorge ourselves on locust bean bits and condemned chocolate with little chance of Granny spotting us from the feeding pens at the other end of the calf house.

A motor horn hooted outside. Out came Granny's

glasses from her pinny pocket, and down went the lid of the feed bin. Today's delivery van was that of Archie the fishmonger from the fishing village of Port Seton just along the coast. Coming from a long line of fisherfolk, Archie possessed that droll sense of humour so typical of his kin. A wiry little man with an impish face, he would probably have been given his own TV show nowadays, so unique and outlandish were his yarns – all of which I'm sure he had convinced himself were true. On a clear day, he would invariably draw attention to the uninterrupted views of the hills of Fife, which could be seen from the Cuddy Neuk farmyard.

'See the Paps o' Fife?' he would say, pointing to the nippled summits (paps are breasts in Scots parlance) of two adjacent rounded hills far over the wide waters of the Firth of Forth. 'Well, Buckie Doddie, the oldest survivin' fisherman in Port Seton, if no the whole world – well beyond a hunder year auld he is, an' still sailin' – well, Buckie Doddie still has eyesight that ye'd hardly credit.' Doddie, according to Archie, could look out from his home harbour and not only recognise the identity of someone standing on top of one of the Paps, but could also tell you what brand of cigarette he was smoking. It had been one Watty MacCraw from Kirkcaldy puffing a Capstan Full Strength yesterday. 'It's true! Ah wouldnae tell a lie!'

Of course he wouldn't. The Paps o' Fife were only about twenty crow-flying miles distant from the quay at Port Seton, after all.

For all his unbridled whimsy and predilection for stretching the truth to breaking point, Archie was still a slave to the many deep-rooted superstitions of the fisherfolk. For instance, if his van contained a salmon (usually poached in wartime!), he would refer to it as 'pink fish', use of the salmon-word being one of several heavy-duty taboos. Similarly, should a minister of the church visit one of the farms which he had called in at, immediately on seeing the reverend gent Archie would shout out, 'Cauld iron!', and touch the metal of his van in order to ward off certain bad luck. But Archie's most endearing quirk was his routine of announcing in song the retail value of his fishy wares of the day. Parodying a Robert Burns verse that is regarded by many as being Scotland's *real* national anthem, the original words paying homage to such historic Caledonian heroes as William 'Braveheart' Wallace, Archie would sing ...

> '*Scots wha hae, wa-ha, wa-hoo,*
> *See the price o' kippers noo;*
> *Herrin's up tae one an' two –*
> *Haddie's one an' sixpence!*'

Archie had other verses to cover whatever types of fish had come off the boats at Port Seton that morning, but I can't remember them now, nor can I vouch for the accuracy of the foregoing prices, quoted in shillings and pence. But you get the idea.

'I'll have a dozen fish cakes, please,' said Granny, playfully specifying the one item not included in Archie's rhyming repertoire today. You could be sure that it would be next time, though.

The yard at Cuddy Neuk comprises a quadrangle enclosed by the house, its kitchen garden and a drying green on one side, and various farm buildings on the other three. An articulated Bedford truck was pulling in as Archie left in his van. Although small by today's standards, the 'artic' had a flatbed trailer unit that was capable, nevertheless, of carrying a fair-sized load of timber for its owners at the local sawmill. But all that was on the truck today was a solitary five-gallon petrol drum. My grandfather appeared round the corner of the steading, propped his dung fork against the stable wall and immediately entered into what appeared, from the other side of the yard, to be some serious negotiations with the driver. Much furtive looking over shoulders and whispered exchanges were the order of the day. After a minute or two, Grandfather nodded his head, strode off into the nearby barn and re-appeared a few moments later with a small cardboard basket of eggs. The truck driver took the basket, deposited it inside his cab, then shook his head, muttering something out of the corner of his mouth.

An exasperated cry of, 'Bliddy thievin' bastard!' resounded over the yard.

The trucker merely smiled a take-it-or-leave-it smile, folded his arms, crossed his legs and leaned back against his trailer. My grandfather, a man of renowned canniness when it came to the art of hard bargaining, had clearly met his match. His face a picture of frustrated outrage, he stomped off mumbling to himself and disappeared into the hen run which was located behind the cart-shed. Minnie and I couldn't see him from where we were standing at the back door of the house, but we could hear the sounds of chaos suddenly emanating from the chicken coop. Cackling, flapping, frenzied squawking and bellowed Orcadian curses – even a few feathers floating up over the cart shed roof.

'Gettin' more eggs for the man,' my sister confidently informed me.

If indeed Grandfather was in there for more eggs, it appeared that he wasn't just gathering them from the nest boxes, but was in the process of physically squeezing them from the nether regions of any hapless hen he could get his massive mitts on.

'Bless me!' Granny gasped, venting her favourite exclamation as she came out from the kitchen to see what all the carfuffle was about. 'Come now, peedie bairnos,' she said, preparing to shepherd us inside the house, 'pay you no heed to yon blasphemous tongue.'

I for one had no idea what a blasphemous tongue was, but I *was* thoroughly enjoying my grandfather's long-distance lesson in swear words. Just as Granny was about to shut the kitchen door on them, however, the sounds of poultry pandemonium suddenly ceased. A victory grin spread over the truck driver's face on seeing his adversary-in-bartering re-entering the yard. A hen, its head lolling about lifelessly at the end of a rubbery neck, its wings spread and still twitching, dangled by its legs from Grandfather's hand.

'Bless me,' Granny sighed. 'Petrol's getting dearer all the time nowadays.'

And so it was. But that was the black market for you. Petrol, desperately needed in the war effort, was strictly rationed for civilians, and although special dispensations were made for agricultural use, there never seemed to be enough available ... legally. So, if an enterprising trucker siphoned off a few pints from the tank of his vehicle every day, he'd soon have a five-gallon can of liquid gold to trade with. The fuel-desperate recipient would be at his mercy, while the truck driver's employers would be blissfully unaware of what was going on.

Without even glancing in his direction, my grandfather barked at the driver, 'And if thoo ever come by here again, boy, I'll tak the bliddy twelve-bore tae thee!' He then unceremoniously flung the hen into the truck cab and grabbed the can of petrol from the trailer. 'Now bliddy well clear off!'

'See ye next week then, Tam,' the trucker grinned as he drove away.

'Skinny owld boiler,' we could hear Grandfather grump once the truck had left the yard. 'Greedy bugger'll be hard pushed tae get even the one bowl o' soup oot o' yon bag o' bones!'

We decided to keep a safe distance from Grandfather for a while, so my sister went off with Granny and our mother to gather brambles along the old road, while I joined Dad and Big Jim for a bit of dung-spreading out in the field. As luck would have it, none of the grown-ups had noticed that I'd wet my pants earlier, so I calculated that, by the time my trousers had picked up a spattering of cow muck as well, my unfortunate misdemeanour would go unnoticed. Unless Minnie clyped on me, that is. But as she hadn't snitched to our parents at the time (thanks only to her being sidetracked by Jimmy Walker's scary ghost story, I suspected), it struck me that my chances of avoiding a humiliating dressing-down were now pretty good. I felt quite proud of myself. If I could get away with pulling the wool over adults' eyes as easily as this, maybe I was catching up with my big sister on the smarts front at last.

'I see ye've pissed yer breeks, Wee Pete,' Big Jim remarked deadpan.

'Yeah,' my father laughed, 'with fright! One of Jimmy

Walker's tall stories. But his mother and I reckoned his troosers would get into an even bigger mess helping you with the dung out here, so …'

My moment of self-satisfaction had been brief.

'Never mind,' said Jim, holding his forefinger out to me. 'Could've been worse. Ye might've shit yersel'. Here, pull *that*!'

I knew what was coming, of course. Jim had put me through this ritual on many previous occasions, yet it never failed to impress me. I grabbed his finger and gave it the required tug, whereupon a loud, pitch-changing rasp blasted forth from the seat of his dungarees. Fanny the horse looked round in amazement from her stance between the shafts of the cart.

'Aye, even the horse would've been proud o' that one, Wee Pete,' said Jim with a wink. 'Don't you try it, though. With your luck you'd likely let off a lumpy one!'

The three of us had a good manly guffaw. Suddenly, I couldn't have cared less about my self-imposed pressure to learn things. A guileless little smout I doubtless was, but thanks to Jim's unorthodox and earthy psychology, I didn't care – for the moment, anyway. I was 'one of the boys', on equal terms with the adults, sharing a rude laugh with 'the lads'. And that's how it was with Big Jim. Whenever we were away from the women of the family, he'd take great pleasure in teaching me things that were not entirely politically or socially correct. Nothing seriously corruptive, I should add – just the occasional mildly dodgy expression, or daft schoolboy pranks like the pull-a-finger-for-a-fart trick. And I'm sure that's why Jim empathised so well with us kids; despite his sharp mathematical brain, he was in many ways just an overgrown schoolboy himself. Tall and slim, but with his father's huge hands and a strength that belied his lanky physique, Jim could do the work of three men when he had to. I held him in affectionate awe, and wondered if I'd be lucky enough to have hands like his some day.

They were certainly being put to good use on this occasion. The cowp-cairt, or tipping cart, to which Fanny was yoked, had been piled high with rich, steaming manure, forked laboriously on board by Jim and his father back at the midden behind the steading. Having removed the cart's tailgate, Jim was now depositing the muck in little heaps spaced an equal number of paces apart across the length and breadth of the field. The hand implement which he was using to haul the clinging matter out of the rear of the cart was known as a 'dung hawk', a fork with its tines bent at right angles to its long shank. This was sore-on-the-arms work, made mercifully a bit less onerous by the simple back-tilting mechanism of the cart – the user-friendliness of the system being diminished, unfortunately, by the need for the operator himself to trigger it by putting his shoulder under the front overhang of the cart, then heaving upwards with all of his strength. No easy feat when the cart was heaped to overflowing with a heavy load.

As Jim got on with his work, my father and I made our way back to the headland of the field and began spreading the contents of the muck heaps over the stubble, my father with a conventional fork or *graip*, I with a toy spade of the seaside variety. My contribution to the job in hand was minimal, of course, but I thought I was doing well, saw myself as a real working man, and my elders were happy to indulge me. If nothing else, it kept me out of mischief, I suppose.

For some strange reason, working with cattle dung makes a chap extremely hungry. To the best of my knowledge, nobody has yet figured out why being wrapped in the ambience of such a reeky substance should whet the human appetite so sharply, but it does. In fact, by the time we started plodding our weary way back to the farmhouse that evening, I could have eaten a scabby cat, as Big Jim had taught me to say. But, fortunately, there was much more wholesome fare than that on offer. On entering the kitchen, the combined aromas of warm fruit, spices and hot dough seduced the nostrils and teased the taste buds with their irresistible charms. Newly made bramble jam and clootie dumpling! Manna from heaven to a seriously sweet-starved Scottish child.

The brambles (or blackberries as they're called outside Scotland) had been gathered by the womenfolk along the old road, where their entwining, prickly shoots wander in profusion among the hawthorn hedges. They're always in plentiful supply in autumn, but how our grandmother managed to get enough rationed sugar or any of the other difficult-to-obtain ingredients needed for her to work her culinary magic, I don't know. It's very likely, though, that one or two more scrawny, 'past their lay-by date' hens had gone to meet their maker in the course of the tough bartering process that would have been involved.

Clootie dumpling, named after the *cloot* (cloth) in which it is made, is a gastronomic treasure of Scotland, which deserves to enjoy much greater recognition beyond its native shores. Yet it doesn't, and perhaps only because Rabbie Burns never got round to immortalising clootie dumplings by composing an ode to one, as he famously did in praise of its more savoury cousin, that world-famous 'great chieftain o' the puddin' race', The Haggis. In country areas especially, the dumpling's simple recipe used to be handed down from mother to daughter, and although the 'mistress' of many a household might have added her own secret 'something special' to the mix, the basic ingredients and method of making the Clootie remain the same ...

Having blended the required amounts of flour, sugar, sultanas, raisins, mixed spice, milk and suet to the required consistency, the resultant fruity dough is wrapped in a piece of damp muslin, lowered into a pot of boiling water, then patiently simmered for upwards of two hours. The resultant steaming hot dumpling may then be served immediately with custard as a sweet or, as was Granny Muir's favoured way, left to cool, cut into chunky slices, griddled until crisply caramelised on both sides, then served as a main course with a fried egg or two on top and a garland of black pudding, bacon and sausages. Sitting round the table by the warmth of the old-fashioned kitchen range on which the food had been cooked, we regarded what was laid before us as a banquet fit for a king. On this occasion, 'steaks' of horse mushrooms the size of saucers, which had been gathered in the hill field early that morning, were also found a place on each plate, along with a generous dollop of clapshot – a traditional Orkney fusion of mashed potatoes, turnips, dripping and maybe some chopped onion.

Not much of this menu would find favour with today's low-fat, cholesterol-obsessed advocates of healthy eating, it has be said. But, as Big Jim might have remarked, they'd soon change their minds if they had a bash at spending a twelve-hour day flinging midden shite with nothing in their guts to sustain them but a meagre bowl of muesli, a glass of carrot juice and a sensible portion of nut burger salad. Working on the land at the time demanded the expenditure of huge amounts of physical energy, and you don't have to be Einstein to work out that what goes out must first be taken in. Put it this way – you never saw an overweight farm-worker in those days, 'unhealthy' diet notwithstanding.

To end the meal with a celebration of the start of the berry-picking season, Granny had prepared her own version of a classic old Scots pudding, best known as cranachan, but which she preferred to call cream crowdie. Deliciously uncomplicated, as many of the best recipes are, this one involves mixing toasted oatmeal with lightly whisked cream and some plump, juice-oozing brambles (or whatever berries are available), all served with maybe just a drizzle of runny honey. The traditional way, I'm assured, is to include a nip of whisky or Drambuie in the blend, but Granny brooked no such intemperance. Naturally, that didn't register as being of any significance to me then, but many years later I would find out the reason behind her strict prohibition of alcoholic drink in the house – even for culinary purposes.

It transpired that, as a young married man back in Orkney, my grandfather, though by no means a habitual boozer, did enjoy a dram or ten of whisky on such essential male gatherings as a winter ploughing match, or at one of the agricultural shows which take place on the islands every August. Arriving back home at Backaskaill late at night in a relaxed state (often, I was told by a contemporary of his, as 'relaxed' as a newt), there would be the inevitable domestic *stooshie*, at the end of which the young Tom Muir would retreat wobbly and defeated to the sanctuary of the stable. There he'd *coorie doon* on the straw in a cosy corner of one of his beloved Clydesdale's stalls, cuddling his dram bottle for comfort, and would drift into a deep, mumbling sleep, the sound of his blissful snoring eventually reverberating round the farmyard until cockcrow. Inevitably, I suppose, this quirky habit must have stretched even the exceptional patience of my grandmother to the limit, and an ultimatum would have been delivered to her wayward husband ...

'Me or the whisky – take your pick!'

He chose wisely, and never wandered from the straight and narrow path of temperance again. Well, not often, anyway!

But none of this was either known by or of any interest to my sister and me. We had tucked into a plain but nourishing farmhouse dinner – a not entirely exceptional occurrence for us, but a luxury denied to many millions of unfortunate victims of the war throughout the world. In our innocence, we just didn't realise how lucky we were to be part of a farming family in a country relatively untouched by such misery. For, despite the restrictions of food rationing, we had enjoyed an unstinting meal prepared almost entirely with ingredients produced on the farm, or gathered from the wild in the surrounding countryside. Such menus may not have been fancy, but we never knew what it meant to go hungry. There was always a new brood of chicks being hatched to set claw on the first rung of the bartering ladder, their busy mothers kept up the supply of eggs for human consumption, the pigs provided the bacon and essential ingredients for the sausages and black puddings, the cows saw to it that we never wanted for milk or cream, and the land yielded up much of the rest.

As kids, we had no inkling that this was a world apart from the life being lived by our mother's sister Renee and her family just then. Several years before the outbreak of war, Renee, who was working in Holland, had married Bob, a young Dutchman with a promising career in banking. In 1937, promotion saw Bob posted to Java in the Dutch East Indies, there to manage the bank's affairs within the expanding economy which the island was enjoying during those pre-war years. Bob and Renee, who by then had an infant son and daughter, lived a life of colonial privilege – blessed with a lifestyle which only existed in Hollywood movies for most ordinary folk. The bank had provided them with a luxury ranch-style bungalow, set in lush sub-tropical gardens, with a palm-fringed swimming pool, and even a staff of servants to see to their every need. It was a far cry from the everybody-mucks-in farming life which Renee had known as a young girl back in the breezy, treeless expanses of a northern Orkney island. And she loved it. For Renee and Bob's little family, life could not have been more wonderful.

Then came the Japanese invasion of Indonesia. At one brutal stroke, their paradise was lost. Their dream home was ransacked by the occupying troops, who summarily condemned Bob to a 'life' of slave labour, while transporting Renee and the two small children to a concentration camp for women in another part of the island. They were forbidden any means of contact with anyone beyond the barbed wire confines of their respective prisons. For the remaining long years of the war, Bob and Renee not only had no knowledge of where the other was, but had to suffer the appalling conditions of their captivity without even knowing if the other was still alive. An exceptionally attractive young woman, Renee must have had to endure unspeakable hardships in her struggle, not just for her own survival, but for that of her two little children as well.

This was a subject not normally discussed in front of

Minnie and me, yet thoughts of Bob and Renee's plight must have weighed heavily on the minds of the adult members of our family all of the time. They knew nothing of the fate of their loved ones, other than what had been broadcast on sketchy radio news bulletins by the BBC – Java had been overrun by the Japanese, and all Dutch nationals not killed in the invasion had been captured and imprisoned. It must have been hard to bear the haunting thought that they might never see Renee and her family again, a chilling source of anguish exacerbated by a total absence of information about their circumstances in some unimaginable hell on the other side of the globe.

But life must go on, and the endless, inescapable cycle of farm work was undoubtedly a blessing in disguise, particularly for my grandparents. Keep busy – that was the best way to keep worry at bay. Music, too, provided a temporary escape from the disheartening uncertainties of a war-torn world. Like most farms in the area then, there was neither phone nor mains electricity at Cuddy Neuk, so our evening meals had been eaten by the light of a paraffin-fuelled Tilley lamp hanging from a ceiling hook above the table, the hissing of the lamp's flickering mantle providing a comforting accompaniment to its meagre glow. From a big valve-powered radio in the corner, the toe-tapping sound of Jimmy Shand's Scottish dance music crackled out through a quickly deteriorating reception, which served as a reminder that the set's bulky battery/accumulator would soon have to be lugged down to Amos's wireless shop in Haddington to be recharged.

The perky swing of Jimmy Shand's accordion music was undoubtedly one reason for my grandfather being in a markedly happier mood than he'd been after his petrol 'negotiations' with the truck driver earlier in the day. But there was something else too. The local vet had confirmed during an afternoon visit that young Fanny was in foal – a piece of news that had set Grandfather grinning till his pumpkin-lantern teeth were exposed in all their randomly spaced glory, his ever-alert pale blue eyes glinting with a sparkle usually reserved for a man who has just been told that his *wife* is pregnant – or isn't! As Jimmy Shand faded into oblivion with the dying electrical current, Grandfather rose from the table and strode purposefully over to the big dresser which stood against the wall where the budgie-breeding enclosure had once hung.

'Weel then, Pate,' he said.

'Yes,' I replied.

'Nah, nah, no thee this time, peedie Pate.' He winked at my father. 'Time for a tune, eh, owld Pate?'

A knowing groan from Granny heralded the appearance of grandfather's melodeon from the depths of the cupboard.

'Get thee on the pianny, Pate,' he smiled at my father, gesturing towards the old upright by the window. He then seated himself beside the range, sticking his right thumb through the leather 'steadying' thong at the melody side of the little squeeze-box, and shoving his left hand through the strap at the bass end. 'We'll gie some owld favourites laldy, boy!'

Long, hard-working days meant that such impromptu soirées weren't all that common at Cuddy Neuk. But no one was more delighted to join in than my father when the opportunity did arise. He was ever ready 'to go his dinger on the old ivories', as he put it, and I had seen him doing just that a few times at parties which the RAF families used to throw in the back room of the Castle Inn at Dirleton. It

71

took little persuasion for him to knock six bells out of the out-of-tune pub piano with his dubious interpretations of ragtime and boogie, and it took Keith Taylor, the jovially-shrewd proprietor, no time to start pulling the pints of beer that grew steadily in demand as the music hotted up. During one of those long, balmy summer evenings when the sun barely sets on the East Lothian coast, I even saw the old Castle Inn 'joanna' trundled outside when the party atmosphere grew too hot for indoor comfort. Regarded as one of Scotland's most picturesque villages, leafy Dirleton has a broad expanse of village green, overlooked by the majestic ruins of Dirleton Castle, and flanked by huddles of pantiled stone cottages. The castle was described by sixteenth-century Edinburgh nobleman Lord Robert Logan as 'the pleasantest dwelling in Scotland'. It is one of several magnificent old fortresses in the area that were vandalised in the seventeenth century by the heavy artillery of Oliver Cromwell's armies as they bulldozed their way through southern Scotland, trying to win the hearts and minds of the local folk. But its still-proud walls rang to a more benevolent sound than the brutal roar of cannon fire during those RAF party evenings, although the fabric of the ancient stonework may well have suffered slightly from the discordant thumps and wild glissandos inflicted on the ivories by my father's pounding fingers.

Musical recitals in the Cuddy Neuk living room were much less frenzied affairs, however – at least to start with. On the rare occasions when the old melodeon was lifted out from the dresser, Grandfather would usually begin with a somewhat stilted rendition of a traditional Scots air, or, as this time, with a chorus or two of an old-time music hall ballad, like 'Love's Old Sweet Song'.

*'Just a song at twilight, when the lights are low …'* Granny quietly half-sang, half-hummed, pretending to be aloof from the proceedings while she and our mother cleared the dishes from the table, and Grandfather loosened up his work-stiffened fingers 'on a peedie slow one'.

'*… And the flickering shadows softly come and go.*
*Tho' the heart be weary as the day is long,*
*Still to us at twilight, comes love's old song –*
*Comes love's old sweet song …'*

But before the dishes had been washed and dried, melodies of lively hornpipes, jigs and reels were fairly buzzing forth from the melodeon's metal reeds, Grandfather's increasingly fluid playing goaded on by the eager rhythm of my father's vamping digits. Minnie and I had seated ourselves on Big Jim's knees, being bounced up and down as his feet kept time to the music, and revelling in the unbridled fun of it all. I was being inadvertently instilled with a lasting love for an infectiously happy form of music that typifies the spirit of our little country – the chance result, perhaps, of a combination of Celtic and Norse blood and cultures, but a unique and much treasured feature of our heritage, nevertheless.

Launching into a spirited version of a catchy old number called (appropriately enough, considering the nature of the day's work) 'The Hen's March To The Midden', Grandfather yelled out a loud *'Hoo-oo-ooch!'*, and dissolved into a fit of cackling laughter, head back, bunnet askew, mouth open wide, tombstone teeth glinting in the guttering Tilley light. Suddenly everyone was laughing. Even Granny abandoned her feigned air of disinterest in her husband's performance. The dishwashing over, she was now clapping her hands to the beat and joining in the boisterous outbursts of 'Hoochin" and 'Wheechin" that such happy-go-lucky music provokes in everyone except the terminally cheerless. Oliver Cromwell, for instance, would not have been a fan.

Watching Grandfather play, I was amazed that such technically tricky tunes were being coaxed out of that tiny apology for an accordion by those huge callused fingers of his. With only one short row of buttons on which to produce the melody, and two 'paddle' keys to provide the bass, a melodeon isn't equipped with much for the player to work with. And to make the task of mastering it even more difficult, the melodeon functions on the mouth organ 'suck-blow' principle. In other words, pressing the same button creates one note when the bellows are being extended and another when they're being compressed. So, to knock a melody out of the instrument, the musician must not only concentrate on which buttons he's pressing, but also has to keep those bellows pumping out and in with absolute accuracy as well. Then there's the added complication of making sure there's always enough air in the thing to produce a series of 'in' notes before the playing of an 'out' note sucks more air in. The melodeon 'running out of wind' and, therefore, running out of sound is an ever-present risk.

But Grandfather's 'peedie box' wasn't being allowed to play such a nasty trick on him as he expertly squeezed and pulled the *bellises* with rapid, jerky movements of his left arm. Impressive stuff. And in a further show of his mastery of the *sook–blaw* technique, whilst never missing a note of the melody he somehow managed to cajole his melodeon into mimicking the clucking noises of the hen as she marched her tuneful way to the midden.

'What grand fun, peedie bairnos!' he shouted out to Minnie and me, delighting in our expressions of admiration for his feats of musical magic, his mighty fingers still scampering over the tiny keys like tap-dancing bananas. 'Ya-a-as, what bliddy fun, eh!'

What fun indeed. An hour or so of simple fireside entertainment of the sort that once brightened up the long, dark evenings in every farm cottage and horseman's bothy in the land, but which first radio and then television progressively banished from most homes for ever. No one back then could have predicted how the advance of technology would one day do so much to enrich our lives, while also, sadly, taking so much of the true richness away.

But tomorrow would be just another day at Cuddy Neuk – another morning which would see our grandparents and Big Jim rise at five o'clock to hand milk up to twenty cows; another day of keeping busy; another day of getting on with life and hoping for the best for absent family. The melodeon was returned to its shelf in the cupboard, the piano lid was closed, the fire in the old range was given a final poke and its cast iron doors closed for the night. It was time for us to make our way back to Gullane, thoughts of a full and happy day warming our way through the chill autumn air, the strains of 'The Hen's March To The Midden' and the sound of laughter still echoing inside our heads.

My request for a second glass of 'National' orange juice before going to bed that night was flatly refused. My mother didn't say why, and I didn't need to ask. If I'd learned nothing else that day, I now at least knew the meaning of the saying, 'Let sleeping dogs lie' …

## CHAPTER FOUR

## MATTERS OF LIFE AND DEATH

Not many boys of four are given their own pipe to smoke. But Big Jim gave *me* one – a proper miniaturised version of the real thing that he'd picked up from an Indian 'lucky' knickers salesman in the pub. These door-to-door traders from Leith's enterprising Sikh community were often to be encountered in the country areas, selling their wares from a suitcase in the days before the advent of out-of-town Sunday markets. Their stock consisted mainly of bargain shirts, loud neckties, pseudo-silk scarves and the like. If you succumbed to their tenacious sales pitch just to get them off the doorstep, and purchased a small item like a packet of hankies, you'd be given a prediction of modestly good fortune in your life, with the gift of a 'lucky' bead as back-up. However, if you really weakened and bought, say, a couple of shirts, some socks and a pair of long johns, the good-fortune forecast would graduate to a massive win on the football pools and the gift might be a pair of passion-killer drawers for your wife.

'Werry naughty knickers, my friend. Oh, most deffinlee,'

(suggestive smirk), 'werry many luck for your lovely laydee!'

The little pipe had a yellow bowl and black stem. And it worked, Jim divulged with a conspiratorial wink. He lifted it down from the mantlepiece above the range one morning when I'd stayed the night at Cuddy Neuk, being fed up of hanging about at home in Gullane, I suppose, now that Minnie was at school. Or maybe it was because my mother was fed up of having me hanging about at home asking the same quarter-hourly question: 'When will Minnie be back from school?' I still couldn't see the point of her being in that miserable-looking place all day. She already knew all there was to know about everything, as far as I could make out, so why waste valuable playing time sitting about in a classroom? I certainly had no intention of doing anything *that* daft – ever.

It was about eight in the morning, and Grandfather was still outside seeing to matters in the byre, while Granny cooked breakfast. Jim had cleaned himself up after the early milking and was preparing for his regular trip to deliver the full churns to the Co-operative bottling plant in Tranent.

'Stick that in yer mooth, Wee Pete,' he said, handing me the little pipe.

Granny glanced round momentarily from her bacon-frying chores at the range. 'For blowing soapy bubbles, is it?' she asked without much interest. 'That'll be grand fun.'

Big Jim said nothing.

I gripped the pipe between my teeth. Jim took a Capstan packet from his pocket, pulled out a cigarette and broke off a half-inch piece which he stuck into the bowl of the pipe. It fitted perfectly, which would suggest that what I had in my mouth was in reality a novelty, right-angled cigarette holder. But that's not how I saw it. To me this was the genuine article – a real *man's* pipe, albeit a wee man's one. I was blissfully ignorant of the fact that it was probably just another bottom-of-the-suitcase trinket that came somewhere between a bead and a pair of outmoded bloomers on the 'lucky' hand-out scale. Jim flicked his lighter and held the flame to my protruding cigarette butt. I could hardly wait. At last I was about to experience the long-admired ritual of breathing in smoke. This was it – in a moment I'd even be blowing it out through my nose just like Grandfather and Jimmy Walker. Ignition – inhalation – delectation!

I was too busy retching my guts up and coughing fit to burst a blood vessel to notice if Granny actually hit Jim with her frying pan. But I'd never heard her losing her temper like that before.

'Good Lord help us and save us!' she piped. What in the name o' the *divvil* was Jim thinking about? 'You'll fell the poor peedie bairno, big gowk that you are!'

Thumping my back, Jim was laughing so much that he couldn't speak. Whether he had set up this little episode to teach me a lesson about the evil of the poisonous weed, or whether it had just been one of his typical acts of schoolboy mischief, I neither knew nor cared. All I was aware of was the horrible burning sensation in my throat and chest, and the sickeningly foul taste of tobacco smoke in my mouth. Manhood, I silently conceded, was still a long way off. About fourteen years, in fact – as far as smoking was concerned, at any rate.

'Quick, quick! Daisy the coo's bringin' hame a calf!' It was my grandfather at the back door, sounding unusually excited. 'Come on, an' bring the peedie boy! He'll be fairly tickled wi' this!'

A cow bringing *hame* (or 'home') a calf, as Granny

explained to me while dabbing the smoke-induced tears from my eyes and wiping the Capstan-flavoured slavers from my chin, meant that a birth was imminent in the byre. Her explanation made about as much sense to me as Grandfather's original back door pronouncement. Bringin' hame? Imminent birth? The scene which greeted us in the byre didn't help my understanding of what all the fuss was about either. The rest of the herd having been turned out to pasture until time for the evening milking, all the stalls were empty except one at the far end of the byre. Daisy was lying on her side on a fresh bed of straw, Grandfather kneeling behind her, holding her tail up and peering at her rear end, from which blood-stained mucus was oozing. Daisy looked round and groaned, the pained expression in her big brown eyes suggesting to me that she wasn't particularly tickled with the proceedings, even if I was supposed to be. Which I wasn't. This all looked distinctly dicey to me.

Grandfather patted her bony hip with a gentleness that I'd only ever seen him bestow before upon his beloved Fanny the Clydesdale. 'There, there now, lass,' he crooned, a note of quiet urgency in his voice. 'Just another peedie shove now. There's a fine-like coo.'

Seeming to respond to his words, Daisy breathed in deeply and gave an almighty heave, a low moan of distress escaping her mouth as her flanks trembled with the effort. Granny was kneeling by her head now, Daisy's muzzle cradled in her lap, an understanding hand stroking her temple. What appeared to me to be a sort of water-filled sausage skin was now protruding from somewhere beneath the cow's tail. Jim joined his father, crouching down behind Daisy and looking anxiously at this strange balloon-like outgrowth, from which a discharge of liquid suddenly spewed out.

'The waters have burst,' he muttered. 'It'll no be long now.'

I stood alone in the middle of the byre floor, watching this disturbing scene from just a few feet away. 'Is Daisy goin' to die?' I asked, seized by the chilling anxiety of childish ignorance.

'Nah, nah, never fret, boy,' Grandfather mumured with deliberate calm, his eyes never shifting from the cow's rear end. 'Just bringin' hame a calf.' He patted Daisy's rump again. 'Tak a peedie rest now, lassie. There now – just tak it easy a while.'

As if obeying him again, Daisy lay still for a minute or two, her breathing less strained, her whole body seeming more relaxed. Magically, she appeared to be experiencing some measure of relief from whatever had been causing her so much torment. Not realising that this was a natural reaction in an animal following 'the breaking of the waters', I marvelled again at my grandfather's ability to control creatures with his words. Then Daisy's flanks quivered again, her rib cage rising and falling with every laboured breath. Clearly, the pain was returning. Both my grandparents and Big Jim began to utter gentle words of encouragement while patting and stroking Daisy to comfort her.

'That's right, Daisy – work hard now. There, there – soon be over now, lass.'

Daisy responded with a pained groan and a visible contraction of her sides.

'Here it comes, Wee Pete!' exclaimed Jim, smiling expectantly and motioning towards two tiny cloven hooves which were emerging from what I thought was Daisy's bum.

What strange magic was this? I wondered, spellbound and totally confused.

'Come on, Daisy,' Jim urged. 'Another big shove, hen!'

Daisy bellowed in pain as the tiny hooves turned into bony forelegs, quickly followed by a pink nose. Then a calf's head appeared. Pausing in her exertions for a moment, Daisy then strained every muscle in a series of supreme efforts, finally managing to expel the calf's shoulders from her body. The rest of the little animal then slithered out comparatively effortlessly – emerging prostrate and motionless from the burst sausage-skin cocoon, its brown and white coat matted and wet. Exhausted, Daisy raised her head, looked round at the cause of all her pain lying there in the straw, and gave a little grunt of relief.

Grandfather lowered his cheek to the lifeless calf's nose. 'No breathin'. Quick, Cheem, lift it up by the back legs!'

Big Jim did as instructed. Grandfather took a handful of straw and began to vigorously rub the calf's sides, while Granny carefully cleared it's nostrils with a single straw, then opened it's mouth an blew into it. The little animal's body twitched, then it gave a snort, a sneeze, took a gasping breath, coughed again, and blinked open its eyes. It let out a bleating little cry as Jim laid it down gently by its mother's head.

'A wee heifer,' he grinned. 'Good one, too.'

A female calf is always what's wanted in a dairy herd, not just because she will one day join the milkers who earn the farmer his money, but because bull calves – particularly in smaller breeds like the Ayrshire and Jersey – aren't particularly suitable to be raised as beef cattle. Not being efficient converters of feed, the smaller examples, known as Bobby calves, invariably find themselves on the pie and sausage makers' slab within a few hours of seeing the light of day. But the primary reason for keeping a cow calving regularly, of course, is to ensure her continued 'in milk' condition, which is a prerequisite of her membership of a dairy herd. After a few days of suckling its mother's milk, Daisy's new baby would be taken to join the other bucket-fed calves in a pen in the calf house, while Daisy's daily milk would end up in a churn on its way to the wholesale dairy along the road in Tranent. The miracle of birth on a farm is, by necessity, harnessed to the harsh realities of business.

Daisy gave a series of contented little moans as she began to lick her new calf dry. Her ordeal having only ended a few seconds earlier, she was already getting on with what her instinct told her to do.

'Come then, peedie boy,' Grandfather said, nodding towards the door, 'we'll leave them for a while now. Ya-a-as, we'll tak another look and see how they're gettin' on after breakfast.'

It was as if no such drama as the one that had just been played out existed in my grandfather's view. All part of the day's work, and much more waiting to be done. I was still transfixed, however, gazing at Daisy lovingly tending to a new little creature that hadn't even existed a few minutes ago. I didn't understand.

'How did the wee calf get inside Daisy's bottom, Granny?' I enquired, sitting at the kitchen table, too fascinated by what I'd just witnessed to be particularly interested in the plate of bacon and eggs that she'd just placed in front me.

She just laughed quietly. Grandfather pretended he hadn't heard my question, busying himself by spreading butter on a slice of toast and stirring several spoonfuls of sugar into his mug of tea.

'Who put it in there, Big Jim?' I asked, hoping that the close rapport I shared with my uncle would result in an answer from him.

Jim cleared his throat. 'Well, ehm, the bull … yeah, the bull put it in there, Wee Pete.'

I started to laugh. Another one of Big Jim's jokes! I mean, I knew the bull – a nasty looking creature if I'd ever seen one, a clumsy, bad-tempered brute that I'd been taught never to go near. And Jim expected me to believe that it had delicately inserted a live calf-in-a-balloon up Daisy's bum?

'You're tellin' fibs,' I told him.

Jim merely shrugged, had a quiet chortle to himself, and got on with eating breakfast. And that was all that was said on the subject. One more mystery of life for me to ponder. I didn't even regard Daisy's giving birth to a calf as being related to how young Fanny the mare happened to be 'in foal'. And, although I didn't realise it, I had actually seen the 'deed' of conception taking place in Fanny's case.

*****

Minnie and I had been told by Grandfather to stay in the yard on the morning the travelling stud stallion called. He was a magnificent monster of an animal, a perfect specimen of Clydesdale muscle and beauty, the same rich bay colour as Fanny, but with more white to his face and legs. The travelling stallion man led him down the ramp of his wagon, and immediately the great horse flared his nostrils and threw his head up, tossing his mane flamboyantly while letting out a deep, rumbling whinny that left no one in any doubt that they were in the presence of an animal which was very aware of his own importance and power. Sniffing the air, he pranced and postured, eyes blazing, massive fore-hooves pawing the ground impatiently. Whatever his business, he looked as if he meant it. Minnie and I huddled in the safety of the barn doorway until the stallion had been led bucking and shying out of the yard, Grandfather a few paces ahead, showing the way, looking as if he meant business himself.

'Dinna thee bairnos be comin' after me, mind!' he shouted back at us. 'No for your eyes, this!'

That was all the temptation we needed. We waited a few moments, then, without saying a word, tiptoed past the stable and on towards the cattle shed, following the sound of our grandfather and the stallion man exchanging grunted words.

'Ready, is she?' asked the stallion man.

'As hot as a hoor's erse on a Saturday night!'

I looked at Minnie for a hint of enlightenment as to the meaning of this last remark. None was forthcoming. Continuing round the corner, we could make out even more excited horsey noises than before, but could see nothing yet. We crept past the front of the cattle shed and stopped at the far corner, Minnie in the lead, glancing at me over her shoulder, forefinger raised to her lips. The mingled sounds of neighing, hoof-stamping and muffled, clipped conversation were very close now. Crouching down, my sister peeped round the corner.

'What's happenin'?' I urged.

Saying nothing, Minnie shook her head, eyes fixed on whatever she was watching. Consumed by curiosity now, I got down on all fours and crawled alongside my sister, straining my neck to see past her and find out what all the commotion was about. There, in a little paddock behind the cattle court, Grandfather was standing holding Fanny by the halter, while the stallion strutted about behind her, his movements so agitated now that his keeper was struggling to keep him under control. The man, no lightweight himself, was even lifted clear off his feet a couple of times by the violent tossing of the stallion's great head. This display of unbridled excitement had clearly affected the normally placid Fanny as well. She was looking round at the snorting giant with a strange, near-hysterical look in her eyes, her hooves beating a dusty tattoo on the dry earth. Grandfather, looking a bit agitated now too, was doing his best to restrain and calm her, but his magic words didn't seem to be working all that well on this occasion. Curling his top lip to reveal a row of long yellow teeth, the stallion was now sniffing at Fanny's backside while doing his own version of her heavy-hooved tap dance. We could hear the rasping of his breath and the rising pitch of his whinnying, could see the rippling of his muscled limbs.

'What's *that*?' I asked my sister, pointing at what appeared to be a fifth leg that the stallion had miraculously sprouted.

'What's what?'

'*That* thing – between the big horse's back legs …'

Minnie pulled a nonchalant shrug then blandly informed me that it was 'just his willie'.

For the first time, I was moved to doubt my big sister's superior intellect. She may have seen five summers to my modest four, but at least I had the natural physical equipment to know better than she that what we were discussing here was no willie! Admittedly, that dangly appendage was noticeably less muscular than the stallion's other four legs, but it looked long enough to need a roller skate to be strapped to the end of it in order to keep it from scraping along the ground. Yes, it was a leg all right, and I told Minnie so. Further deliberation was halted, however, by the next stage in the ritual dance that the two horses were now completely engrossed in.

'Look,' I hissed, 'that big horse is trying to get on Fanny's back! Why's it doin' that?'

Minnie offered no answer, mesmerised as she clearly was by what was happening. The stallion's great barrel of a chest was resting on Fanny's rump, his bared teeth gnawing at her mane. We both looked on goggle-eyed as the horseman took the stallion's fifth leg in his hand and guided it under Fanny's tail.

'What's he doin'?' I whispered.

'Just wipin' Fanny's bottom,' Minnie replied, her normal confidence in her grasp of general knowledge suddenly restored.

Granny's voice calling us from the back door of the house spared us both further confusion – mine admitted, Minnie's veiled. And despite having contemplated many times the bizarre scene which we'd clandestinely witnessed behind the cattle shed that day, I still didn't relate it to Big Jim's breakfast table assertion that the bull had been responsible for Daisy's new calf. In fact, the thought couldn't have been farther from my mind that morning as we returned to the byre to see, as Grandfather put it, 'how the owld coo an' her peedie heefer are doin' now.'

Though scarcely half an hour had elapsed since the trauma of the birth, both mother and daughter were already on their feet, Daisy murmuring her little sounds of maternal bonding with her new baby as she tried to nudge it gently towards the source of its first feed. The calf, her coat licked clean and looking perfectly groomed, was tottering on spindly legs at Daisy's side, pointing in approximately the right direction, but trying vainly to suckle her mother's back leg. With just a little guidance from Granny, however, Daisy Junior was soon plugged in to her own personal milk bar and was chugging away hungrily while her mother got stuck in to a well-deserved munch of hay.

I'd seen the cows being hand-milked often enough to know what the calf was getting from its mother's udder, but what I didn't understand was why this particular calf wasn't already in the calf house and being bucket-fed like the others.

'Ah weel, that's because all peedie caffs need tae sook their mother's teats for a day or two,' Grandfather explained. 'The coo's first milk after caffin' – beesmilk it's caa'd – full o' goodness and things tae set the calf on the right road.' He chortled quietly as the calf, already confident in its budding suckling technique, began to greedily butt Daisy's udder while it selected one teat after another. A milk bar with four spouts – Shangri-La! 'Ya-a-as, the peedie caffo's doosin' Daisy's teats tae mak more milk come. A fine-like heefer, this one. Aye, boy, she'll do just grand.'

Confused as I still was about how the little animal had come to be, I was so enthralled by this heartwarming scene that I sat on an upturned bucket like Oor Wullie, Scotland's favourite comic-strip character, and looked on for a good half hour after the grown-ups had left the byre to get on with the rest of their morning's work. I had watched the marvel of new life for the first time. I had seen how a so-called dumb animal endures the rigours of giving birth and, through instinct, attends immediately to the needs of her offspring. The calf, too, had taught me how quickly the young of certain animals learn the essentials of survival. Instinct again – deep-rooted and primaeval. I've seen this same miracle take place countless times since then, but my fascination remains undiminished, my feelings for the special attachment that exists between mother and calf as warm and child-like now as then – though tempered by the commercial reasons behind our breeding and rearing of farm animals. For, as strange an anomaly as it may seem, no farmer with a heart (and surprisingly many do have extremely soft hearts) would do anything but regard his livestock with respect and, in most cases, with real affection. Just try getting one to admit it, though!

As the months passed and the time for the birth of Fanny's foal drew closer, the young mare was given lighter and lighter work to do, until she was leading a life of relative leisure, pampered and fussed over by our grandfather in a way that Granny often said he'd never done for her during her five pregnancies.

'Good God Almighty, Mary Muir, horse is delicate-like beasts!' was how he dismissed such thoughtless remarks.

Britain, like other Allied nations which were considered vital to US defence, had an agreement during the Second World War by which desperately needed equipment, food and materials were lent or leased by America to bolster the war effort and help sustain the people of those beleaguered countries. I presume that it was via some particular channel of this arrangement that my grandfather managed to procure, for his fifty acres and a few annually rented fields nearby, two brand new American tractors to replace his clapped-out old groaner of a Fordson, when some farms ten times the size had to get by with their one tractor, which they'd probably had for years as well. Maybe it was because he had turned over as much of the Cuddy Neuk land as possible to the intensive growing of vegetables to help supply the insatiable demand of military cookhouses in the area, or maybe it was just because his canny Orcadian guile had guided him towards the right strings to pull. Then again, most of the larger farms still had several pairs of horses and the relevant manpower required to get the work done without tractors, so perhaps it had simply been Cuddy Neuk's modest one-horse status (and the horse pregnant at that!) which had swung the benefits of the United States' Lend–Lease Act in the required direction. Whatever the reason, a gleaming orange-red Allis-Chalmers tractor arrived from America – a small machine by today's standards, but quite capable of pulling a two-furrow plough and all of the other tasks required of it with the converted horse implements then available. A few months later, the Allis-Chalmers was joined in the yard by a bright yellow Minneapolis Moline ('MM' for short) – a three-wheeler especially suited to row-crop cultivations and just what was needed, therefore, to work the fields of cabbages now being grown on the farm.

Despite purporting not to share Big Jim's enthusiasm for these new-fangled contraptions – 'They mak for a muckle burst boil standin' there thegither' – Grandfather was quick to learn how to operate them. Moreover, he delighted (before the novelty wore off, at any rate) in sitting atop one of his new tractors, tearing up and down the spring fields towing a set of harrows, his coat tails flapping behind him like a flag in a gale, paraffin smoke belching from the little machine's *lum*, dust billowing up from the land, sparks flying from the Woodbine jutting from the corner of his mouth. For him, this was all 'grand fun', but he knew in his heart of hearts that scooting about on a tractor would never replace the deep sense of satisfaction which he derived from the unique relationship which existed between himself and his Clydesdales. He was just marking time, having a *guise* with these new toys until young Fanny foaled. Then he would relish the joy of seeing her nurse her first offspring, watch the foal take its first wobbly steps, marvel at how quickly it would be frisking around the paddock, running with its mother, carefree and beautiful in the sheer exhilaration of life. Those were magic moments that could never be replaced by any machine. And training the young horse too; patiently introducing it to the feel of harness, helping it get used to pulling a log at first, teaching it the rules of the reins, reassuring it as it was backed into the shafts of a cart for the first time – nothing that you could do with a tractor could ever come close to the rare pleasures that a horseman derives from that. Deep down, he pitied the younger generation, impatient for the speed and efficiency that the dawning age of mechanisation would bring to the farms, blindly eager to turn their backs on a priceless bond that had existed between man and beast since time immemorial. No tractor would ever induce him to forsake such a priceless heritage, tempt him to turn away from an inbred feel for a life that was dictated by nature instead of the engineer's idea of 'progress'. Young Fanny and her peedie foal would see to that.

It happened on a late May morning. A Saturday morning. I remember that because Minnie wasn't at school, both of us having stayed overnight at Cuddy Neuk to allow our parents to enjoy a rare Friday evening together at one of the dances Dad used to organise in the Gullane village hall, raising funds for the local junior football team which he helped to run. It was early, a mist hanging lazily on the brow of the monument hill. We had just got out of bed when Big Jim rushed into the bedroom, fixing the straps of his dungarees over his shoulders, patently agitated, a strangely dark look on his face.

'Now, don't you pair even *think* about coming outside!' he barked at us. 'Just bloody well stay where ye are, right!'

Minnie and I looked at each other, thunder-struck, even a bit scared. We had never known Jim to speak like that to us before. These were the first harsh words that we'd heard him utter, to anyone, ever. What had we done to deserve this? Feeling both confused and hurt, we ran to the window as he slammed the back door behind him. Outside, Grandfather was getting out of his little black Ford Eight as another car swept into the yard and crunched to a halt. A man with a small leather case got out and quickly followed Grandfather and Jim to the stable, where Granny was standing just inside the door. Their expressions were strained, their movements hurried.

'It's just Fanny havin' her baby,' my sister assured me after a few moments.

But I sensed from her frown and from the anxious look in her eyes as she stared over the yard towards the stable that, subconsciously, instinctively, Minnie knew that something was wrong. My thoughts returned to the vision of pain and struggle which the drama of Daisy's calving had stamped indelibly on my mind.

'She'll be fine,' I said without thinking, and also without conviction. 'Just the waters breakin'. Fanny and the wee foal will be fine now.'

After a while, Granny and Jim emerged from the stable with the stranger, none speaking, their faces ashen and distraught, their heads bowed. The stranger handed Granny the towel with which he had been drying his hands and arms, then got into his car. A few quiet words were exchanged, then he drove out of the yard, slowly, no sign now of the rush that marked his arrival.

Grandfather buried Fanny and her foal in a grave at the side of the drying green, near the house, where he would always see from the kitchen window the two apple trees he planted by their heads. Those trees are still there, old and bent by the wind now, leaning into the yard, their branches reaching towards the stable door. It had been a breech presentation, we heard them saying. Minnie and I didn't understand what that meant, of course. But we knew that, because of it, both Fanny and her foal had died. Grandfather never mentioned it, never once showed any outward sign of the hurt that he must have been feeling. But even as young children, we realised that Fanny's death had meant much more to him than just the passing of a friend. For him it was also the end of a way of life that he cherished more than anything.

Here are some lines that my father wrote at the time –

YOUNG FANNY'S ELEGY
– With apologies to Burns –
(The following verse concerns a prize mare owned by Mr Tom Muir of 'Cuddy Neuk', West Garleton, by Haddington ...)

*The partridge and the ramblin' hare*
*On Garleton's braes besport nae mair*
*Wi' lightsome hearts; instead they bear*
*A heavy heid.*

*They've lost a friend – a bonny mare:*
*Young Fanny's deid.*

*A finer mare would ne'er be got*
*Between the reins o' plough or float;*
*And no for gold could she be bought*
*A show to lead.*
*Her value now, alas, is nought,*
*For Fanny's deid.*

*From Orkney came her forebears' strain,*
*Where horse are bred to plough and chain.*
*'Twas there Tam Muir had aye his ain*
*Big strappin' steed:*
*And such a one, wi' flowin' mane,*
*Was Fanny – deid.*

*On Garleton's slopes she played her part*
*Wi' zealous pride, more zealous heart;*
*Doon heavy fur's she aye did face*
*Wi' youthful speed,*
*And ne'er a hoof put oot o' place*
*Did Fanny – deid*

*The mornin's sun, or drizzlin' wet,*
*Will greet no more Tam's horse and pet:*
*The noble beast, still-foal did get,*
*And broke the thread.*
*No cheer for Tam Muir, so bereft –*
*Poor Fanny's deid.*

CHAPTER FIVE

## THE DEVIL OF MONUMENT HILL

Buying a farm during a world war, the successful conclusion of which was still far from certain, could be regarded as being either a tad foolhardy or exceptionally shrewd; depending, I suppose, on the eventual outcome of that war, and then with the benefit of hindsight. But, driven by either impetuosity or astuteness (or maybe a combination of both), in 1944 that's exactly what our grandfather did. As far as he was concerned, the realities of farming viability had always dictated that he would have to procure a much bigger place than Cuddy Neuk sooner or later. He opted for sooner, the uncertainties of war tilting the scales of risk in his favour, as he saw it. Land values were depressed. He bought the farm of Morham Braes, 185 acres or thereby, as the ad in *The Scottish Farmer* newspaper stated, for the princely sum of £3,000. The neighbouring Morham Home Farm, a much larger spread with a gracious Georgian farmhouse, could have been bought instead for only £7,000. But Orcadian sagacity (and perhaps a nervous bank manager)

94

limited the 'gamble' to the purchase of the more modest of the two farms.

As Morham Braes was almost six miles distant and on the opposite side of Haddington, Grandfather's inclination now was to relinquish the tenancy of Cuddy Neuk. Transporting implements back and forth between the two farms would be impractical, he reckoned, and equipping each unit separately would be both too expensive and would result in inefficient use of the implements involved. Fortunately, Big Jim disagreed. His considered opinion was that fifty acres *was* fifty acres after all, and, while hardly likely to be profitable on its own in normal times, the Cuddy Neuk land would provide a much-needed addition to Morham Braes' 185 acres – still only a marginally viable amount of land in an area where 400 acres was considered the optimum. And so it was decided – we would give up the little house in Gullane and move to Cuddy Neuk when my grandparents and Jim took over the larger farm. The equipment problem would be partly solved, for the short term at least, by a compromise. A 'skeleton' inventory comprising the old Fordson tractor (suitably patched up), a trailer, a plough, a land roller and a set of harrows would be left at Cuddy Neuk, and whatever other implements might be required from time to time would be 'borrowed' from Morham Braes.

Interesting times beckoned. Even as children, Minnie and I sensed the excitement that this speculative expansion of the farm business was generating. Grandfather obviously wasn't a man to let the grass grow under his feet, although that admirable trait was to give him the fright of his life when he did eventually begin farming Morham Braes. But there was still plenty to do that summer before taking over at Morham on 28 November, the date of the beginning of the Martinmas Term, traditionally the day when farm-workers in Scotland would be engaged for a six-month 'term' of employment, but also a favoured entry date for the new proprietors when farms were changing hands.

First there was hay to make – all too often a chancy operation in Scotland's unpredictable summers. While timing is of the essence, and an inbuilt sense of forthcoming weather invaluable (though invariably unreliable!), good luck is still the most prized gift that any hay-maker could wish for. Lady Luck and her friend the sun certainly looked as if they'd be smiling on the Cuddy Neuk hayfield that summer. Before operations could commence, however, the old horse-drawn mower first had to be converted for towing behind a tractor.

There was a blacksmith's shop, a smiddy, in every village and at many crossroads in those days, the nearest to Cuddy Neuk being in the hamlet of Athelstaneford, about three miles away on the eastern flanks of the Garleton Hills. Having lashed the mower's horse-yoking shaft to the back of the little Allis-Chalmers with a rope, Big Jim set gingerly off, the mower rattling and slewing about behind, its metal wheels crunching and squealing over the tarmac, the lethally pointed fingers of its cutter bar raised vertically for the safety of other road users. As if it weren't difficult enough to control this highly suspect coupling of machinery, Jim had yielded to my pestering to be allowed to go with him, and had seated me on his lap.

'Fancy a go at drivin', Wee Pete?' he said, having eventually found a slowish forward speed that minimised the mower's erratic movements.

I never needed to be asked this question twice. So, with

a four-year-old at the wheel and his laid-back uncle on the pedals and gears, the Allis-Chalmers proceeded steadily eastwards along the twisting road towards Athelstaneford. Jim lit up a cigarette as we skirted Giant Hill.

'Fancy a drag o' the fag, Wee Pete?' he asked, offering me his Capstan.

I was too delightedly preoccupied with 'driving' the tractor on a public road to answer. Plus, I hadn't forgotten my earlier 'lucky' pipe experience in the Cuddy Neuk kitchen, and I didn't relish the prospect of making an infantile fool of myself in front of my hero uncle again *quite* so soon. I'd get to grips with the technical intricacies of smoking eventually, I was sure, but for the moment I'd concentrate on mastering one manly skill at a time. I steered the Allis-Chalmers studiously. Jim chuckled knowingly, flicking his cigarette ash into the slipstream with a deft popping of his fingers. This was another art I'd have to master one day. That seemed to be the trouble with life, I began to conclude – the older you get, the more there is to learn. It was a daunting thought then, but still seems as valid to me today!

Away to our left, the lush agricultural plain of East Lothian rolled gently down over field and farmstead to the sea, the coastal villages of Aberlady and Gullane picked out by the June sunlight as smudges of red-over-white on the edge of a vast canvas of soft summer hues. Grey warships of the Royal Navy, ever exercising for battles still to come, stalked and circled each other on the still waters of the Firth of Forth. From this distance, the great ships looked like tiny lead toys gliding slowly over a sheet of glass. But we could see the explosions of white smoke bursting from their guns, followed by a menacing, distant rumble. Those were no toys.

Although the gentle landscape unfolding before us lay as sleepily peaceful as ever, the big East Lothian skies above were as busy as the sea with reminders that any impression of peace was purely superficial. From our elevated position it was easy on a clear morning like this to see Drem Airfield, some three miles to the north. Down there, processions of Mosquitos, so far away that they looked like twin-engined flies, practised take-offs and landings on the long grass runway, while thousands of feet above, the exhausts of a dozen Spitfires scribbled vapour trail graffiti across the sky as their young pilots engaged in mock dogfights with their chums. It may have looked, from the ground, like wizard sport for the chaps, except that at any moment the sound of sirens could herald the real thing, and a few of these trainee heroes might be soaring to an even higher place – forever.

Above us and to our right, the tree-cloaked slopes of Byres Hill climbed steeply to the summit, from which rose the lofty stone finger of the Hopetoun monument, only its cup-and-saucer top visible above the dense woods from this angle. The musty smell of leaf mould filled the air, that attractively dank odour of deciduous woodland, spiced here by the tang of whin bushes which flecked the hillside with gold where tree gives way to pasture. Without warning, the twittering of birdsong was silenced by a deafening mechanical scream, and we looked up to see a Spitfire playfully 'dive-bombing' the monument. We instinctively ducked as its pilot levelled the plane out at treetop height, then treated us to a hedge-skimming barrel roll while he sped homeward to Drem.

'Bloody maniacs, these guys,' Jim grunted. 'Bunch o' stark ravin' loonies, the lot o' them.'

There was a slight hint of admiration in the way Jim had made that lightly disparaging comment, and I was about to find out why. As we approached a crossroads, the first vehicle we had seen since setting out from home came broadsiding at full tilt round the corner. It was a little open-top MG roadster, late-1930s model, British racing green and immaculate. Biggles was at the wheel. Oh yes, it was Biggles all right – I could tell by the flowing white silk scarf, leather bomber jacket and vintage goggles. The only concession to non-Biggledom was the headgear – a loudly chequered cap instead of the fictional flying ace's distinctive leather helmet. Big Jim stood on the tractor's brake and clutch pedals and knocked the gear stick into neutral. The little MG came skidding to a dust-raising halt alongside us.

'Hey, hi there, Jimbo!' Biggles breezed, raising his goggles Rommel-style over the skip of his cap. 'One of yours?' he enquired, jerking a nod in my direction while smoothing his luxuriant mouzer with kid-gloved forefinger and thumb.

'Nah, nah, Humph,' Jim chuckled, 'this is Wee Pete – sister's sprog. Strictly not guilty for producing any bairns, me.'

'You disappoint me, old chum. Been firing blanks from your old Spitfire, have you? Arf! Arf!' he guffawed, seal-style. 'Hell's bells, that'll never do! Hey, tell you what, though – why not mosey on down to Greywalls House in Gullane this Saturday night. We have a, well – a sort of off-base mess for us flyin' wallahs there, y' know. Shipping in a bevy of girlies from Edinburgh this weekend – frisky types – game for a laugh (wink, wink) *and* a few other things. Arf! Arf! Arf!'

Still 'arfing' merrily, Biggles replaced his goggles, crunched his MG into first gear and took off in a swirl of silk scarf, tyre smoke and flying gravel.

'Who's that man?' I asked.

'Him? Oh, just Humphrey Whatsizname – Spitfire

jockey from the 'drome at Drem. Daft as a brush, but a good lad. Likes a good bevvy.'

That was twice the word 'bevvy' had cropped up within a few seconds, and I hadn't grasped its meaning in either case. Big Jim was no help either, replying to my request for elucidation with a shrug and the advice that I'd learn to enjoy them both soon enough. And that, although it was years later before I could understand the significance, was a clue as to why Jim had got to know and, in a certain way, admired those devil-may-care young pilots.

On leaving Orkney to begin his accountancy studies, Jim had moved in with my father's parents in Edinburgh. My mother and father, both of them civil servants at the time and still working in the same department in Edinburgh, thought that young Jim's first taste of city life might be less traumatic if he had a 'home from home' to return to every evening. My father's folks would take him under their wing and look after him until he got over what must have been quite a culture shock. A perfect arrangement ... or so they thought!

Big Jim took to the bright lights of the city like iron filings to a magnet. This was the life. No more would he be trudging behind a horse-drawn plough through gales and sleet in a lonely field in the depths of winter. No more would he be mucking out stinking cattle sheds with a fork while the makers of the muck were lying chewing the cud in a sunny field. No more would he be leaving a cosy bed in the middle of the night to hand milk cows by the light of a storm lantern in a draughty byre. No, for Jim the city with all its decadent distractions and temptations was just what the doctor ordered. And so what if his studies were suffering? Time enough to concentrate on them once he'd let his hair down for a while. God knows he deserved to grab some serious big town high jinks after spending the first eighteen years of his life on a farm. That was his attitude, and he indulged himself with a vengeance.

The outbreak of war and Jim's consequent return to the farm and family home may have put an end to his profligate ways in Edinburgh, but it didn't dull his taste for a way of social life that he'd now become accustomed to. The trouble was that there wasn't much of *la dolce vita* to be found in the sleepy old East Lothian countryside … unless you were in with those daredevil young pilots, that is. They all lived for today, for the simple reason that they never knew if they'd see tomorrow, and that outlook suited Jim just fine. And who could blame him? He was young and healthy, he worked damned hard, there was a war on, and if he could live it up occasionally with fun-seeking people of his own generation, why shouldn't he? So, whether in the opulence of Greywalls, one of Gullane's finest houses, which had been requisitioned by the RAF for the off-duty comfort of its flying chaps, or in the officers' mess at the aptly named Macmerry Airfield near Tranent, or even at a 'knees-up' in any one of several pubs favoured by his new-found chums, young Jimbo got his kicks. There was only one snag, though. Even modest hedonism costs money, and as he was living with and working for parents for whom financial prudence was of necessity second nature, no such extravagance would be entertained. Nor, given the modest wages which his father paid him, could Jim afford to keep up with Humph 'Biggles' Whatsizname and his well-off mates in any case. But where there's a will there's usually a way. Jim certainly had the will, and it would emerge that he didn't have much trouble in finding ways either.

Set amid rich, open farmland, Athelstaneford is a tiny settlement which, apart from a clutch of relatively modern houses on the periphery, hasn't changed in centuries. Pretty little stone cottages snuggle beneath red-pantile roofs and face each other across the grass-bordered road which passes through the village and constitutes its only street. There's a church, a village hall, a primary school and, at that time, there was still a little post office and, of course, the smiddy. Said to have been built originally to house the families who worked on the lands of the surrounding Gilmerton Estate, Athelstaneford's drowsy timelessness does, however, conceal a much more dramatic past. The names of close-at-hand places like Camptoun and the Chesters bear witness to what must have been a considerable Roman presence in the area, and the ruins of other more recent forts overlook the village and its approaches from the ancient highway which once ran along the Garleton Ridge that dominates the horizon to the south.

Although not flauntingly publicised and therefore attracting little in the way of tourist interest, Athelstaneford is considered by many historians to be the birthplace of the Scottish nation, no less. In the ninth century, this was the scene of a fierce encounter between a great invading army of Saxons and the 'hopelessly outnumbered' forces of the native Picts and Scots. There were no aircraft vapour trails in those distant days (as far as we know!), yet a white St Andrew's Cross did appear in the blue sky high above the village on the morning of battle. Taking this to be an omen, the Picts and Scots swore then to embrace Andrew as their patron saint should they be granted victory over the enemy. Athelstan, the Saxon king, was eventually slain near a ford over the nearby burn, his army was routed, and the Saltire, with its diagonal white cross over a blue ground, was duly adopted as the national flag of Scotland.

More pragmatic matters were on the minds of the blacksmith and his motley assembly of customers on the June morning that Big Jim and I drove up on the little Allis-Chalmers, however. Not only was every smiddy the implement-repair and horseshoeing centre for its surrounding farming community, but it was also a hive of male gossip and banter to rival the most tittle-tattling of ladies' hairdressing salons. And now that the tractor was starting to compete with the horse for the smith's skilled attentions, ostensibly good-humoured barbs were increasingly directed back and forth between the members of both camps while they passed the time of day waiting their turn by the smiddy door.

'Where the hell d'ye get the poofy-lookin' yoke, son?' was the pithy greeting fired at Big Jim by one old pipe-puffing horseman, leaning against the smiddy wall while one of his Clydesdales was being shod by a farrier lad. 'Christ, Ah wouldnae see ma pair o' horse deid in a field beside the likes o' yon!'

If, as he claimed, he cared for little else about farming, Jim did like tractors and was particularly proud of the two new ones which had recently arrived at Cuddy Neuk.

'Fresh in from America, Shug,' he said, patting the Allis-Chalmers' rounded nose. 'Latest model.'

Shug bent down to retie one of his nicky-tams, pieces of twine tied just below the knee to keep the cuffs of a horseman's trousers out of the mud, and (although no self-respecting farmhand would own up to it) to prevent fieldmice from running up his legs. 'Aye, latest model, right enough,' he scoffed, spitting a tobacco-coloured gob out of the corner of his mouth without removing his pipe. 'Latest model, bucket o' shite!'

'Could pull the arse-end off that couple o' moth-eaten nags o' yours, anyway. Aye, and that's wi' the brakes on!'

'Away an' boil yer heid, laddie!' another hoary old horseman chipped in from his lounging position against the wheel of his cart. 'Ah've yet tae see the tractor as could match a horse for grip in the dirt an' glaur, never mind yer pullin' power. What the fuck's the point in a' yer pullin' power if ye havenae got the grip? Just tell me that, eh – smert-ersed young bugger!'

His pal Shug immediately agreed with him, and Jim left the two worthies to cement their joint loathing of tractors while he went into the forge to explain to the blacksmith what he wanted done to the drawbar of the hay mower.

'Nae bother, freend,' said the smith without need to even glance up from the nugget of white-hot metal which he was hammering on his anvil. 'Stub pole instead o' the horse pole. Easy. Come back the morn's mornin' an' it'll be ready for ye.'

Back outside, old Shug and his crony were now engaged in heated and foul-languaged debate with another tractor – *not* with the tractorman, who had wisely headed off to the post office to buy a packet of fags, but with the tractor itself.

'Look at ye!' spluttered Shug, running disapproving eyes over the defenceless machine. 'Stinkin', greasy lump o' scrap! An' what's a' this ten horsepower, twelve horsepower shite? Ah wouldnae give *one* fuckin' Clydesdale for any amount o' yer mingin' paraffin horses!'

Shug's pal nodded in unassailable agreement. 'Bastard!'

he grunted at the tractor, then delivered a hefty hobnailed kick to its back wheel. 'Dirty, oil-pissin' bastard!'

King Athelstan had probably had it easy in comparison to the doing which that poor machine was about to get.

Big Jim hauled me aboard the Allis-Chalmers and made swift our departure while the going was good. We made swift our return journey too, the little tractor 'goin' like shit off a shovel', as Jim put it, now that it was no longer encumbered by the old mower. But our progress was halted abruptly as we rounded the last bend at the foot of Byres Hill. There, by the gateway to the woods, were two of our neighbours, Dick and Joyce, waving frantically at us to stop. Dick farmed a little spread at Blackmains just over the rise on the way to Haddington, while Joyce's old father Frank had a little one-field holding next door. Joyce, in her early twenties and a real tomboy who could work and curse along with the best of the farm men, earned a living by helping her father or any other of the small farmers in the vicinity who needed a hand. On this occasion she had been assisting Dick herd a few calves down the road, when they heard a commotion coming from the direction of the monument on top of Byres Hill.

'Fair set the hairs standin' on the back o' ma heid,' declared Dick, never one to underplay a dramatic situation. What Dick lacked in height, he more than made up for in his ability to make a tall story (and a long one) out of the most insignificant of happenings. He'd have been about fifty then, his long top lip and sparkly little beads of eyes giving his face a mischievous, elf-like appearance beneath the peak of the essential *fermer's* bunnet which, like my grandfather's, he was never seen without. 'Terrible howlin' an' roarin', it was – just like the Devil himsel', it sounded like tae me!'

'No half,' said Joyce, forsaking her usual 'Dinnae talk

such bloody tripe!' response to Dick's frequent overstatements. 'Tellin' ye, Jim – near scared the breeks off me!'

John, our nearest neighbour at Cuddy Neuk, had just arrived on the scene, his eyes lighting up on hearing Joyce's last statement. Unmarried and living with his spinster sister, John was a quiet man, old-fashioned, unsophisticated and shy, and totally dedicated to working his little farm. He also fancied Joyce something rotten and would doubtless have dreamed many times of getting the breeks off her, if only he had the know-how and courage. Joyce used to chaff him mercilessly.

'An' dinnae you be getting' any horny ideas,' she told him on noticing the glint in his eye. She nudged Big Jim with her elbow. 'He widnae ken how tae tackle a nice fanny even if it jumped oot o' his porridge in the mornin', eh no?'

Jim smirked as John blushed and Dick studied his feet while forcing out an embarrassed cough. Just then, a hollow-sounding bellow echoed down through the trees.

'There it goes again,' whispered Dick, moving close to Jim as he stared pop-eyed at the monument high above. 'Just like the Devil himsel'!'

I felt a shiver run down my spine. I gripped the sleeve of Jim's jacket. 'It's the giant,' I warbled. 'Him that steals the monument durin' the night.'

If I needed any further convincing, Joyce drew our attention to the rocky outcrop of Giant Hill rising up only a few paces behind us. 'First time I've heard o' the big bugger comin' out durin' the day, though.'

'Nah, nah. Old wives' tale,' Jim pooh-poohed, realising that Joyce was trying to wind me up, and remembering what the consequences might be. Taking no chances, he instructed me to have a pee in the hedge-back. We'd be going up the hill to see what was making all the racket, and he didn't want any 'accidents' if we happened to encounter something scary. Not that he expected to, he added. John headed back home to fetch his shotgun – just in case.

It's a stiff climb up Byres Hill, particularly with the short legs of a four-year-old, so I had to be dragged up the tricky bits between Jim and Joyce, my feet hardly touching the ground at times. Never having been up the hill before, the first thing that struck me when we eventually cleared the woods near the summit was how awesome the monument is close up. Its cylindrical stone bulk looms over you in a menacing sort of way, the strange feeling of threat exaggerated on this occasion by the clouds above it drifting away in the opposite direction, and giving the impression that the great tower was toppling down on us. We hadn't heard the weird noise since starting our climb, and I deeply hoped that whatever monster had made it had gone on its way in the meantime. I could see that Dick and Joyce shared my feelings of trepidation, glancing nervously about as they were. The three of us froze in our footsteps as a mighty roar reverberated round the clearing.

'It's comin' from inside the monument,' Jim said, striding ahead. 'You guys stay here and I'll go and check it out.'

'Maybe ye'd better wait till John comes wi' his twelve-bore,' said Dick, stepping behind a whin bush.

Joyce and I joined him as the roar rang out again, seeming eerily amplified and distorted as it escaped the slits built into in the monument's stonework to lend some light to the narrow spiral staircase inside. My heart was in my mouth. I genuinely feared for Big Jim's safety. He disappeared through the doorway at the tower's base, and the monster bellowed again.

'Maybe it's a dragon,' I said to Joyce, my voice quivering with terror. 'Maybe it's eaten Big Jim.'

'Naw, Jim'll be OK, never fear,' she replied unconvincingly. 'No dragon wi' any taste would take a bite out o' yon big arsehole.' Joyce had a comforting way with words.

'He's takin' a long time,' said Dick, glancing anxiously at his pocket watch. 'Maybe we should go an' fetch the polis.'

'Just you stay put, feardie breeks,' Joyce told him. 'Women an' children first, remember? C'mon, Wee Pete – let's get the hell outta here!'

Our retreat was nipped in the bud by the arrival of John.

'What's happenin'?' he panted, clambering up from the depths of the woods, shotgun at the ready. 'Where's Jim?'

'Inside the monument,' said Dick. 'Ye'd better go an' see how he's getting' on.'

John cast him a 'get-stuffed' look and took up station behind us. Just then, we heard another roar – but this time it was unmistakably Jim's voice blasting out from one of the slits in the monument's masonry …

'Ye dirty bugger!' he yelled. 'I'll cut yer bloody throat!'

A couple of moments later he reappeared in the doorway, the front of his dungarees smeared in what looked suspiciously like fresh cattle dung – green, slimy and evidently smelly.

'It's a bloody cow!' he shouted, holding his nose while grabbing a divot of grass to wipe the clinging muck off his clothes.

'A *coo*?' exclaimed Dick, stepping out from behind the whin bush in a sudden rush of bravery. 'Up the stairs?'

'Yeah – halfway up the monument. Jammed solid, she is. I tried pullin' her back down by the tail, and *this* is what I got for my trouble. Filthy hoor skittered all over me!'

This was proving to be a highly educational day for me, my knowledge of the proper use of swear words being enhanced considerably. And there was more to come.

'Did ye try shovin' her up the way?' John meekly enquired.

'He said she's jammed solid, ye dingly eejit!' Joyce snapped. 'Like the plumber says, ye cannae stuff a six-inch shite through a four-inch pipe!'

'And ye'll never get her tae come backwards doon the stairs,' opined Dick. 'No keen on walkin' backwards doon stairs, coos.'

Jim shook his head. 'Nah, we'll never shift her.'

'Cannae just leave the poor beast there,' John said. 'Better send for the fire brigade.'

'Aye, and the vet,' said Dick. 'Put her oot o' her misery.'

But Big Jim had other ideas, and neither the fire brigade nor the vet featured in them. Joyce was to take me back down the hill, drive me home on the tractor, make sure I went into the house and stayed there, then hitch up a trailer and come back smartish with certain 'tools' on board. He didn't specify what tools he meant, but a nod and a wink to Joyce seemed to get his message across. We heard a muffled 'bang' coming from the direction of the monument when we were halfway down the hill, but no more ghastly bellowing, no more spooky roaring.

The episode of the cow stuck up the monument was never mentioned again, not even when her owner turned up in the Cuddy Neuk yard the next day asking Jim if he'd seen a stray Friesian thereabouts lately. But it was an open secret within the Garleton Hills community that certain neighbouring families had dined well on beef for several weeks thereafter – the Cuddy Neuk household included. And it was a foregone conclusion that a few juicy joints would have been converted into hard cash on the black market to subsidise the architect of the caper's occasionally prodigal lifestyle.

Dick's 'devil', as the proverb goes, had apparently looked after his own.

## CHAPTER SIX

## THE NOISY PASSING OF A QUIET WAY OF LIFE

Our grandparents' final summer at Cuddy Neuk turned out to be a good one. Grandfather's early morning tapping and checking of his trusty barometer in the front hallway confirmed what he 'felt in his water' about a settled spell of June weather, allowing haymaking to be tackled in near perfect conditions. Following Fanny's untimely death, he had bought another horse from a dealer he chanced to meet at Haddington Auction Mart. Duke was a young Clydesdale with a truly noble head, a confident, almost cocky look in his eye, and a lustrous brown coat which Grandfather kept so beautifully groomed that he claimed he could shave his face in it in the morning. Duke was indeed a strikingly handsome animal, and he knew it, picking up his white-feathered legs with real style, whether trotting freely round his paddock or putting in a hard day's work in the field.

Now that the old mower had been converted for towing behind the tractor, Duke's services weren't required in the hay field until after the hay was made. After cutting and being left to wilt for a couple of days, manpower was what was required to flip the hay over so that the underside of the swath was exposed in turn to the drying warmth of the sun. Tractor-hauled mechanical 'tedders' and hay spreaders were already being used for this purpose on some of the larger farms, but at Cuddy Neuk the traditional method was still the order of the day. And when there were four or five acres of a heavy hay crop to turn and scatter, it meant that a lot of pitchforks had to be brought into play – a labour-intensive operation involving every available pair of hands. Neighbours like John, Dick and Joyce were willing volunteers, knowing that the favour would be returned without question. Even some of the men from nearby big farms would lend their services for a few hours whenever their bosses' work schedules permitted. Time, as ever, was of the essence as long as the sun shone on the hay field. All country folk knew that, and a spirit of keen co-operation prevailed.

Young kids like Minnie and me would have been more of a hindrance than a help, even if we'd wanted to get involved, which we'd probably been strongly advised against anyway. Flipping over thick wads of long grass looked easy enough when being done by a line of expert forkers, but it was hard work too, particularly when the hay was still 'raw'. Not a job for children. But we had our uses, nonetheless. Working folk need to be fed, and the thirst which comes with toiling away in perfect haymaking weather has to be regularly quenched. In the days before fridges and freezers became taken-for-granted items in every farmhouse kitchen, a bucket of drinking water was somehow kept cool, in the absence of ice cubes, by the curious practice of sprinkling a scattering of oatmeal over the surface. My sister and I didn't have the strength to lug full pails of water all the way from the house to the field, of course, but we could just about cope with a couple of billycans apiece, and by maintaining a fairly steady shuttle service managed to satisfy demand. At mealtimes, or at 'minute' time mid-morning and mid-afternoon, our mother and grandmother would accompany us, carrying baskets of freshly made sandwiches and flasks of sweet, piping hot tea. Just how the latter has a refreshing effect on an already overheated human body is another of those perplexing mysteries, but it does, and the sugar content of the brew gives an instant energy boost into the bargain. Clever country commodities, oatmeal cold water and sugary hot tea. And the stronger the better, as far as the tea was concerned. 'No bliddy use unless thoo can race spiders on it,' was Grandfather's firm judgement.

Nellie the collie regarded haymaking time as one of her favourite periods on the farming calendar. It was a suitably busy time for an incurable workaholic like her. She was always there when the mower was slicing through the last strip of standing hay in the field. She knew from experience that there was every chance that a hare (a complete cretin of a creature, in her opinion) would be lying in there, confused and terrified, as the reciprocating knife of the cutter bar rattled ever closer to its defenceless lair. And Nellie was lightning-quick to give chase at the long-awaited moment when the hapless animal burst forth from the last square yard of sanctuary. She never caught the hare, though. Stupid as the hare may have been, it was smart enough and, more importantly, fast enough to outmanoeuvre and outrun Nellie as it made its zigzag dash for the cover of a convenient hedgerow. But in her own mind Nellie was doubtless convinced that she had done a good job. She had seen off an interloper – just one of the many jobs that a diligent mistress of all trades had to see to in the course of an industrious day.

She was an ever-present in the field during hay turning operations as well; head lowered, barking at every inverted swath and paying scant regard for the points of pitchforks flashing past her nose. There might just be a rabbit or a field mouse or two lurking under there, and she'd be the one to show them a clean set of teeth. But she never caught a rabbit or a mouse either. Pathetic vermin of ludicrously sub-collie IQs they certainly would have been in Nellie's view, but they weren't so daft as to hang about waiting when a dog barking loudly enough to be heard a mile away was on their case.

But all that essential work makes a dog hungry too, so Nellie made sure that she took a break with the rest of the labour force whenever sandwich baskets arrived on the scene. And what better place for man or dog to take rest and sustenance than sitting on a windrow of fragrant, almost-cured hay on a balmy summer's evening? You could almost hear the warm rays of the sun doing Nature's work to help make safe the forthcoming winter's supply of fodder; pale golden blades of the drying grass rustling and crackling beneath bottoms shuffling to make a comfortable cushion on which to enjoy a welcome respite. Without the invasive clatter, roar and smell of machinery to assault our senses, we were sitting once more in a scene that had been repeated unchanged at haymaking time through the centuries. Even the pervasive growl and howl of distant aircraft engines was curiously hushed. Quietly exchanged words and the occasional burst of laughter as someone cracked a pawky joke were the only sounds to compete with the animated chattering of sparrows in the hawthorn hedges along the old road and the lazy cawing of crows flying home to roost in the tall trees of Byres Hill.

Over the watery expanse of the Firth of Forth and its spreading hinterlands, the June sun is never in a hurry to set. It seems to hang blazing red and motionless in a sky that will reflect that same warm light till morning. For on midsummer nights, the sun only dips behind the distant hills of Fife for an hour or two, before rising again from the shimmering waters of the North Sea at an hour when only insomniacs and poachers are yet awake. And in early evening the heat seems to intensify as the sun arcs almost imperceptibly towards the western horizon – a time when hay-makers bless the smile of Lady Luck, while wiping sweat from tanned brows and dipping enamel mugs into a bucket of cooling water.

It was time now to finish 'rowing up' the crop for the night, said Grandfather, first on his feet to start working again, as usual. Gathered into windrows, as much of the hay as possible would be protected from the falling dew at sunset. And tomorrow, once the warmth of the morning sun had dispelled that dampness, the next crucial stage of the routine would begin. This was when Duke would be called upon at last to earn his corn, albeit while engaged in one of the most pleasant tasks of the year – as long as the weather held, that is. Sitting atop a horse rake, a malicious-looking contraption comprising a row of claw-like tines with a big metal wheel at either end, Grandfather coaxed Duke along each windrow, pulling a lever to deposit small heaps, or 'huts', of accumulated hay every so often. Next day, Duke was yoked to an old-fashioned hay sweep, a simple tool, attached to the horse's harness by means of two chains, and with long, horizontal teeth which skidded over the ground to gather several huts together. These were then deposited at convenient points throughout the field, there to be piled into larger ricks to complete the curing process of the hay. The curved sides of these 'kyles', as they're called locally, were carefully raked to help shed any rain which might fall in the meantime. But, rare though it was, there were no such weather worries that year. Soon, the kyles would be loaded onto trailers a forkful at a time and carted to the farm, where the hay would be built into larger stacks, thatched with straw and roped down to guard against the ultimate arrival of inclement weather.

Through the eyes of a child, it had all seemed so easy, this haymaking business. But then, I hadn't had to do any of the muscle-busting, back-aching work involved. I hadn't had to face the financial implications of failure. For how different the idyllic-looking job would have been if the weather hadn't been so uncharacteristically benevolent. I'd find out one day how cruel the exposed location of Cuddy Neuk can be at times, and how the summer weather in Scotland can have a scowl as angry as its smile had been kind during that exceptional season, when even Spitfires and Hurricanes hummed a more hopeful tune. Times, and the course of the war, were changing. And so were our lives, though little did we know it then.

★★★★★

In the weeks before haymaking, the Gullane area had been bustling with military activity. The place was buzzing with rumours spawned by 'inside gen' whispered to locals by servicemen and women in hives of gossip like Bisset's bar.

This was all very unusual at a time when national security was paramount, and 'careless talk', particularly by members of the armed forces, was solemnly warned against in government notices posted everywhere. Nevertheless, it soon became an open secret that the influx of wave after wave of extra troops, and flotillas of DUKWs (amphibious transport vehicles nicknamed, logically, 'ducks') landing on Gullane beach were all part of a huge military exercise codenamed 'Fortitude North'. The beach and its 'bents', deep folds of sedge-covered sand dunes that skirt the sweeping foreshore of Gullane Bay, were declared out-of-bounds for civilians during these operations. And the troops, most of them billeted in tents on the grassy links above the dunes, were forbidden in turn to venture into the village. An 'invasion' armada of something like seventy vessels lying at anchor over towards the Fife coast, and the sight of scores of troop-transport gliders being towed by Halifax bombers above the East Lothian shoreline only added to the speculation that something big was afoot. The hush-hush Operation Fortitude North, it eventually leaked out, was a run-through for a forthcoming Allied invasion of Norway that was to spearhead the liberation of Scandinavia.

It ultimately transpired, however, that the spread of such rumours had all been encouraged as part of a skilfully orchestrated propaganda campaign intended to dupe the opposition into maintaining their large military presence in Scandinavia. The Allies were, in fact, preparing for an incursion hundreds of miles further south. Operation Fortitude North had really been a massive dress rehearsal for the D-Day landings in Normandy on 6 June 1944, a bold action that was to turn the tide of the war in Europe. And, to the credit of the military strategists, the beaches of

Northern France turned out to be remarkably similar to those of Gullane Bay. So much so, indeed, that one veteran of the campaign is on record as saying that, despite the fearsome realities of combat, he and many of his comrades could almost imagine that they were still clambering over the Gullane 'bents', harbouring thoughts of sneaking away to Bisset's for a sly beer or two at the end of the day.

Back in Britain, although an early restoration of peace was still far from a foregone conclusion, the threat of the country being invaded was receding by the week, and a welcome feeling of optimism was in the air. By the time the grain harvest was in full swing in early September, it was beginning to look increasingly as if Grandfather might well be proven right in having made the decision to buy the larger farm of Morham Braes. The oat crop, because of its later maturing, was the last of the cereal varieties to be cut, and with the shortening of the days was always liable to be the trickiest to harvest successfully. But the Fates looked favourably upon the Cuddy Neuk slopes yet again that year. Grandfather didn't think the good weather had anything to do with alien mythical goddesses, however. According to him, we were being looked after by the farm's very own hogboon, a benevolent little spirit fellow who had followed him down from Orkney to live under one of the knolls on the hill field. Naturally, Minnie and I believed him, and actually went so far as following his advice to pour milk on one particular hill field mound as a reward. Though the continued fair harvesting conditions were proof enough that our gesture had been appreciated by the hogboon, to our deep disappointment he never did make an appearance to thank us in person.

'Dinna thoo ever forget tae give him a sup o' milk when

things are goin' weel, mind,' Grandfather told me. 'And the peedie hogboon will never let thee doon.'

Once the barley was safely 'in' and stacked at the farm awaiting the autumn arrival of the travelling threshing mill, the old reaper-binder was greased up for the last time that summer. Before its conversion by the Athelstaneford blacksmith, the binder – to give it its more commonly-used abbreviated name – had required two horses to pull it, but now its newly adapted drawbar could only be yoked to a tractor, like the old hay mower and an ever increasing range of ex-horse implements on so many farms.

In those days, before the widespread use of combine harvesters had become established, and suitable earlier-maturing varieties of oats had been bred, the practice was to cut the crop with a binder while the straw was still slightly 'green', and allow the heads to complete their ripening in the stook. This speeded up the maturing process, reduced the risk of the grains shedding prematurely, and saved valuable time when the onset of autumn weather was rapidly approaching. Miss a harvesting opportunity now and you could easily find yourself struggling for weeks to save a sodden crop laid flat by wind and rain. Grandfather knew better than most farmers in East Lothian about that potential nightmare. With the shorter summers of Orkney, all too often he'd had to battle the Sanday elements with some of his oat crop still uncut and lying rotting on the ground as late as November. Even peedie hogboon's have their limitations, it seems.

I can appreciate now how men of our grandparents' generation must have felt the first time they saw a tractor instead of horses hauling the binder. For me back then, it was an exciting experience, a chance to watch an innovation in action; walking alongside the tractor, feeling the heat of its engine on my face, smelling the whiff of its burnt paraffin fuel, hearing the groaning whine of its engine over the rattling of the binder. For a small boy it was a delight. But, for Grandfather and his contemporaries, it would have seemed like just another nail in the coffin of a cherished way of life – a reflective time, made more sufferable, perhaps, by the knowledge that the advance of new technology would eventually improve the farmer's lot. Ah, but would it? Indeed, has it? Whatever the answer to that, there are still old farm men alive today who yearn for a return to traditional ways. A forlorn hope? Almost certainly. A dream sweetened by the passing of too many years? It may be. But, for all the physical hardships that had to be endured in the days before the internal combustion engine became king of the land, few would doubt that there is still nothing to compare with the magnificent sight of a team of workhorses nodding their heads to the steady rhythm of their step, sure hooves plodding the ground, coats gleaming, harness jingling, muscled legs straining as they pull a binder through a corn field on a fine September day.

Yet, whether the binder was drawn by horse or tractor, man's work in the harvest field remained basically unchanged. Pulled gently over the binder's shuttling reaper blades by the arms of a revolving 'reel', the cut corn was then carried by a series of canvas conveyor belts up to a deck where a system of packers and butters compacted it into a sheaf-sized bundle. Next, another mechanism looped the gathered straw with a length of twine, knotted and cut it, then kicked the bound sheaf out onto the stubble. But all this automated wizardry still had to be overseen and, at certain stages, helped along by someone sitting onboard the binder where the horseman had previously sat.

During the long haymaking days of June, it was always assumed that at least a few neighbours could be counted on to help out, but now, in the less generous daylight hours of September, most were usually too busy trying to complete their own harvest to have time to lend anyone else a hand. So, with Big Jim driving the tractor and Grandfather on the binder, it was up to Granny and Mother to gather up the sheaves and set them into stooks. This was work that, while not particularly heavy, needed to be undertaken with some urgency while the weather held, so our father always tried to wangle as much time off as he could in order to be on hand at this crucial time as well.

The reason for stooking the sheaves quickly was twofold. Firstly, the longer they lay on the stubble, the more they would draw dampness from the earth, and the more they'd be exposed to any dew or rain that might fall overnight. But the main object of the exercise was to raise the heads of the corn into the optimum position for speedy ripening, while also assembling the sheaves in a way that would best shed rainwater. So they'd be set together two-by-two, one bunch of corn heads leaning against the other, four sheaves on either side of a stook of eight. As more and more took shape, they looked just like rows of little straw tents in an ever-expanding camp site, their 'gable' ends open to allow the drying air to flow through. And the direction in which the stooks faced was of real importance too. It wasn't simply a case of grabbing armfuls of sheaves and balancing them together willy-nilly. The ridge of each stook had to point south-to-north, thereby allowing the ears of grain on either side equal exposure to the sun as it traversed the sky during the course of each day. The folk on every farm knew certain prominent features on both horizons which they would use as landmarks to help them judge this essential angle correctly – say a hilltop in one direction, a strip of woodland in the other.

With the whole family engaged in the Cuddy Neuk oat harvest, there was no one in the house to cook meals. So that problem had been solved by taking the food and a little Primus stove into the field when setting forth in the morning. The Primus, a handy kitchen stand-by before the availability of mains electricity and gas in country areas, could best be described as the paraffin-burning forerunner of the bottled gas mini-cookers so popular with campers, trekkers and the likes today. It worked on the same basic principle as the Tilley lamp, in as much as the base (like an upturned bowl) was actually the fuel tank, with either the cooking ring or lighting mantle attached to the top. The pressure required to atomise the paraffin and make it burn efficiently was achieved by the frequent employment of a little hand-pump device set into the base.

My sister and I, whose only contribution to the job in hand had been to play Cowboys and Indians inside and around the stooks – which we took to be as near to being real wigwams as made no difference – were quick enough to take our place beside the adults when harvesting operations drew to a brief halt for the midday *denner*. A previously cooked pot of thick Scotch broth would be re-heated on the Primus stove, while everyone tucked into sandwiches filled with scraps of cold meat, or maybe just spread with butter and jam. These were, and still are, called *pieces* (short for 'pieces of bread', I suppose), the latter variety being known in Scotland as *jeely pieces*, a staple in

122

every workman's and school kid's *piece bag* when leaving
the house in the morning. If Granny or our mother had
had time to bake the previous evening, there might even
be an apple pie or some scones to accompany mugs of tea
or fresh-from-the-cow milk after the soup was finished.
Simple stuff, but wholesome and more enjoyable than the
pricey contents of any highfalutin picnic hamper to hungry
harvesters – *and* their junior hangers-on.

Sitting on sheaves and leaning against the tractor's big
sun-warmed tyres, it felt good to be part of a family's three
generations gathered together in a common cause – the
essential tending of a business, undeniably, but much more
than that as well. Working together and sharing simple food
in a field, be it in fair weather or foul, in summer or in
winter, were as much an embodiment of close family ties
as they were mere prerequisites of a job that *had* to be
done. It was all part of a lifestyle dictated by the cycles and
vagaries of nature, a way of life that depended entirely on
folk's dedication to good husbandry and their common love
of the land. And, needless to say, we were far from alone in
that respect. All around, similar scenes were being played
out on farms large and small, where farmers and farmhands
alike put the safe winning of the harvest before personal
comfort or leisure. That was the rural world in which we
lived, and unwritten rules of survival and co-operation were
adhered to without as much as a second thought. For the
greatest pleasures of all, whether for rich farmer or the
humblest of his hired help, came from taking a pride in his
work, followed by the satisfaction of seeing a good job well
done.

Although we, like others on the smaller farms, were
obliged to get on with the harvest with whatever of our

own family help was available, on many of the large spreads round about, as many as ten families of workers would be involved in the same tasks. And right now, every man and his wife and every one of their children who was big enough and strong enough would be out in the fields playing their part. From where we were sitting waiting for Grandfather, our Dad and Big Jim to finish smoking their post-*denner* ciggies, we could hear just such a team of families working in a field on Byres Farm immediately below us. We couldn't see them for the thick hedges, but we could picture them. Stooking may well have seemed repetitive, monotonous, even boring work to the unacquainted onlooker, but the sounds of banter and raucous laughter drifting over the old road told a different story. Most field jobs that were required to be done manually by squads of workers, whether *singling* turnips, cutting cabbages, turning hay or, indeed, making stooks, could fairly be described as repetitive and may well have become boring if it hadn't been for the company and the often shamelessly raw humour of the participants. I had already become familiar with the strong language that was an integral part of the jokes and jibes that were bounced back and forth between the likes of the old horsemen Big Jim and I had met along at the Athelstaneford smiddy, but hearing it emanating from women's voices was a comparatively new experience. An experience that the gruff guffaws and high-pitched cackles of hilarity rising from the neighbouring field suggested was an enjoyable one for both sexes alike.

'Away an' screw yersels!' one female voice jovially piped. 'Ah wouldnae pee on ye if yer erse wiz on fire!'

The roars and screams of unbridled mirth which then erupted were masked by Granny's shocked reaction.

'Come now, peedie bairnos,' she called to Minnie and me, clambering to her feet and taking us by the hand, 'come you and play away up the field there now.' All of a fluster, she turned then to Big Jim: 'Start up yon tractor again and make a noise. Bless me!' she gasped. 'I never thought to hear such muck from a woman-body's mouth. And in front of her menfolk too!'

Big Jim and I exchanged manly winks as he stood up and carefully stubbed out his cigarette end with the heel of his boot. Such everyday lingo was no big deal to us.

And so the work progressed until the crop was cut and every sheaf stooked. After a week or two, when the grains had been checked for ripeness by 'nipping' a few between the fingernails, the stooks would be dismantled and the sheaves transported to the farm on whatever carts or trailers were available. Then the skilled task of building the sheaves into big, weather-proof stacks would begin – warm, back-aching work in the September sunshine for all the able-bodied men that could be mustered. And urgent work, too, with autumn creeping ever nearer. Yet the long harvesting routine wouldn't be truly over until the corn was threshed by the travelling mill some weeks or even months later. Compared to today – when the same task is completed in one go by a man driving a satellite-linked combine harvester, with another man conveying the grain back to a diesel-fuelled drier in a 'rig' made up of a giant tractor and bulk trailer – the harvesting job of over half a century ago seems unthinkably arduous, labour-intensive and prolonged. But it had its blessings. The countryside was full of people – country people, not the big city commuters who have now taken over most of the farm cottages, and even farmhouses (where two or more farms have been amalgamated in the name of efficiency), from the folk who lived on and worked the land in the way of their forefathers. The countryside was a vibrant place, a busy place, where most of the population could afford few material possessions, but nonetheless enjoyed a healthy outdoor life and the camaraderie of neighbours and workmates of kindred spirit. No one wrote to their local newspaper complaining of the smell of farmyard manure being spread on the fields back then! Dung was the natural food of the soil long before anyone had even thought of the term 'organic'. And so what if it stank to high heaven? That was a sign that it was good, strong stuff – just what a field of hungry land needed.

With the harvest safely 'home', the traditional way of celebrating in southern Scotland, as in most parts of the country, was by organising a *kirn*, or barn dance, usually held in a hayloft above the cart sheds of one of the larger farms in the area. Music would invariably be provided by a ceilidh-type band comprised of an accordionist or two, a fiddler, a drummer, a bass player, and, *if* a heavy upright piano could be manhandled up the narrow outside stairs to the loft, a pianist as well. This was long before the invention of the portable electric keyboard! Like the harvest itself, a kirn was something for the whole family to be involved in, so everyone from the smallest toddler to the oldest codger in the neighbourhood would be there to join in the thanksgiving fun. By the time a dram or two of whisky had been quaffed from discreet quarter bottles by under-age ploughmen, the wooden floor of the loft would be shaking to a hundred feet stomping wildly through 'The Eightsome Reel', 'Strip the Willow', 'The Dashing White Sergeant' and a breathtaking programme of other Scottish country dances well known to all present. Wartime rationing or not, the provision of food for the revellers was never a problem. For weeks in advance of the kirn, the women of every family would have been setting aside enough of the essential ingredients needed to bake a modest donation of cakes, scones, biscuits or pies for the big occasion. Lovers of intoxicating drink were also adequately catered for – on the unlikely off-chance that they hadn't brought their own hip-pocket supplies. Powerful punches, home-brewed beer, and even strange wine-like concoctions made from turnips, or any other fermentable substance that was readily available on a farm, would share the groaning trestle tables with the appetising array of eats. Many's the horse or cattle beast that was tended by the walking dead on the morning after a good-going kirn.

Big Jim turned into just such a zombie on one memorable occasion. Some full-grown Aberdeen Angus bullocks were due to be brought from the field into their winter housing – usually a simple enough operation, provided all relevant gates and doors are either opened or closed in advance. In his woozy, sleepless state Jim unfortunately got it just a wee bit wrong, and Granny just happened to be on the receiving end of his dropped clanger. She was awakened from a rare lie-in by a cold, slimy nose sniffing one of her cheeks, while a rough tongue slobbered the other. Her scream of alarm on opening her eyes to a close-up view of two coal-black bullocks staring at her spooked the poor animals so badly that they turned tail, only to be confronted by their own reflections in the wardrobe mirror. They evidently didn't like what they saw, because they promptly made a mad dash for the door, bellowing as they went and spraying the wallpaper with a stinky brown dapple of digested grass. And as if that hadn't made a big enough mess, Nellie the collie did her superior-intelligence act by chasing the escaping bullocks back into the house for a second bash at interior decorating.

Granny never did own up as to whether her verbal response was limited to the customary 'Bless me!' Jim, conversely, was notably less reticent in admitting what he exclaimed when arriving panting into the bedroom to see what the damage was. He was left in no doubt that the smell of dung, as I had already discovered to my own cost, does indeed improve with distance – just as bullock-shifting while nursing a post-kirn hangover isn't really the brightest of ideas. And anyone who knows how hard it is to remove even fresh grass stains from the knees of a pair of jeans will have just *some* idea of how many coats of white distemper Jim had to slap onto those bedroom walls – and that's after he'd scraped off and bucketed out the extensive range of the bullocks' avant-garde wallpaper patterns.

*****

*Toot, toot, toot!* piped the distant whistle.

'Now then, that'll be them comin' tae get ready for the mornin',' said Grandfather. 'We'll just have time tae hap this load o' neeps afore they arrive. *Tschk! Tschk!* Giddup there, Duke!'

It was almost dusk on what had been a sharp, clear November day. Behind us, the setting sun was projecting our silhouettes into long shadows along the rutted surface of the old road ahead. Grandfather, Big Jim and I were sitting with our legs dangling over the front of the cart, which was heaped high with purple-skinned Swedes. Not Scandinavian people who'd been out too long in the frosty air, I hasten to add, but Swedish turnips, or neeps, as they're known in the fair land of haggis and tatties. Duke pulled us along with an unhurried gait, the shafts of the cart creaking under the weight of the load, the bearings of the big wooden wheels squeaking as they turned, bumping through potholes, lurching over bumps.

'It'll be a fine day the morn,' said Jim, glancing up at the reddening sky while lying back on the neeps and taking a deep, leisurely drag of his fag. 'Aye – fine day for the job, by the looks o' things.'

Whatever, no point in raising your blood pressure about what might happen tomorrow when the completion of today's work is governed by the pace of your horse. Duke was in no hurry, and no one expected him to be. He knew that. Going at any more than a steady plod with a heavy load on a rough old track would do nothing but court the very real danger of landing in the ditch in a heap of neeps, splintered wood, broken limbs and flailing horse hooves. Everybody knew that. Grandfather started to hum 'Comin' Through The Rye' to the rhythm of Duke's unhurried step. *Toot, toot, toot!* piped the distant whistle again, though a little less distant now, and sounding a mite more urgent too. Duke snorted a noteless whinny that you could easily have imagined harboured a certain touch of disapproval. 'What's the hurry?' it seemed to say. 'Take it canny-like and ye'll get there just the same.' Sound advice, straight from the horse's mouth, but an age-old country maxim which 'progress', as symbolised by the approaching whistle, had started to erode irreversibly almost two hundred years before. I doubt if Duke knew that, though.

Just as we rounded the bend at the top of the hill on the main road, we saw a thick plume of black smoke rising above the trees at the Athelstaneford road-end about a quarter of a mile up ahead. Then a couple of puffs of white steam heralded the next *toot, toot!*, which reached us on the still evening air a split second later. Not a word was spoken by Grandfather or Jim, but as young as I was, I could sense their growing feeling of tenseness as we wheeled through the Cuddy Neuk gateway. There was a distinct air of anticipation about them now – even the hint of a need to get a move on, a mood of urgency which had been so palpably absent only a moment before.

'*Wheesh! Hup*, lad!' Grandfather growled, briskly flicking Duke's reins to hasten him up the little rise into the stack yard and beyond to the 'neep pit', the turnip clamp, to which the cart was quickly backed up. The load was duly tipped out onto the open end of the long heap, and the thick 'hap' of straw which would protect the stored neeps from the winter frosts was extended over the top of the newly deposited roots. Job done – and just in time.

There, coming down the road only a hundred yards away now, was the procession of machinery that comprised Messrs R. Wyllie & Sons' travelling threshing mill. And what a spectacular procession it was. It was the first time I'd ever seen the likes of it, and I was as enthralled as any small boy would have been. Leading the grand parade was a mighty steam traction engine, the polished brass 'belts' girding its great cylindrical body glinting in the sunset, its tall chimney belching smoke and sparks into the twilight sky. I could catch the beautiful old machine's sooty smell now, hear the grinding of its huge metal wheels on the surface of the road as the driver did something with the controls that caused the steady chugging beat of the engine to speed up momentarily before settling back into its normal rhythm. Seeing us watching him, the driver waved his hand and sounded his whistle in a flamboyant series of *toots* which, compared to the impression of sheer power that the magnificent machine exuded, sounded strangely puny and more suited to a toy train.

Hitched to the back of the traction engine was the threshing mill itself, a long, bulky and complicated-looking rectangular box bristling with belts, pulleys, spouts and chutes. The entire contraption was topped by an overhanging wooden platform, and all of this rolled along on four metal road-wheels. It was an impressive and daunting piece of agricultural tackle. The mill in turn was towing something that looked like a slightly smaller version of a railway goods van which, I was told later, served both as a home-from-home for the mill men and as storage for their machinery's essential accessories and spare parts. To me, this all looked as magical and exciting as would the arrival of an itinerant circus or funfair to a city kid.

'Stand thee yonder by the front o' the cattle court, peedie boy,' said my grandfather, shooing me out of the way. 'Mind an' keep weel back now. Bairnos and mills is a bad-like mix.'

I could see what he meant, and I didn't have to be told twice to keep my distance. The concentration and skill needed to turn that cumbersome cavalcade off the road and to negotiate a non-destructive way through the farm gateway had me in instant awe of the driver. At that moment in time, I definitely wanted to be like him 'when I was big'. And the desire increased as the machine progressed up the incline into the stack yard. Standing on his platform alongside a huge, rapidly spinning flywheel that would have converted him into instant mince had he stumbled against it, the driver leaned this way and that, checking his angle of approach to the first corn stack, furiously twirling the steering wheel with one hand, constantly adjusting mysterious levers with the other. And all the while his mighty iron steed responded to his every command, venting steam and smoke like the breath of a reined mechanical stallion, while the thunder of its fiery heartbeat echoed round the yard. I was doubly smitten.

With darkness quickly falling, the driver shouted that he'd better 'put the yoke tae bed where it stood for now'. Final lining up of the mill beside the stack, he told Grandfather and Big Jim, could wait until morning, when the baler 'and the other lads' would be arriving on site as well.

'Fine that, boy,' Grandfather shouted back. 'Fine that. We'll see thee first thing the morn's mornin'. First thing, mind!'

In the dim light of gloaming, I watched Jim go over to give the mill man a hand to do whatever had to be done to 'put the yoke tae bed', while my grandfather wandered off alone in the other direction to unhitch the patiently waiting Duke from his cart, then to lead him away to the stable for a good rub down and a well-deserved feed. Though meaning nothing to me in my childish innocence then, I have often thought since that this one little scene in the stack yard at Cuddy Neuk at the end of that November day encapsulated almost perfectly the parting of farming ways that were destined never to meet again. But, with only the cup-and-saucer on top of the Hopetoun monument now catching the last of the sun's rays, and a full moon already showing the tip of its head above the dark summit of Byres Hill, I made my way back to the house and supper with no thought in my mind but the morning and the show that it would bring. And what a show it turned out to be.

***** 

'Moon's on the wane,' said Grandfather, glancing up at the pale orb floating like a transparent balloon in the dawn sky above the stack yard. 'A grand time for the threshin'.'

'What's a wane?' I asked Big Jim.

'It's a Grasgow bairn,' he replied, straight-faced.

I struggled with that conundrum for a moment, then it dawned on me. 'The man in the moon's bairn!' I proclaimed, pleased as Punch.

'Ye've got it in one, Wee Pete,' Jim said. He gave me a pat on the head. 'Nae flies on you, eh?'

I checked my hands and clothes. He was right. No flies. I couldn't let on, of course, but I was now more confused than ever about this 'moon on the wane' stuff. Some years later, however, when he reckoned I was old enough to understand, my grandfather explained to me how the old ways of judging the best time for doing tasks on the farm depended on synchronising them with the appropriate phases of the moon. Anything that corresponded to growing or reproduction, for instance, would be best done during the waxing moon, whereas things relating to conservation and the likes should be tackled during the waning phase. It made perfect sense, he said – plants would grow better or animals would breed better if the 'sowing of the seed' was done while the moon was growing. Conversely, the making of hay or the threshing of corn, even the castrating of calves, should be timed to coincide with the moon's decline. Positives, negatives – the ebb and flow of the tide – that was what it was all about, boy. The energies o' Nature's rhythms – follow them and thoo'd never go wrong.

The stack yard was already abuzz with activity. A good head of steam had been built up in the big traction engine, and its driver was completing the job of positioning the threshing mill at the optimum position relative to the first barley stack in the row. Telling me to take up my 'weel oot the road' place at the front of the cattle shed again, Grandfather and Jim went off to remove the ropes and thatching from the stack. Meanwhile, one of the miller's men unhitched the traction engine, then the driver steered his mighty steed round the yard and halted it facing the front end of the mill. To me, dwarfed as I was by these huge machines, this had the look of a pair mechanical behemoths squaring up for a duel.

And the two giants were indeed to be joined, though not in mortal combat. A long, continuous belt was looped round a drive wheel on the steam engine, with the other end looped round a pulley on the mill. The engine was then carefully reversed, inch by delicate inch, until just the right tension on the belt had been achieved. Too tight and it would damage the bearings in the mill – too slack and it would fly off once in motion and risk whipping the head off anyone within twenty paces. With the two machines finally chocked in place, adjustments were made to the mill's operating settings, then a lever on the engine was pulled to engage its belt pulley. The sleeping threshing mill came gradually to life as the speed of the drive belt was increased. First, as if the machine was starting to breathe, there were the wheezing and whirring sounds of fans and blowers, then in quick succession the rattle of riddles and the chatter of conveyors, sieves and shakers, all increasing in volume and tempo until full working speed had been reached. Now the mill was a living thing, shuddering and vibrating with pent up energy as the final lever was pulled and the threshing drum itself started to revolve with a deep rumble from within the very heart of the mill. With the steam engine now running at full tilt, the noise in the stack yard was tremendous.

Grandfather had been watching operations from a somewhat precarious position between the mill and the traction engine, apparently oblivious to the speeding drive belt flapping and flailing about just inches from his head. He turned and exchanged thumbs-up signs with the engine driver, then yelled out to all present:

'RIGHT, BOYS! LET'S GET BLIDDY THRESHIN'!'

The engine driver pulled his whistle string, and with a final *toot!* that released a jet of steam skywards like a white flare, the last phase of the year's harvesting operations finally commenced. I don't know how long I sat there watching from my straw bale seat by the cattle shed doors, but I do know that looking at that old threshing machine working gave me a bigger thrill than all the circus acts and fairground attractions put together ever could. For this was real, it wasn't make believe, yet it was as spectacular and memorable a show as any I've seen. That said, it was also hard, incessant work for the protagonists. The threshing mill had a voracious appetite that had to be satisfied steadily, carefully and ceaselessly if its mechanical digestive system wasn't to be seriously upset.

Big Jim was on the stack, rhythmically forking barley sheaves onto the platform on top of the mill, where a man cut the twine on each sheaf before passing its contents to his mate, who fed the straw – grain heads first – into the mill's hungry mouth. Feed it too much at a time, and the threshing drum would complain with a muffled 'gulp' – feed it too little, and the same mechanism would make its displeasure known with an angry clatter. Once in dining mode, a threshing mill becomes a pernickety customer for its waiters.

At ground level, Grandfather had taken up position at the 'business end' of the mill, the end where the corn spouts were located. The quality of the threshed grain was his priority, but checking that was the easy part of the job. The grain also had to be bagged off as it flowed from the spouts, then the full sacks had to be manhandled aside, weighed and sewed up – a never-ending cycle that kept three men hard at it for every moment the machine was working. At the other end of the mill, the straw from which the corn had been threshed was tumbling out to be forked into a baler where four men were seated, two on either side, threading and tying wire round each bale as it was formed. Add to this concentrated hive of activity the men who were barrowing the full sacks to the barn and those stacking the straw bales and you had a perfect example of what could fairly be described as factory farming, though in the most worthy sense of the term.

The farm cats and Nellie the collie were as interested in the proceedings as I was, but viewed them at much closer quarters. The two cats sat patiently watching every sheaf that was lifted from the stack in hopes of spying a mouse scurrying out. And a few mice did, to their permanent misfortune. Nellie, of course, was after bigger game. As the stack diminished in size, she dug away at the bottom of it with her front paws, growling and barking in anticipation of flushing out the rat that she instinctively knew was in there somewhere. And she was right – there *was* a rat in there, except that it had the savvy to escape from the side of the stack opposite to the one where Nellie was making all her racket. Nellie just never seemed to learn, but she apparently didn't care either. There were plenty more stacks and rats still to come. And next year there would be plenty more hares in the hay field, plenty more rabbits under the stooks of corn. And if she failed to catch any of those, there would still be plenty of cattle and horse heels to nip, and the two cats, the hens or even the postie's van to round up if things got really quiet.

The lasting memory I have of the end of that November day in the Cuddy Neuk stack yard is a picture of man and machine working in perfect harmony, each depending on the efficiency of the other to achieve the desired goal. It was a picture that would be replaced eventually by one in which the development of machines had seen the need for human partners diminish to the point of near extinction. The glow of the setting sun was reflected once more by the mellow stone of the monument's cup-and-saucer crown, a long smudge of coal smoke from the steam engine's chimney drifting past it on the evening breeze, the threshing mill below shrouded in a cloud of dust and billowing chaff. Soon, the engine's whistle sounded again, signalling the end of threshing for the day. The mill sighed its final breath as its belts, chains and wheels wound down to a stop, the steam engine coughed out a last puff of smoke as its driver damped down the boiler's fire for the night, and weary men, a dog and two cats made their way to their respective places of rest.

Big Jim ambled over to me, lighting up a long-craved-for cigarette while wiping the sweat from his brow and picking barley awns from the neck of his shirt. He glanced up at the rosy hue of the twilight sky. 'Well, Wee Pete,' he said, 'it'll be a fine day the morn. Aye – another fine day for the job, by the looks o' things.'

As we crossed the yard to the house, Duke the Clydesdale looked on through the open top of his stable's half doors. If the sky and Big Jim were right, tomorrow, paradoxically, would be yet another day without a job for him to do.

## CHAPTER SEVEN

## A PEEDIE PIECE O' PEACE

Tucked away down a narrow lane that winds through thick woods off the road between Haddington and the village of Gifford at the foot of the Lammermuir Hills, Morham Braes had the air of a farm that time forgot. Nothing appeared to have changed in a hundred years or more. And if that was true of the old stone and pantiled steading, complete with a tall brick chimney rising above the barn where a corn mill would once have been housed, it was equally so of the farmhouse itself. Built in typical Georgian style, it had a southerly façade of dark red sandstone, and beyond the gravel sweep two sturdy stone pillars stood either side of a flight of steps leading down to the front lawn. Well, it must have been a lawn at one time. Now it was just part of a rough grass field which sloped away into a little glen overlooked on the far side by the woods on Linplum Hill. It was a handsome house of unfussy appearance, sheltered on both sides by stands of mature trees – beech and oak mainly, but with an old walnut tree taking pride of place opposite the western gable. It must have been a very gracious home in its prime, and it would be again, one day. But that would take some tender loving care and *a lot* of work.

Granny took an instant dislike to the place. Not because of the neglected state of the house, for she could see the potential just waiting to be realised, but because the farm was situated in a wooded, hilly area – an undeniably beautiful landscape, but totally alien to someone used to the wide open spaces and treeless horizons of the Orkney Islands. She felt hemmed in at Morham Braes, and I can only suppose that our grandfather had bought the farm without consulting her. But there was no point in her complaining now. 'Dammit all, Mary Muir,' would have been Grandfather's typical reaction, 'it's a grand-like hoose, so just thoo roll up thee sleeves and shak thee feathers!' And that's precisely what she did. It couldn't have been easy for her, though, even with the occasional help of our mother and her younger sister Tomina. It was a big, rambling house, with two 'best' rooms either side of the front entrance hall and an elegant stairway leading to the first floor bedrooms. But there was no electricity, running hot water or even a bathroom, so the grand-like hoose did have its drawbacks, particularly for those trying to clean it up. The absence of a telephone line, the remoteness of the location and the fact that she couldn't drive must have added to Granny's disenchantment. But she never complained. She was a farmer's wife and she had already weathered many worse storms than this.

The heart of the farmhouse was, as ever, the kitchen, and in Morham Braes, that was a big single-windowed room with a flagstone floor, hooks in the ceiling for hanging hams, a scrubbed-pine table in the middle and the ubiquitous black iron range. That range must have been as old as the house, and it had been well used over the years. It still worked well, though. It had to. For, in addition to its essential food-cooking functions, it also had to heat all the water (in pots and pans) needed for everything from washing clothes to filling the zinc bathtub that was stored in an outhouse until being brought into the kitchen when required – every Friday night in Big Jim's case, but probably once a year in Grandfather's. Taking too many baths, in his considered opinion, took all the protective grease and vital oils out of your skin, weakened you, and therefore invited illness. He was never ill. Case dismissed. Washing his feet in the kitchen sink occasionally with a bar of carbolic soap and a kettleful of hot water would do him just fine.

The jewel in Morham Braes' jaded crown was undoubtedly the big walled garden hidden away behind the house. Even Granny loved that garden. The moment you walked into it through the pantry door next to the kitchen you were enveloped by the heady smell of boxwood. The dwarf hedges that bordered the pathways around the garden had somehow retained a reasonably trimmed appearance amidst the surrounding neglect. Yet it was a neglect that, in a strange way, seemed to suit the place. Empty vegetable plots, broken cold frames and tumbledown greenhouses evoked images of a time when the farmer could have afforded to employ a gardener to grow everything needed for the table of a large family. Although it had obviously been years since they'd been pruned, aged fruit trees dotted about the garden still looked healthy enough, and Minnie and I couldn't wait to sample the damsons, plums and greengages that we were assured would eventually appear in profusion. Also, the inside surfaces of the high surrounding walls were laced with cordons which, although bare in their winter slumber, would produce apples, pears and even figs come summer. For 'utility' kids like us who'd never seen any fruit more exotic than brambles, the summer couldn't come quickly enough.

But it was only early December, the war continued, and there were more important things on Grandfather's mind than 'bliddy plums'. The government was still paying subsidies to farmers to plough up old grassland, and there was plenty of that on Morham Braes. In fact, the whole farm consisted of old grassland. Until then it had been run as a stock (mainly sheep) farm, and its one-hundred-and-eighty-plus acres of permanent pasture hadn't been ploughed up in living memory. Never one to let the grass grow under his feet, Grandfather instructed Big Jim to make ready for ploughing most of it under without delay. However, the grass under his feet, or rather the land below it, had a surprise in store for him.

The little Allis-Chalmers tractor, trailing its two-furrow plough, entered the 'lawn' field. Jim stretched back from the tractor seat, pulled the plough's trip lever, the ploughshares entered the ground, and the tractor stopped dead, its rear wheels spinning on the squelchy turf.

'Buggeration, shite and abortion!' grumped Grandfather from his stance atop the stone steps leading down from the house. 'What the bliddy hell's ill wi' it?' he barked at Jim.

Jim didn't bother to answer, but instead had another go at opening up the first furrow – then a third go, one more, and yet another. Within a couple of minutes the Allis-Chalmers was up to its axles in a sticky-looking quagmire of yellow clay, stuck fast and going nowhere.

'We'll need tae dig her oot, Cheem boy,' Grandfather shouted. 'Unhitch the ploo an' I'll go an' fetch a couple o' spades.'

Jim didn't bother to answer this time either. He jumped down from the tractor and trudged off muttering incoherently towards the steading.

'Fetch a hantle o' sacks an' all for under the wheels,' Grandfather shouted after him, marching down to inspect the marooned tractor more carefully. 'Would never have happened wi' a pair o' horse,' he mumbled, his turned-down wellies sinking into the boggy muck oozing from around the tractor's wheels. 'Bliddy useless-like machine!'

A minute or so later, the sound of another tractor starting up rasped over from the steading, then the little yellow MM three-wheeler appeared in the field, Jim driving, his expression dark. He reversed up to the nose of the Allis-Chalmers, pointing to a heavy tow chain hitched to the drawbar of the MM.

'Hook that up to the front o' the Allis.'

His father did as instructed, climbed aboard the bogged-down tractor himself and revved up the engine.

'Steady on the throttle, for Christ's sake!' Jim snapped. 'Ye're no tryin' t' take off in a bloody aeroplane!'

'Dinna thoo shout at me, boy!' Grandfather snapped back. 'Show some damn respeck!'

The generation gap had opened up again, and this time its teeth were beginning to show. It took an hour and the full range of expletives to haul the Allis-Chalmers out of the mire. It then took both tractors hitched in tandem to a single-furrow plough to turn over the heavy, stale-smelling mud that lay beneath the grass of the 'lawn'. And much of the rest of the land on the farm proved to be of little better quality. After the light, sandy soil of his native Sanday, Grandfather could scarcely believe that such stiff, unyielding stuff existed. He had bought a chunk of land now notoriously known as the Humbie Series of clays which runs east to west for several miles through that part of the county. And he'd thought the relatively friable loam of Cuddy Neuk had been 'heavy-like dirt' in comparison with what he'd been used to in Orkney! The reason why the land of Morham Braes had previously been left unploughed despite the attraction of government hand-outs was now glaringly obvious.

'Dung,' piped up Granny, never one to be discouraged by what appeared to be insurmountable adversity.

'Basic slag,' Grandfather replied.

'How dare you!' Granny retorted.

'No, no,' Jim intervened, 'he means the high phosphate powder ye get from the steel mills. Great for heavy land like this, and plenty of it about these days, what wi' all the arms bein' made and everything.' That, together with better drainage, and the application of the farmyard manure which Granny had suggested, would be the way to improve the bad land on Morham Braes.

'Cheem's right enough,' Grandfather concurred, giving no credit to his wife. 'Sharn, slag an' field drains – that'll mak decent-like dirt oot o' the claggy grund on this place.'

The generation gap had closed again – at least for the present. But all of a sudden, a shadow of doubt had appeared over our grandfather's hitherto flawless reputation for business astuteness. Instead of cashing in on the increased volume of vegetable production that the purchase of Morham Braes had been intended to make possible, he was faced with a situation which would require a considerable input of capital and work before any profit at all would be forthcoming. Even dung doesn't come cheap. You need to have the livestock to make it, and cattle cost money. A quick shift in farming policy was called for, but Grandfather was up to the task. The dairy herd at Cuddy Neuk was sold off and the proceeds invested in young beef cattle for stocking Morham Braes. Improving the drainage was a trickier problem, however. That would take manpower, very little of which was available in wartime. And digging drains was hardly a job for the city girls of the Women's Land Army who had been drafted in to work on farms while so many able-bodied country fellows were serving in the armed forces. Then Lady Luck smiled on Grandfather once again.

An increasing number of prisoners of war were now being interned in camps throughout Britain, and one of those camps just happened to be on the outskirts of Haddington, in Amisfield Park, hardly three miles from Morham Braes. A recent government directive had decreed that approved prisoners would be allowed out of camp during the day to work on local farms, and Grandfather wasn't slow to exploit this timely new source of 'value-for-money' labour. Enter 'the German boys', as he called them. He was correct on one point – they *were* just boys, in their late teens or early twenties at most, yet veteran soldiers all. They were, however, not Germans but Austrians, who had fought with Rommel's forces during his ill-fated North Africa Campaign. The cold, sticky clay of Morham Braes was a far cry from the searing desert sands they had so recently ploughed through with the tanks of the Panzer Division, but as many of them were actually country-boy conscripts, they took to the task of breathing life into the stale Morham land with genuine enthusiasm. And Granny Muir took to them like a mother hen to her chicks. She knew that those 'peedie bits o' boys' just wanted to be back home, wherever that was, and with whatever members of their families were still alive. She had a daughter, a son-in-law and two grandchildren languishing in some unknown prison camps on the other side of the world, after all, so she could empathise with these lads, few of whom could speak more than just a few words of English. But they rewarded Granny's kindness with unstinting hard work in the fields. Grandfather, in turn, eventually persuaded their camp commandant to allow four of the POWs to 'live out' during the working week, and a cottage on Morham Braes was made available to them to turn into their own little home far away from home. The war may still have been raging throughout the world, but at least one small gesture of peace had already been made and gratefully accepted in a quiet little corner of Scotland.

My sister and I got on really well with these young men too. I suppose we were fascinated by the strange language they spoke, and I know that we enjoyed listening to their folk songs and nursery rhymes, some of the melodies matching those English language versions with which we were already familiar. Maybe we reminded them of nieces and nephews or younger brothers and sisters back in their homeland, but for whatever reason, they showered us with little gifts at every opportunity. These were usually just simple things they made with whatever materials were to hand. For Minnie, there would be corn dollies made from straw, or a ring for her finger fashioned from a shard of Perspex from the windscreen of a Mosquito aircraft which had tragically crashed nearby. For me, they carved tiny cars and tractors from bits of broken fence posts, even a miniature

Panzer tank, which they assured me in their broken English was really an American Sherman. '*Boom! Boom! Sehr gut das Sherman in der sand, nein?*' They always had a good laugh after saying that, and although I didn't understand why at the time, it did prove that they not only had a sense of humour, but a self-deprecating one at that. There was no doubt about the identity or nationality of the gift which they gave me that Christmas, however. It was a Lancaster bomber, also carved from an old post. With a wingspan of fully two feet, it had been painted silver and was perfect in every detail, right down to the RAF roundels on its wings. I couldn't have been more thrilled and delighted had I been given the most expensive factory-made toy imaginable.

Quick as ever to recognise a talent that could be put to good use, Grandfather then harnessed the woodworking skills of 'the German boys' for the purpose of building a new implement shed at Cuddy Neuk. And to their credit, that shed is still there, standing as true and solid as when it was built from second-hand materials almost sixty years ago. The results of their labours on the tough land at Morham Braes were not so immediately apparent, of course. It would be years before any significant difference in the quality of the soil would show. That was simply a fact of life. But the foundations were being diligently laid, and a happy working relationship was now established between 'employer' and his 'guest workers'.

With the dairy herd gone from Cuddy Neuk, more grass had been ploughed up and cabbage production correspondingly increased. Our father, now that we had moved from Gullane to Cuddy Neuk, had even managed to buy himself an old car to help speed his journey between the farm and the Dirleton radar station. Everyone was working harder than ever, but progress and a fair amount of money was being made.

Then Dad was posted to India, and Nellie the collie started having fits.

The two happenings weren't directly connected, at least as far as we knew, but Dad found a way of getting round his problem, whereas poor Nellie couldn't – not on her own, at any rate. In a dog's world, even collie power has its limitations.

'Your grandfather always made me put too much old bread in her bucket,' said Granny the first time we watched Nellie writhing about on the ground, foaming at the mouth, her eyes staring rabidly. 'Bad for dogs, too much stale bread. They need plenty meat as well. Protein, you know.'

'Bliddy eejit,' said Grandfather. 'Damn dog was never right in the heid.'

Nellie would survive, though. Granny and the vet's fees, paid out of her secret 'housekeeping savings', would see to that. Our father's predicament was going to be a tad more difficult to overcome, however. A posting to India wasn't going to be averted by a prescription of tablets. Or was it? Usually, a heavy cold is the bane of everyone's life. Nobody ever relishes the arrival of a runny nose, sore throat, thumping headache, or any of the other symptoms of man's simplest yet most incurable of ailments. But they came as a blessing in disguise to Dad in that fateful winter of forty-four. It wasn't that he was a cowardly man. Far from it. He wasn't one to look for a scrap, but he'd take on anyone if he had to. That applied to his outlook on the war as well. He had volunteered for military service before the outbreak of hostilities because he recognised that the well-being of his family would be under threat should the worst come to the worst, and he wanted to be there to do what he could to protect them. That meant being at *home* to protect them, not being in India, or anywhere else for that matter. His wangling prowess had seen him right so far, but notice of the posting to India had come from a higher authority than his latest 'tame' commanding officer, and the long flight eastward was extremely imminent – one week away, in fact. Rabbits and cigarettes were the only solution; maybe a partridge or two and a roe deer as well. So, with Big Jim's assistance, the shotguns provided the game, the game provided the money, and the money (via the black market) provided the fags. As many of them as Dad could smoke during his waking hours.

Within a few days he was in hospital, his head cold having obligingly descended into his chest, the overdosing on cigarettes having done the rest. Although not quite having merited administration of the last rites, he *was* deemed to be seriously ill. He even overheard one Polish nurse telling someone outside his room to be quiet as there was a young airman dying in there. Her regular supply of antibiotic pills being thrown out of the window to coincide with further clandestine inhalations of a small plantation of tobacco leaves ensured that his fitness for a move to the tropics was given the official thumbs-down. Someone else would be enjoying vindaloos next week, while our father, once he'd survived the pampered hardship of recuperating in the opulence of Gullane's Greywalls House, would still be radarring at Dirleton and ploughing at Cuddy Neuk. Mission accomplished.

*****

So the war drew to an end and, with the demobilisation of so many troops, the county gradually returned to its former quiet state. Bittersweet farewells were said, not just by members of the Allied Forces returning to happy homecomings after five years away, but also by many of the prisoners of war who were being repatriated to countries ravaged by the conclusive blows of conflict. Because of the apportionment of the spoils of war between the victors, some of the young men who had become friends of the local country folk during their time working on the farms would never see their homelands or families again. They would join the many thousands of displaced persons forlornly wandering a battle-scarred northern Europe in search of a new life.

Although luckier than most of those unfortunate souls, the survival of our mother's sister Renee and her family hadn't come about without a heavy price being paid either. They arrived at Morham Braes wearing clothes made from blankets. Every material thing that they once had was gone. The life of comfort and privilege that they'd enjoyed in the Dutch East Indies before the war was now just a distant memory, and whatever the future held for them back in Holland would have to be built from scratch. But they were alive, and to them that was all that mattered. They would never forget the privations they had suffered in the concentration camps of Java, but neither did they dwell on or even talk about them. For the first time, one of the 'best' front rooms in Morham Braes farmhouse was opened up to welcome them home – a rare honour indeed. For the occasion, Grandfather even abandoned his straw-filled wellies in favour of his good black leather 'funeral' boots. With the whole family once again together, the old melodeon was taken from the cupboard, Dad was instructed to 'get thee on the ivories, boy', and for an hour or two at least it was as if the war had never happened. At last, the sound of music and laughter had taken the place of the wail of sirens and the drone of warplanes. It sounded good.

## CHAPTER EIGHT

## INTO THE REALM OF THE GYPSY KING

The whole idea of going to school had never appealed to me, and, still three months short of my fifth birthday, being deposited there by my mother on the first day came as quite a shock. I had never been left by her anywhere before, except at our grandparents' place, which never failed to be a pleasure. But they weren't here, nor was Nellie the dog, or even Big Jim – only crowds of other kids, none of whom I knew. Even the tall oriel windows of the old Victorian schoolroom were set too high to see out of, so the cheery sounds of life passing by outside only added to the torture.

Miss Peacock was a schoolmarm of the old-style career spinster variety, dressed in a frumpy twinset, with a calf-length skirt of 'hairy' Harris Tweed, and a few bristles on her chin to match the ginger hue of the cloth. She distributed 'musical instruments' in a brave effort to make all of us newly entrapped nippers feel less cut up at being cooped up in a charmless room that smelled of stale chalk dust, fresh pencil sharpenings, a lone hyacinth and bewilderment-induced piss. I had a triangle, the boy next to me a skinless tambourine, the girl beyond him castanets. Miss Peacock thumped out an intro on an old upright piano, then soprano'd the words of a song called 'The Merry Shepherd' (who was she kidding?), while conducting each and every one of us with flamboyant hand gestures that were intended to make us hit, shake or rattle our respective 'instruments' bang on cue. It was twenty-piece pandemonium.

Within the first minute of the performance I got a splinter in my backside from shuffling about on the bench attached to the ancient desk I was imprisoned behind. Too timid and embarrassed to ask the teacher to help me, I had to endure the discomfort of my spiked bum until my mother tweezed out the offending *skelf* when I got home that evening. By that time, given that Minnie and I had to walk the three miles from the Haddington school to Cuddy Neuk, the tiny sliver of wood felt like a telegraph pole, and my inflamed behind was throbbing to the unsteady but unforgettable rhythms of Miss Peacock's 'Merry Shepherd'. If that was what school was all about, they could keep it!

But no such luck. Everyone had to go to school, my father explained. Minnie had to, he'd had to – our mother as well. Everybody. 'Don't worry, Paderooski,' he said, giving me the customary pat on the head, 'you'll soon get to enjoy it. In no time you'll really look forward to going to school. Honest.'

Instead, I shat myself in the playground the very next morning. Humiliation had been heaped upon disaffection – already. My sister shepherded me into a cubicle in the girls' toilets, there to hide from the sniggers and guffaws of the older kids until a teacher was summoned. I was mortified. Unlike the time when I'd wet my pants at the punch line of Jimmy Walker the roadman's ghost story, I knew there was no chance at all of concealing the evidence of this latest mishap. When you're wearing short trousers and waddling about like a bandy midget with rickets, such crafty acts of subterfuge are definite non-starters.

'Why didn't you ask Miss Peacock to let you go to the loo?' Minnie enquired through the cuff of her cardigan sleeve.

'Didn't need to go.'

'I think you *did*,' said Minnie, glancing sidelong at the proof of the matter. She stifled a retch.

'No, I didn't,' I gamely protested, trying to put a brave face on things while struggling to hold back the tears. 'Just needed, uhm … just needed to go when the playtime bell went.'

'Well, why didn't you go to the loo *then*?'

'Wanted to show a boy Big Jim's pull-a-finger-for-a-fart trick first.'

'Hmm, and you filled your breeks instead.' Minnie was not impressed. 'Serves you right for showin' off then!'

The teacher on playground duty wasn't impressed either. Although she seemed quite grown-up to me, she'd only have been about eighteen – an aspiring student keenly getting in a bit of work experience before starting her first term at teacher training college. The look on her face when she opened the cubicle door, however, suggested that a shift in career direction might already be worth serious consideration.

'What are we going to do with you?' she gagged.

'At home, Grandfather would just scrape him down at the midden, miss,' said Minnie, her customary air of superiority returning for the teacher's benefit.

'You must come from a very strange home,' the girl muttered. She turned to me. 'Come on, kiddo, let's get you to a bucket of water. Yuck!'

The memory of what happened immediately after is blotted from my mind, as so often happens following such ghastly experiences. But I do remember returning to the classroom some minutes later to see everyone already seated at their desks, bored to distraction while listening to Miss Peacock droning on about 'A is for Apple', or something equally tedious. The faces of my classmates lit up when they saw me, though. In place of the neat grey flannel shorts I'd been wearing earlier, I was now decked out in what (unbeknown to me) the teaching staff mischievously called the 'Primary One Pooper Pants', a stock wardrobe item kept ever handy in the staff room cupboard for the salvation of 'Pooper of the Day'. They were made from a matted jersey-like material that had probably once been brown but had been washed so often that the colour now resembled that of the wrinkly lisle stockings worn by Miss Peacock. They were the colour of a dead, or extremely sick, donkey. To make matters worse, the springy texture of the cloth meant that the seat of the pants clung to your buttocks, while the legs, which looked as if they'd been crudely reduced in length, rippled out into a sort of scalloped flare a couple of inches above the ankle. With my socks having joined my trousers in the laundry bag, I must have looked like a distressed version of one of the Bisto Kids without his flat-cap. The outburst of laughter from my new school peers was both spontaneous and unrestrained.

'Now, now, children,' scolded Miss Peacock, 'we must remember our manners. No mocking the afflicted.' Not a flicker of humour appeared on her face. She'd have seen it all often enough before, of that there was no doubt. So, instead of being directed to my previous desk in the middle of the room, she ushered me at arm's length to a lone spot by the window, which she quickly opened wide. I'd be back at my normal place tomorrow, she assured me after all the hilarity had died down. Once I was, uhm … *better*.

I've often wondered since if those ridiculous Pooper Pants had been specially designed to generate the maximum explosion of mirth from the other kids, just to make the wearer feel so humbled that he'd never put off asking to go to the bog again. Whether or not, that's certainly how the experience affected me. After that, things at school could only improve. I'd been in the shithouse once (literally), and I wasn't about to let anything like *that* happen again. And getting the chance at lunch times to explore parts of Haddington that I'd never been to before was to prove unexpectedly educational too, albeit in an odd way at first.

With a population of about seven thousand, Haddington seemed huge to me after the intimate village atmosphere of Gullane. I'd been in the town often enough before, of course, but usually only to go to the livestock market with Grandfather on Mondays, or to the pictures with Big Jim on a Friday night, so there was a lot yet to see – and hear.

★★★★★

'Aye, gadge. D'ye wun'ae deek ma joogal?'

This puzzling question was put to me by wee Eck Broon after memories of the Pooper Pants episode had long since waned. Wee Eck sat in front of me in class and lived in the Nungate, at that time a fairly run-down district located 'ower the Panny', or, as some would say, on the 'wrong' side of the river that snakes through the town.

'He's a barrie joogal. Stone radge, mind. Dead shan. But he'll no mar ye, like – fur he disnae scran chavvies.'

I'd never heard any of these strange words before meeting Eck, and neither had most of the other kids who'd come to Haddington infant school from the surrounding countryside. Eck explained that a *gadge* or *gadgie* was the Nungate term for a male person, while *deek ma joogal* meant 'see my dog'. *Panny* could either be used to refer to 'water' in general, or the river in particular. *Barrie* was the word for 'good', *radge* meant crazy, *shan* was the word for 'untrustworthy', *scran* could denote either 'to eat' or simply 'food', and *chavvies* were children. So, what Eck had really said to me was ...

'Hi, man. Would you like to see my dog? He's a good dog. Completely crazy, though. Absolutely untrustworthy. But you'll be fine, as he doesn't eat children.'

And Eck had actually been watering down the Nungate lingo for me! He had an impressive command of it, and it hadn't taken long for me to pick up some key words myself. Soon, even some of us out-of-town kids could carry on simple conversations which nobody who wasn't wise to the cant would understand. This ability to *mang the can* came in very handy, for example, when arranging within earshot of a teacher to go and *chore yaps* (steal apples) with your pals at playtime, and deciding which one of us would keep an eye open for the *stardies* (the police). It has to be said that the use of these words was roundly condemned by school staff and many parents, who saw the language of the Nungate as nothing but vulgar gibberish that wasn't fit to be spoken by anyone but tinkers and tramps. That disparaging attitude, together with the gradual dispersion of the old Nungate families and the ever-increasing influx of people from other parts of the country, has resulted in the diminution of a fascinating way of speech, to the extent that most of the words have now fallen into disuse. And how wrong the original toffee-nosed detractors have turned out to be.

By the time serious students of linguistics stumbled upon the fact that the essence of this so-called uncouth slang was rooted in Sanskrit, an ancient literary language of India, it was already too late. Most of the elderly local speakers of it had already passed away. Despite a couple of recent attempts to compile a dictionary for the preservation of the vocabulary, its use continues to decline, except for a few words like *radge*, which turn up occasionally in such unlikely works as *Trainspotting* – though in that case the word has been turned from an adjective into a noun. Evidently the cant doesn't now travel as well as it once did, because the twenty miles that separate Haddington from the Leith of *Trainspotting* is but a tiddlywink jump compared to the thousands of miles and many centuries through which the language survived on its way to the Nungate in the first place. For it's the ancient tongue of the Romanies, the gypsy peoples who set out on their nomadic exodus from northern India a thousand years ago, eventually arriving in Britain some five hundred years later.

Because their language was one of oral rather than written tradition, the Romany ways, beliefs, skills and superstitions were passed by word of mouth from generation to generation throughout their endless travels. And during those wanderings, words from the languages of the many lands they passed through also found their way into the Romany lexicon, so that by the time the first gypsies reached southern Scotland their tongue would have acquired a rare cosmopolitan richness. But the basis of the Romany language was and still is Sanskrit – many of the words virtually unchanged in several millennia. The character of Haddington's Nungate is all the less colourful without the everyday use of its own particular version of the gypsy cant.

Yet colourful is hardly the adjective I'd use to describe the place itself when wee Eck first took me there back in the forties. We approached the Nungate via the eponymous stone bridge which links two of the most ancient parts of the history-steeped town of Haddington. I was still too young to be interested in any of that, however, and a picture of decay was all I could see ahead of me as we crossed the Tyne, a lesser-known namesake of the famous river which flows through Newcastle ninety miles to the south. The bridge, which is built close to an even older ford, is said to have been there in one form or other since Roman times. Nobody really knows its age, although there's certainly evidence that it was already known as 'the auld brig' as far back as the thirteenth century. Some of the Nungate houses looked as if they'd been around almost as long, such was the advanced state of their creeping dereliction. But most, if not all, still seemed to be occupied.

I didn't like the look of where Eck was leading me. To a hitherto cocooned village kid like me, the place had an unwelcoming air about it. The message it sent out seemed to be 'Strangers keep out, or enter at your peril.' Clearly feeling absolutely at home here, Eck clambered up onto the parapet of the bridge and scampered over the worn coping stones, oblivious of the twenty-foot drop to the fast-flowing water below. I looked nervously around, wishing now that I'd stayed safely in the school playground. So preoccupied was I that I even failed to notice the wide grassy bank on the Haddington side of the river, the *haugh* known as the Ball Alley, that sweeps beguilingly away to the part-ruined grandeur of St Mary's Parish Church, standing serenely in the old graveyard behind a sentinel of spreading trees. All I saw was the apparent squalor of the Nungate ahead.

I ran to catch up with Eck, who had jumped down from the parapet and was skipping down a flight of stone steps leading to a row of ramshackle cottages skirting the far bank of the river. I'd noticed a really unpleasant stench hanging in the air since crossing the bridge – a putrid smell that did nothing to improve the ambience of the place. I drew Eck's attention to it. It was just the tannery, he said, pointing in one direction, and the slaughter house, pointing in the other. You got that *boggin' guff* here all the time, he assured me, smiling quite proudly at this disparaging comment on the air quality of his own neighbourhood. 'Ye should smell it when the Panny floods and the drains are overflowin', but,' he added with a cheery wink. 'And ye wouldnae believe what it was like afore the brewery closed doon!'

Eck then threw a handful of pebbles at an upstairs window of one of the cottages. A tousled head looked out, so Eck chucked some stones at another window. A few more unkempt heads appeared. Eck made a rude gesture at them and yelled an even ruder-sounding insult in diluted Nungate-ese, the key English words of which appeared to be 'Paddies', 'shag' and 'donkeys'.

'*Nash*, gadge! Run like stoor!' he shouted at me, leading the way back up the stone steps.

'Away wit' ya!' one of the heads shouted after us. 'Feck off, ya little bastards, or oy'll loop yer feckin' bollocks in a feckin' half-hitch, so oy will!'

Eck was thoroughly enjoying the sport of introducing a

green little country guy like me to the subtleties of how the town kids had fun. The heads at the windows, he informed me, belonged to a small community of itinerant Irish farm-workers who squatted in such semi-derelict cottages between spells of lifting tatties, digging ditches, or doing whatever other casual work they could find in the area. They sounded tough, he said, but they were mostly harmless. Oh, they got into plenty fights, right enough – especially on Saturday nights when they were the worse for drink after being thrown out of the Long Bar round the corner. But they usually only fought with each other, so nobody bothered that much.

Secure, then, in the knowledge that our private parts weren't going to be knotted together after all, I ambled with Eck down the slope from the bridge towards the heart of the Nungate, passing between stone-built buildings showing varying degrees of decay caused by past floods and untold years of general neglect. Some were still habitable, whereas others already appeared beyond repair. One building whose condition fell somewhere between was, according to Eck, the last surviving of two Nungate 'model lodging houses'. Rather than being 'model' anything, these were rough-and-ready establishments where, for a few coins, wandering labourers, not lucky enough to have a roof over their heads like the Irishmen we'd just seen, could doss down for the night. Their beds would probably be nothing but chaff-filled mattresses on the dirt floor, the stuffing most likely already inhabited by familes of mice and attendant fleas. Eck said that, on weekend nights when customers outnumbered mattresses, unfortunate latecomers would have to settle for a 'penny *hing*' (the dubious luxury, for the price of a penny, of draping their inebriated bones over a rope suspended above the floor). I thought he was pulling my leg, of course, but I've since been assured on good authority that the 'penny *hing*' (or 'hang') was indeed a familiar and accepted 'amenity', not just in that lodging house, but in others of its ilk throughout Britain. The alternative for the Nungate latecomers was to go and seek shelter under one of the arches of the old bridge.

The lodging house looked a grim and desperate place. Even Eck gave its open door a wide berth. From the interior drifted the smell of cooking – a sour whiff of fish, of stewing mutton fat and boiled cabbage, a pungent aroma that blended disturbingly well with the stench from the nearby tannery. As we passed gingerly by, a witch-like cackle echoed through the dark doorway, followed by a gruff curse and the clatter of what sounded like a tin plate being thrown against a wall. The food obviously tasted as bad as it smelled.

'They eat bairns like us in there,' Eck told me, putting on a suitably serious look.

I believed him, and despite his encouragement to *nash* on a wee bit further so that he could introduce me to his dog, my instinct was to turn and run away as fast as my little legs would carry me. Eck's mother spared me the shame of having to resort to this, however.

'Where the hell d'ye think *you're* goin', gadge?' she barked, suddenly appearing smack in front of us as we rounded the corner at the pub. Eck's reply was rewarded with a swift clip on the ear. If he didn't get out of there and back to school smartish, she warned, she'd kick him all the way round to the tannery and have his useless hide made into a shopping bag.

I never did get to meet Eck's *joogal*. I did get to know

more about the Nungate and its people as time went by, though. There was no doubt that its character-rich population included an element of notable hard cases. The melting-pot nature of its shady history had seen to that. You'd have needed to be able to look after yourself to survive, particularly if you happened to be at the wrong end of the advantage scale. Having sprung up at a place where two ancient routes from the south meet at the crossing of the river, the Nungate had become a stopping place for all manner of people en route to the heartlands of Scotland. Some, like the abbesses and their reverend sisters of medieval times, whose historical importance is reflected in the Nungate's name, had put down permanent roots. Others, like the troops of warring Scots, English and French armies, had, in the main, fought their battles and moved on. However, as happens in the wake of all military conflicts, the evidence of the troopers' temporary presence would be present in local genes for ever. Then there would have been the drifting farmhands and cattle drovers, seeking simple sustenance and shelter on their travels – most staying for only a night, but some lingering longer, a few for a lifetime.

So, when the Romanies finally arrived in their caravans from the south in the sixteenth century, they must have regarded the unprejudiced old Nungate and the adjacent grassy banks of the Tyne as being a perfect place to set up camp while plying their wares in Haddington and the surrounding countryside. Forty miles to the south, the tiny Borders village of Yetholm had already been chosen as the seat of the Gypsy King and, therefore, the hub from which his subjects would disperse to exploit whatever opportunities might exist in this latest land to be reached in their millennial wanderings. The Nungate, ideally placed on the road to Edinburgh city and its teeming thousands, soon became the most important satellite base for the Romany people in south-east Scotland. From here they could set out on their seasonal travels, while remaining within easy contact distance of their overlord in Yetholm.

No one knows how long the gypsies stayed, but their recurring presence in the Nungate probably lasted several centuries, and even in the mid 1940s their legacy remained in the dark-haired, swarthy good looks of some of the Nungate children I encountered for the first time when starting at Haddington school. And their skills of survival in the countryside had been inherited by the well-kent poachers still making a living by following the 'trade' on the riverbanks and in the fields, woods and hills within a moonlight ramble of their Nungate homes.

But there was also a close community spirit among the families who had lived there for generations. They had an inherent pride in their neighbourhood and a will to see its modest lot improve, as indeed it would … in time. As would the fortunes of the somewhat threadbare old 'lady' on the other side of the Nungate Bridge – Haddington, one-time capital of Scotland, birthplace of a Scottish King, heart of the country's most fertile farming lands, an ancient settlement with the richest of histories, yet a town that had the look of having seen better days. And when the good times did eventually return to Haddington, that renaissance was linked in no small way to the contribution made by those who lived on the 'wrong' side of the river – the good folk, native and newly arrived as ever, of the Nungate. The *barrie gadgies*.

Who, of all the many thousands who pass today through

Haddington's colourful and bustling streets would imagine the changes brought about during a relatively short passage of time? They can admire the town's lovingly restored old buildings, or enjoy the timeless serenity of its hidden valley location between the Garleton and Lammermuir Hills. They can savour the sylvan beauty of its riverside walks, or stroll through manicured gardens and churchyards that transport you back to times past, both turbulent and tranquil. Or they can cross the auld brig to the Nungate. There they'll sit in the sunshine outside a fashionable waterside restaurant, sipping cool drinks or enjoying an alfresco meal, blissfully unaware that not so long ago the same cottages which now form this trendy hostelry used to house poor homeless labourers who were glad of the porous protection of crumbling wet walls and fungus-sprouting roofs. And no more do scruffy wee boys like Eck goad the gathered grown-ups with taunts and stones. The most belligerent sound visitors will hear now is the squabbling of ducks dashing for scraps of bread thrown into the gently-flowing water by well-heeled bistro clients, while swans glide regally by, aloof and silently graceful. Even the smelly old tannery has disappeared, to be replaced by a development of bijou apartments, a modern centre of learning has been built where the slaughterhouse once stood, and the motor cars of the bistro's discerning clients are parked in a flowery open space where the dingy rooms of the 'model lodging house' used to provide comfort of sorts for wretched souls.

On the other side of the Tyne is that same broad spread of 'Ball Alley' grass where Romany caravans once huddled and on which gypsy ponies quietly grazed, but where now the plaintive song-stories of a nomadic heritage are replaced with the carefree laughter of picnicking families and the playful yapping of pet dogs that will never know the need to catch a rabbit.

I could not have imagined such idyllic scenes as I scampered back schoolward over the Nungate Bridge with wee Eck on that stolen lunchtime adventure back then. Post-war times were still hard, and a lot of water would pass beneath those same ancient arches before most of us would know anything much better.

And, of course, the lingering language of the gypsies was still very much alive.

## CHAPTER NINE

## BENDING WITH THE RISING
## WINDS OF CHANGE

Ever the early bird, Grandfather was the first in the area to acquire a new type of tractor that was to herald the rapid demise of the little petrol/paraffin machines which, not so long ago, had put the initial nails in the coffins of the heavy workhorses. The Field Marshall was one of the earliest diesel-fuelled tractors, and its gutsy, unflagging power would soon see off not only competition from its precursors on the land, but even the old steam traction engines that had hauled and driven the threshing mills for as long as anyone could remember. With engineering manufacturers now freed from having to satisfy the insatiable appetite of war, energies were being redirected towards developing machines that would improve the quality of life of a population at peace. Yet the speed and nature of such advances would not have been thought possible just a decade earlier. Those same urgent needs of the war machine had turned industry around from the more relaxed ways of the past, and had pointed it firmly in the direction of efficient mass production. Agriculture would be one of the main beneficiaries of this new industrial revolution, although those with their hearts set in the old ways would go to their graves mourning the fact. A new era in farming had dawned, nevertheless, and the Field Marshall was in the vanguard of that change in Britain.

It was a relatively small tractor by today's standards, but standing alongside the little Allis-Chalmers and MM in the yard at Morham Braes on the morning of its delivery, the Field Marshall looked enormous. Also, it had a truly modern look about it, a muscular chunkiness that had been lacking in tractors up to then. From the aggressive bullnose of its dark green cowling to the tip of its sturdy exhaust pipe, rising from the engine like the smoke stack of a cowboy movie locomotive, the Field Marshall looked the business. It exuded a rugged confidence that suggested that no task would be too much for it to tackle successfully. The heavy land of Morham Braes would put it to the test, however, for to cope with that was precisely why it had been bought.

'Ya-a-as, she's a fine-like machine,' Grandfather said, standing appraising his latest purchase and trying not to look too pleased with himself. 'Kindle her up, boy!'

Big Jim scanned the operator's manual for a moment, then said, 'Well, there's the easy way or the hard way. The hard way is to hand-crank that big flywheel on the side there till the engine fires up. Hmm, and that's the cheapest way too.'

'Hand-crank away then, Cheem,' Grandfather directed, taking a couple of steps back from the tractor and not even bothering to enquire what the more expensive starting-up option entailed.

Paying no heed to his father's typically 'canny' instruction, Jim opened a little tool box fixed to the footplate beneath the driver's seat. He pulled out a hammer and what looked very like a twelve-bore shotgun cartridge.

'What's yon for, boy?' Grandfather asked, taking another step backwards. 'Thoo'll best no shoot the bugger till thoo sees if she'll draw the ploo first!'

Again Jim said nothing. Deep in thought, he removed the cover of a small opening in the side of the tractor's engine block, consulted the manual again, then inserted the cartridge-like thing into the hole, leaving its brass head exposed. Leaning over sideways, he then took aim with the hammer.

'Bide thee well oot the way, peedie boy,' Grandfather told me, almost knocking me over as he backed even farther away from the silent green monster.

Having passed my seventh birthday now, I couldn't understand why anyone who was almost an adult should still be referred to as a 'peedie boy', but being as much in awe of my grandfather as ever, I humoured him and did his bidding. With his eyes firmly closed, Jim swung the hammer, missed the head of the cartridge and knocked a chip of paint off the engine casting.

'Tak care, Cheem – thoo'll brak the bliddy thing!'

Muttering to himself, Jim drew the hammer back again and, eyes open this time, gave the brass cartridge cap an almighty wallop. There was an instant explosion inside the engine, a puff of black smoke shot out of the exhaust pipe while Jim fiddled nervously with unfamiliar controls, and the machine came alive. *Chug-a! Chug-a! Chug!* it went in a slow metallic knock, the engine's single cylinder seeming reluctant to be roused from its sleep. Jim was already in the driver's seat, tweaking the throttle lever, desperate to coax the engine into sustainable life before it decided to go to sleep again. His efforts worked. *CHUG-a-chuga-CHUG!* the engine went – *chuggidy-chuggidy-chug-chug-chug!* – the beat of its roused heart quickening, plumes of diesel smoke belching upwards from the exhaust stack. Venturing into the unknown, Jim selected a gear, released the clutch, and the Field Marshall lurched clumsily forwards, its diesel clatter reverberating round the yard. I felt the heel of Grandfather's welly trampling on my toes as he stumbled back out of the path of this lumbering mechanical beast. We landed in an untidy heap on the ground, arms and wellies flailing. Noticing us at the last moment, Jim wrenched the steering wheel of the now-speeding tractor to one side, succeeding – only just – in saving us from a squelchy, diesel-powered death.

'What fun, peedie boy!' Grandfather shouted to me, glancing round with his tombstone teeth exposed in a forced grin, his eyes wide and panicky, his bunnet askew. 'Ya-a-as, what grand bliddy fun! A fine-like machine, right enough, eh!'

That was the closest I ever saw him getting to the Field Marshall. Its arrival would do to the earlier tractors what they in their time had done to his Clydesdale horses. Progress was on the march again, and although he didn't like how it was pushing his cherished farming ways into oblivion, our grandfather was, nonetheless, a shrewd enough businessman to exploit its advance – provided he didn't have to go too near that gunpowder-eating mean green machine. But the Field Marshall was up to the task expected of it, and its brute strength, combined with the action of more advanced tillage equipment, soon made a significant contribution to the ongoing improvement of the Morham Braes soil.

So-called progress was already being manifested in

another way, though. As efficiency improved in tandem with increased mechanisation, bigger was becoming beautiful in farming. Less manpower was required to work a given area, and new buzz words like 'cost-effectiveness' were starting to creep into the farmer's vocabulary. Within a year, Morham Braes had been sold, and a spread more than twice the size bought.

Although we all thought that Granny Muir would have been delighted to leave a place that she'd never really felt comfortable in, when the time came she appeared more philosophical than overjoyed. 'Hopefield Farm,' she mused on the day of the move. 'Ah well, I suppose you can't get a more optimistic name for a place than that.' Bonnyrigg, the name of the town where the farm was located, had a nice ring to it too, she thought. But there was something less than totally convincing about the way she said it. Did she have a premonition of future happenings that were neither particularly hopeful nor bonny? Only time would tell. But for the moment, the purchase of Hopefield was about to have its effect on all of our lives – changes that would trigger a sequence of events stretching far into the future.

Hopefield was all of eighteen miles from Cuddy Neuk; too far, in Grandfather's view, to make running both farms as one business a viable proposition. Because of the greater travelling distance involved, the system of sharing key equipment, which had turned out to be a workable enough arrangement between Morham Braes and Cuddy Neuk, would no longer be practicable. Besides, our father, now demobbed from the Air Force, realised that the wartime advantages of his 'vital' connection with the family farm would no longer prevail. He had to earn a secure and honest living, and that meant committing himself to a full-time civilian career. Trying to combine that with even a caretaker's role at Cuddy Neuk was clearly a non-starter. And returning to the civil service was never going to be an option either, because this would have meant exposing himself to the possibility of being posted here, there or anywhere in Britain at the whim of some faceless personnel officer in London. God knows he'd expended enough energy wheedling himself out of that very situation in the armed forces during the war, without succumbing to its potential deprivation of his freedom now. So there was only one thing for it – we would stay on at Cuddy Neuk to keep an eye on things for Grandfather until the current crops were harvested, then the tenancy would be surrendered and we'd all get on with our new lives.

Sadly, the little farm that had provided our Orcadian grandparents with a toe-hold in East Lothian, and whose fertile acres had helped them earn the wherewithal to expand their farming enterprise so quickly and so significantly, was to be forfeited. The cosy wee house, the familiar fields, the magical views, the good neighbours, the old road, the sources of so many memories both happy and sad, everything that was associated with the place that had come to be regarded as the family's true 'home' would be handed over to others.

But what of Big Jim in all of this? He was now approaching thirty years of age, and any notion which he might have harboured about resuming his accountancy studies had already been scuppered by his father's purchase of Morham Braes before the end of the war and Jim's essential participation in the place's subsequent development. Now, whether his heart was in it or not, his future was inexorably tied to his parents' new farm. His involvement in running Hopefield was doubtless taken for granted by them just as much as was his help in working the place. One day, it would all be his, after all. Why else would they be taking on such a formidable new financial commitment at their time of life? Naturally, it was presumed that Jim would never rebuff such an opportunity, particularly as he had worked so hard for so long to make it possible. Imagine, then, the consternation in the kitchen of Morham Braes farmhouse when Jim announced to his elderly parents on the last morning of their tenure of the farm …

'Incidentally, I won't be coming with you to Hopefield.'

For the first time, I witnessed Grandfather struck speechless. He just looked up at Jim from his easy chair by the old range, where he was enjoying a well-deserved cup of tea. The livestock and farm machinery had already been loaded up and transported to Bonnyrigg, and all the household things were packed and ready for the arrival of the removal van. Surely Jim wasn't going to let them down now, Grandfather's stunned expression seemed to say.

'But – but there are three cottages at Hopefield, Jim,' Granny said, almost pleadingly, the colour draining from her cheeks. 'You can have one of them. I mean, you don't have to live in the farmhouse with us. I never thought – I mean, I should have realised you'd want to be on your own now that you're –'

'No, a cottage won't do,' Jim stated firmly, though obviously finding it painfully difficult to confront his mother in this way. 'Thanks, but … no, that wouldn't work.'

Granny was clearly devastated, yet her only thought was urgently to repair this totally unexpected breach which appeared to be opening in her little family's hitherto impregnable walls. 'But bless me, Jim – I, we, your father and I,' she stammered, '*we* can live in one of the cottages, if you want, and *you* can have the farmhouse. I mean, one of these days you'll want to get married and –'

Jim shook his head. 'No, it's not that. I don't want the farmhouse. I don't need it. I just want to have a bit of independence now, that's all.'

'And how the bliddy hell are thoo goin' tae pay for that, boy?' Grandfather snapped, his initial shock supplanted by anger. 'If thoo leaves the ferm noo –'

'I'm not talking about leaving the farm,' Jim cut in. 'As I said, I just want to have a bit of independence. And don't worry, I'll still do my fair share of work for you at Hopefield. But …'

His parents stared blankly at him, confused, wondering what was coming next.

'Spit it oot, boy! Dinna had us among the nettles!'

Jim cleared his throat. '… I want to hold on to the tenancy of Cuddy Neuk.'

'Good Lord Jesus Christ Almighty, Cheem boy,' his father exploded, 'has thoo tak'n leave o' yer damn senses! I've already put written word tae the landlords that we're quittin' the bliddy place!'

Jim pursed his lips and shook his head. 'No you haven't. I never posted the letter.'

You could have cut the silence in the kitchen with a knife. But not another single word was spoken on the subject. His parents, more obviously so his mother, were clearly disappointed that this one aspect of family unity – namely their close bond with Jim, which they had tried so hard to protect for so long – was about to be weakened, if not ultimately broken. They must have known that there was no point in debating the matter with Jim, as he had a habit of getting his own way in such things, as witness the previous retention of the Cuddy Neuk tenancy against his father's wishes. And, truth to tell, it had been their own determination to smooth Jim's path through life that had nurtured that particular trait. Ever since moving initially from the island of Sanday to the Mainland of Orkney in order to obviate the need for Jim to live in lodgings during the secondary school terms as his sisters had done, they had devoted their own lives to looking after their only son's best interests. Hadn't they even followed him all the way down to southern Scotland? Hadn't their resultant hard-working involvement in a farming enterprise much smaller than they were accustomed to provided him with a legitimate means of avoiding military call-up and all the unknown perils that might have ensued? Now, out of the blue, he was saying that 'I just want to have a bit of independence.'

Perhaps this was the first materialisation of Granny's suspected less-than-positive feelings about the move to Hopefield, but in my own selfish way, I was just delighted to hear that Cuddy Neuk would still be in the family. I loved the place, as I'm sure all of us did, including our grandfather (although he'd never admit it), and particularly Big Jim. I was determined to enjoy every day of our own remaining time there. Although we'd soon be leaving, Jim's taking over would at least ensure our continued connection with the little farm, would guarantee the whole family's ties with 'home'. A cherished element of our lives which we'd resigned ourselves to losing had been restored to us at the eleventh hour.

And who could blame Jim for adopting what, on the face

of it, could have been regarded as a purely self-centred attitude? He had been happy enough, after all, to carry on with his accountancy training at the outbreak of war, even if it had resulted in his being conscripted into the forces. It had been due to his mother's insistence, and his closeness to and respect for her, that he'd found himself tied to a life of farming that he had never sought. That many others, myself eventually included, would have given anything for such an opportunity, was beside the point as far as Jim was concerned. For the most selfless of reasons – as a mark of respect for his parents and his heritage – he had sacrificed the life and career that he had chosen for himself. That was how he saw it. In the process, however, he had put down roots, had made friends, had become accustomed to a certain lifestyle in East Lothian, and he believed he'd earned the right to start playing, in a way that suited him, the cards that fate had dealt him. And as none of this would interfere with his commitment to lend support to his parents' farming business, he felt he was doing the right thing. Because, when all was said and done, he had his own life to live, and the fact that he'd be doing so in a line of work not of his own choosing wouldn't be allowed to stop him having a bloody good time whenever the opportunity arose. For Big Jim, happy days were here again!

For us, moving into a new home – one in a gap-tooth row of houses set on the brow of a brae on other side of Haddington – hadn't been as traumatic a change as I'd feared. We may not have been living on the family farm any more, but we *were* still surrounded by fields, we weren't too far from school, and best of all, there were plenty of other kids to play with. It was still strange not having our grandparents living up the Gifford road at Morham Braes, but we soon got into a routine of travelling along to Hopefield to visit them most weekends, and Big Jim was only just over the Garleton Hills, whose outline we could see undulating along the northern horizon on the far side of town.

In his new job, Dad had managed to stay in close touch with farming, using his local connections built up over recent years to help develop a business supplying oil fuels and lubricants to the farms and little fishing ports of the county and beyond. It was an enterprise ripe for expansion in the atmosphere of growing post-war optimism, and he relished the challenge. Being out there driving around the countryside in his car, meeting people and swapping stories and gossip with local characters, suited his gregarious nature perfectly. He was happy in the freedom of his new life, and nobody would be able to send him away from home again – ever. Not if he could help it, anyway.

Big Jim, meanwhile, was settling nicely into his new pattern of life as well, equally happy with the particular brand of freedom available to him for the first time. He'd been going along to Bonnyrigg on most days to help set things up on the new farm and to play his part in hiring and 'breaking in' the farmhands needed to work the increased acreage involved. But now that he would also be running Cuddy Neuk single-handedly, a change in husbandry policy was essential there. The emerging trend towards abandoning traditional crop-rotation regimes in favour of the simpler (though highly contentious) new practice of continuous cereal production was eagerly embraced by him. Rampant weed infestations, crop diseases and ruined soil structure were what he was courting, according to older and wiser local heads. And without livestock to provide the essential dung to feed it, the land would suffer even more.

'Aye, it'll never pay, son,' predicted doleful Dick from up the road at Blackmains.

'Auld bugger's right, Jimmy,' agreed Dick's neighbour Joyce, never one to stand on undue ceremony. 'Ye'll rue the day ye stopped spreadin' shite!'

Maybe they'd be proved right, but Jim wasn't all that bothered. He didn't have much choice. Pulling his weight on Hopefield's 400 acres, as well as farming Cuddy Neuk's fifty on his own with a minimal amount of equipment, was going to keep him as busy as any man needed to be, *and* he had a long-neglected social life to get stuck into with a vengeance. Under the given circumstances, the long-term welfare of the Cuddy Neuk land would have to take its chances. He wouldn't be losing any sleep over it – not *just* yet, anyway. Time enough to worry if and when there was reason to; that would be his farming maxim from now on.

Of more immediate importance to Jim was the fact that he had a lot of lost time to make up for on the fun front. He'd had to creep into the house in the early hours of too many weekend mornings trying not to wake his sleeping parents over the past nine years. The good old times of RAF officers' mess parties had ended with the war, and the necessary frugalities of the subsequent few years toiling away at Morham Braes had limited the scope of his nightlife to village hall dances and after-hours drinking and poker-playing sessions in the Crow's Nest Bar of the George Hotel in Haddington. Now, though, there was a welcome mood of celebration emerging in the more affluent coastal towns and villages, where the well-heeled owners of big houses that had been requisitioned by the military had gradually returned to pick up the pieces of their former enviable lifestyles. The pretty little fishing-cum-golfing town of North Berwick, once dubbed the Biarritz of the North by the London socialite set who'd discovered its charms and had placed the town firmly on their summer 'season' calendar back in the early 1900s, was once again the 'in' place to be. Jim was drawn to North Berwick, just a ten minute drive from Cuddy Neuk, like a bear to a beehive. Its attractions were certainly sweet, but the danger of being painfully stung was ever present too, as Jim would discover to his cost in the fullness of time. But for the present, only the lure of the honey pot was evident, and Jim intended to enjoy his share of its contents to the full.

However, it takes money to mix with money, as the old saying goes, and the modest income now being earned from the simplified Cuddy Neuk cropping system alone would hardly have covered Jim's bare living expenses, far less subsidise even a part-time involvement in *la dolce vita*, East Lothian style. But the larger farm business centred on Hopefield was thriving, thanks in no small measure to Jim's considerable work input, and as a partner in that business, he was entitled to draw on his share of the profits. And he did. The custodians of those profits, though, were his quiet-living, financially prudent parents, without whose inherent thriftiness the success of the Hopefield venture would never have come about in the first place. The generation gap was showing again. A marked difference in attitudes and agendas had started to emerge. On the one hand were the adherents to the typical Orkney canniness that had seen the Muirs grow from humble crofters to farmers of some substance, on the other the ultimate beneficiary of the sacrifices that had bought that success, the loveable prodigal who wanted to enjoy its fruits today, instead of nurturing the seed of that fruit for tomorrow.

The wind of change was rising, but would even Grandfather be able to lean against this unfamiliar blast?

## CHAPTER TEN

## BAGPIPES, BOOGIE AND BULLOCK BREATH

Not all Scottish boys take up bagpipe playing. In fact, it's been calculated that less than a quarter of one per cent of the male population of Scotland actually learns to play the country's national instrument. I was one of the few. With my sister Minnie already having piano lessons and making good progress, I had been under pressure from my father for some time to take up the violin. It was a three-quarter size instrument that had been handed down to him by his grandfather, an eccentric old coal miner who played the fiddle with the index finger of his left hand pointing stiffly heavenward – the result of a badly aimed swipe with his hewing pick in some claustrophobic black burrow thousands of feet beneath the waters of the Firth of Forth. They say that, during his typically spirited renditions of Scottish jigs and reels, a piece of string tied to the end of that rigid digit would sway perpendicularly upwards like the tricky rope of an Indian illusionist, so fierce was the draught created by his remaining three fingers as they scurried over the strings. It was a legend that intrigued me.

For some reason, however, the prospect of learning the fiddle did not, and I quietly rejoiced when news of the aged local violin teacher's death was announced just a couple of days before my first lesson. On the rebound, I decided to join the learners' class of the town's pipe band before another fiddle tutor could be located.

On Wednesday evenings, a handful of us younger kids would assemble in the same infants' classroom that had trembled to the racket of Miss Peacock's jarring percussion 'orchestra' on my first day at school about five years earlier. Things were much better organised in the pipe band, though. Under the tutelage of two veteran ex-Regular Army pipers, Davie Macleod coaching us novices, and Pipe Major 'Pat' Patterson developing the skills of the older, more experienced lads, everything was run with military-like precision. I was instantly hooked, and watching and listening to the band practising its counter-marching drills in the playground at the end of my first lesson, I longed for the day that I'd be able to join in as a *real* piper, a fully kilted, sporran-dangling, buttock-swinging member of the Haddington Boys' Pipe Band.

I'm afraid, though, that our immediate neighbours soon grew to wish that I'd opted for the violin instead. The screeching, scraping and caterwauling sounds produced during practice sessions on that instrument would have been but soothing lullabies compared to the deafening howls, growls, screams and groans squeezed from a set of blood-curdling Highland war pipes by a ten-year-old rookie. It had been all right in the beginning, when learning the fundamentals of bagpipe music on the practise chanter. This little wooden pipe, held and blown in the manner of a tin whistle, has the same finger holes and playing technique as the full-blown chanter on which the melody is produced on the bagpipes, but, as opposed to the hair-raising wail of the real thing, the practice chanter emits only a gentle, nasally humming buzz. On this inoffensive instrument I had diligently learned the basic scales, gradually progressing through the execution of 'grace notes', 'doublings', 'grips' and 'throws', then on to the mastering of ever more demanding quirks and sleights of fingering, until at last I was deemed proficient enough to tackle a few simple tunes.

Keen as a stropped razor, I would sit on my bed for hours on long winter evenings, the music propped up in front of me, puffing my way falteringly through popular pipe marches like 'Scotland the Brave', 'Highland Laddie' and 'The Barren Rocks of Aden'. Then, when I reckoned I'd just about mastered whatever tune I was currently tackling, I'd rush downstairs and cajole my father into playing along with me on the piano. He usually didn't take much persuading. Any excuse to tickle the ivories was still good enough for him. The trouble (or the boon, as it would eventually turn out to be) was that Dad just couldn't sit and pound away on the piano in strict march tempos for very long.

'Boring, *oom-pah*, *oom-pah* military crap,' he would call it after a minute or two of rhythmic restraint. 'Let's hep it up, Paderooski!' He'd then bash out a raving four-bar boogie-woogie or ragtime intro, cueing me in with a precisely timed nod of the head.

Now, the scope of the bagpipe chanter's scale is quite limited, in that there are no special keys attached for producing semitones, as have more sophisticated orchestral woodwind instruments, like the clarinet, for example. So, when the repertoire of those impromptu duets with my father inevitably graduated (or degenerated) from 'square' marches to more 'swingable' numbers like 'The Saints' or even 'When You and I Were Young, Maggie', a certain unorthodox intonation technique had to be improvised in order to 'bend' true notes into blue notes. I discovered that it was a matter of blowing the chanter harder or softer according to the effect desired at any given point in the music. Not easy, but I cracked it. My piping teacher, old Davie MacLeod, would not have been impressed, but before long Dad and I were ad-libbing away like crazy in bizarre chanter-and-piano jam sessions that had even the stuffiest of neighbours grinning and foot-tapping merrily when dropping by for a shindig at Hogmanay.

Grins were conspicuously absent from everyone within half a mile when I ultimately brought home my first proper set of bagpipes, however. Davie Macleod and Pipe Major Patterson had painstakingly instructed me on how to 'season' the pigskin bag with a mixture of syrup and warm water; how to set and adjust the reeds of the chanter and three accompanying drones; how to inflate the bag with endless, eye-popping lungfuls of air; how to punch the beast into skirling, submissive life; how to squeeze the living bag under my left armpit; and finally how to reach up and tune the drones to the pitch of the chanter without letting the whole squawking caboodle wriggle free and escape to the hills. The cliché'd old jokes aren't wrong – you have to be a human octopus to get to grips with this tartan-wrapped giant squid of a musical instrument. Old Davie and the Pipe Major umpired the unequal struggle for as long as their nerves and eardrums could stand it, then retreated to the pub, sending me home to 'sort it out yersel' afore next Wednesday night, laddie!'

'The dog's just aborted her pups!' the lady next door hysterically sobbed.

'The cat's bolted up the roof and she'll no come doon!' the man two houses along announced with an irate shake of the fist.

'I'm on night shift,' the nursing sister at No. 4 whimpered, dabbing tears from her black-ringed eyes, 'and I think I'm having a nervous breakdown!'

My hapless mother and father cursed the selfish death of the fiddle teacher.

Minnie, apparently deaf to all the fuss, plonked away stoically at the chordal complexities of *Träumerei* and *Liebestraum* on the family piano in the living room.

Meanwhile, I continued to wrestle with my bagpipes in the deafening confines of the front lobby, my thoughts drawn back to that unfortunate 'accident' in the school playground those six years or so earlier. Ah, if only I'd had the precise sphincter control then that I'd now have to master in order to negate the ever-threatening consequences of bagpipe blowing – particularly when I started wearing the kilt … My musings were brought to an abrupt end by the front door flying open and my father bursting into the hallway.

'That's it! Cease skirlin', Paderooski! The neighbours are threatenin' to form a lynch mob if you don't jack in that bloody banshee yowlin' right now!'

I started cycling up to Cuddy Neuk to practise in the now-empty byre on any evenings when I'd managed to finish my school homework quickly enough. Big Jim, I noted, always headed circumspectly out of earshot on my arrival. 'Never did fancy the sound o' a pen o' pigs bein' slaughtered,' he'd muttered the first time he witnessed me struggling, purple-faced and perspiring, to squeeze melodic resonance from my reluctant chanter and drones. So I persevered with my exertions in the echoing loneliness of the byre, with not even a hard-of-hearing mouse for company.

Matters took a turn for the better the next Sunday we visited my grandparents at Hopefield, however. Well, they did eventually. While the rest of the family went into the house for the customary afternoon tea and a chat, I gathered up my bagpipes from the boot of the car and made for an open-sided hay shed, where I reckoned the combination of a curved tin roof and a wall of straw bales would provide just the right acoustic conditions for productive practise. And I was right. Once I'd eventually succeeded in getting the pipes aired up, I was delighted with the effect that the surroundings were having on their tone, albeit that I was still only managing to produce one intermittent note from the chanter, and the three drones were completely out of tune both with the chanter and themselves. This was a modicum of progress at last, nevertheless, and I was wallowing in it. A couple of minutes later, Grandfather appeared round the corner of the shed, fingers in ears, his face contorted into a tortured grimace. I stopped blowing, raised my elbow from the bag, and the pipes wailed their death throws in a pitch-descending cacophony of groans and squeaks. As my ears adjusted to the silence, I heard a choir of dogs howling from a housing estate on the other side of a nearby field.

'The sergeant o' police has been on the phone, boy,' grunted Grandfather, clearly miffed. 'And if thoo dinna stop that deef-makin' noise right noo, he's comin' tae arrest thee for breach o' the damn peace!'

Without saying another word, he took me by the elbow and marched me round to the far side of the steading and into an old stone-walled cattle court. I could skreel awa' to my heart's content here, he told me. Nobody from the town would hear me inside this place, and the cattle beasts were daft enough to listen to my bliddy racket without complaint. Besides, they were locked in. He then quickly left.

But he had been absolutely correct about the cattle. I'd half expected them to take off on a mini-stampede around their straw-bedded yard at the first squawk of the pipes, but instead they just pricked forward their ears, suspended their cud-chewing, and stood staring at me through heavy-lashed, trusting eyes. Whether it was the confidence boost given to me by the groupie adulation of a couple of dozen black Angus bullocks, or whether it was the damp warmth of their breaths combined with the heat rising from the dung compressed deep beneath their hooves that did it I don't know, but for the first time ever the bagpipes started to sing out in glorious unison. No stop-start grunts and yelps, no angry growls and strangulated screams, just the steady descant voice of the chanter ringing out over the bass and tenor thrum of the drones. I was giggling so much I could scarcely hold the end of the blowpipe between my teeth. This was pure magic – easily the biggest thrill I'd experienced in my life.

As if of its own volition, my brain launched my fingers into creating the sequence of notes required to produce the melody of 'Scotland the Brave'. Then my brain set my feet and legs in motion, and I was marching up and down the feed passage of the yard, my enthralled audience gawping at me over the top of their line of troughs. For the moment,

I was leading five hundred massed pipers and drummers over the floodlit esplanade of Edinburgh Castle in front of a crowd of cheering thousands during a gala performance of the Edinburgh Military Tattoo. After I'd segued into the only two other tunes I knew, I played the final few bars of a reprised 'Scotland the Brave' with a flourish of fingers and a snappy military-style 'halt' step that kicked up a puff of dust from the feed passage's dirt floor. Instead of the roar of the Tattoo crowds, I heard a lazy burp, and glanced sideways to see twenty-four black Angus faces resuming the circular jaw motions of formation cud-chewing. One bullock in the middle of the line gave me a knowing wink, though, and to me that was as good as the Queen herself taking the esplanade salute.

In fact, I did eventually get to play on the Edinburgh Castle esplanade, and my marriage to the bagpipes, which had been consummated on that silage-smelling Sunday in the Hopefield cattle court at Bonnyrigg, was to produce the most unexpected and unique of musical offspring many years after that. But that's just one more of those 'other stories' still to be told ... and all in the fullness of time.

CHAPTER ELEVEN

## GOOD FORTUNE FOUND,
## A TREASURE LOST

'I've just been an' bowt a bliddy coal mine!' had been how Grandfather first announced his purchase of Hopefield to us. And indeed he *had* bought a coal mine – located as it was within the boundary of one of the farm's far fields. It had been disused for years, although a scatter of pithead buildings remained, semi-derelict now, but affording welcome protection from the weather and the prying eyes of the police for gatherings of Pitch-and-Toss players who assembled there from far and wide every Sunday. This simple game of chance involved one 'thrower' pitching two coins in the air, while the dozens (sometimes hundreds!) of onlookers bet among themselves as to how the coins would fall – heads or tails. Substantial amounts of money were known to be won and lost in the course of a few hours. Such clandestine gambling 'schools' were still illegal in Scotland, but it was rumoured that the local police turned a blind eye to the Hopefield one as long as no other more serious crime was being committed by the participants.

189

'Plowterin' aboot' on his land was a serious enough crime to warrant the immediate intervention of the forces of law and order as far as Grandfather was concerned, however, and he told them so in no uncertain manner. In fairness to the police, they did make a token appearance at the far end of the pit field the following Sunday, making themselves look as conspicuous as possible until the alarm had been raised by the kid 'keepin' shot' at the pithead, and the assembled hoard of gamblers had scattered to the four winds. But all the pitchers and tossers were back again the following weekend, and Grandfather's attempt to take the law into his own hands by striding into their midst and roaring at them to clear off his land or he'd shoot the bliddy lot o' them was greeted with rowdy contempt. A barrage of good-natured abuse was hurled at him, followed by a clearly stated declaration that: 'Some o' us have been comin' here since the days we used tae work shifts in the pit here. So fuck off, ye soor-faced auld bastard!' Game, set and match.

By a similar token, the proximity of that housing estate with the bagpipe-sensitive dogs turned out to be another bane of Grandfather's life, but also his gateway to unexpected financial gain. The Hopefield farmhouse and steading had originally stood a good half mile from the centre of Bonnyrigg, a former coal mining village just south of Edinburgh. But by the time Grandfather bought the farm, the inexorable advance of urban sprawl in that area had seen the village grow into a town, with its western extremities already reaching to just one field's breadth away – three hundred yards at most.

After the comparatively remote and hilly confines of Morham Braes, Hopefield's proximity to Edinburgh, and the open, softly rolling aspect of the surrounding landscape had been greeted with much enthusiasm by Granny. And the fact that she was now within easy walking distance of Bonnyrigg's bustling shopping centre was an added bonus. The farmhouse, too, had transported her into another era. It was what today's estate agents would describe as an elegant Victorian villa, with tall gables reaching up from generously proportioned walls of beige sandstone. Typically, the hub of the interior was the large kitchen, with the usual pantries and sculleries, and, of course, the mandatory black iron range. Like most farmhouses in the region, there were two large 'best' rooms at the front, with all the bedrooms upstairs. In that respect, it was actually fairly similar in layout to the house she'd just left. But what set the Hopefield farmhouse apart from the one at Morham Braes was that it had a telephone, electricity, hot running water *and* a bathroom. And if all that hadn't been enough to set Granny's heart a-flutter, Grandfather even said that, to relieve her from the daily drudgery of black-leading, stoking, raking out and generally being a slave to the old range, he would buy her a 'grand-like' newfangled electric cooker – *when* he could manage to find one at a 'fair-like' price. She would have a long-like wait!

Much higher on Grandfather's shopping list was a new car, a model that would reflect his new-found status as owner of one of the vicinity's larger farms more accurately than the little Ford 8 which he'd had since arriving at Cuddy Neuk from Orkney all those years ago. And that very field which separated the house and farmyard from the town would pay for it – and much more. The field had been designated as a site for future house-building by the local council, and their immediate plans called for a strip amounting to about three acres to be built on right away. The price to be paid for the land was set at the going 'development' rate, many times greater than the agricultural value Grandfather had paid for it. He was a happy man, despite his stated reluctance at having to reduce his acreage by even that small area, and regardless of his deep distaste at having to pay the 'damn heathen tax' on the handsome profit realised. His distress was instantly alleviated by the delivery of a spanking new, dark blue V8 Pilot, the biggest car in Ford's UK range – a 'braw-like machine' that would provide him with the means of an appropriately impressive arrival at Edinburgh's Gorgie livestock market every week, not to speak of elevating his image in the eyes of those 'bliddy ill-trickit toon folk'.

He was referring in particular to the men who lived in the housing estate on the other side of the 'development' field, most of them decent working chaps, whose only offence against Grandfather was to take a short-cut over the corner of one of his fields occasionally. They were doing no harm, but he still didn't like them taking what he regarded as a liberty. In his view, they were just as guilty of trespassing as were the gamblers at the old mine, or the poachers who roamed about his land at nights with their 'clarty greyhound tikes'. Gates to fields where cattle were grazing had been left open, barley crops trampled and fences damaged. The culprits had been warned often enough by Grandfather, and on more than one occasion they'd even felt the draught of his shotgun pellets whistling past their ears. But all to no avail. The more he confronted them, the more he antagonised them, and the less they respected the inviolability of his property. This was the price he would have to pay for making capital from his farm's proximity to a built-up area, and cruising through town in his big new Ford Pilot would do little to change his perceived image among the locals. Quite the reverse, in fact, particularly when purposely parking his impressive V8 outside the bank, only to step out in his rolled down wellies with straw sticking out the top.

But a peaceful enough co-existence was destined to prevail, Tam Muir being regarded by the good citizens of Bonnyrigg as at best a harmless if somewhat eccentric old character, and at worst a raving loony who took pot shots at people walking their dogs, and probably slept in a coffin at night. In any case, Grandfather soon had worries nearer to home that would take his mind off the intrusive habits of the 'ill trickit toon folk' for a while.

No sooner had Big Jim seen his father's new car than he ordered an identical one for himself. He wasn't about to be left behind in the spending stakes. And so began what could well have developed into a classic tit-for-tat buying competition between two business partners. But it was a contest that was bound to have only one winner – Grandfather's steadfast thriftiness and Big Jim's apparent ambition to become one of the Last of the Big Spenders saw to that. After the novelty of the new car wore off, Grandfather soon settled back into his old dedicated-to-the-farm ways, and financial prudence once again became his criterion, if indeed it had ever ceased to be. But something had changed in his father-and-son relationship with Jim. The seeds of a parting of the ways that had been sown when Jim decided not to move to Hopefield with his parents had slowly sprouted, and their little green shoots were beginning to emerge. From now on Big Jim's contributions to the common cause would be concentrated bouts of hard work at Hopefield and Cuddy Neuk (combined with his now-established presence on the East Lothian social scene), while his father's was to shrewdly consolidate the solvency and future viability of the family business. Within a couple of years Grandfather had bought not just one but two combine harvesters for Hopefield, two of the first Massey Harris machines in the area, whereas Jim had bought a couple of stylish cars and was developing a penchant for continental holidays. Grandfather, like generations of his family before him, lived to farm. Big Jim, conversely, was making no secret of the fact that he was only farming to live, and to live as enjoyable a life as possible into the bargain.

For her part, Granny positively thrived on the new freedom afforded her by being able to catch a bus to Edinburgh at the end of the farm road. She'd still be up in the morning with Grandfather a full hour before the farmhands started work, preparing breakfast and single-handedly attending to the various chores that were involved in running a large house. Employing housekeeping help never even entered her mind. Not having to rise in the middle of the night to milk cows was luxury enough for her. With only the housework, shopping, cooking meals, hen feeding and egg collecting to take up her time these days, life was sweet, and those easy bus trips to Edinburgh were the icing on the cake. Yet she never seemed to buy anything – nothing other than the bare household essentials, that is, and certainly never any extravagances for herself. Having to look after the pennies and let the pounds take care of themselves had been her way all of her life, and she wasn't about to change now. Although always an elegant dresser when venturing beyond the farm gate, her modest range of 'stepping-out clothes' had been in her wardrobe for years and smelled more of mothballs than even the discreet splash of eau de Cologne which she allowed herself when making a trip to the city. Modesty and moderation in all things were her bywords.

Sometimes she would take us kids along, usually to visit a travelling carnival, circus or menagerie inside the covered expanse of Waverley Market by the railway station. She obviously felt that we'd see *something* there to broaden our outlook and contribute to our further awareness of the world at large. Lions, elephants and even ridiculously made-up clowns provided children in the early fifties with glimpses of exotic creatures only ever previously seen in old picture books or black-and-white newsreels at the movies. That was all very positive. But what witnessing suspiciously static displays of outlandish monstrosities like the dismantled lady (complete with heaving breasts and batting eyelids set several feet apart), or the two-headed man who could play saxophone duets with himself, would contribute to our long-term enlightenment was unclear, yet Granny was pleased to give us the chance to study them, anyway.

Sometimes, in the evening, she'd take us along to spiritualist meetings. These were held in a basement in Edinburgh's New Town – a spartan room filled with stale air and other elderly ladies who smelt of mothballs sitting solemnly on wooden benches facing a dimly-lit platform draped with black velvet curtains. The mystic performance of the medium and her histrionic delivery of 'messages from the other side' probably seemed even less plausible to kids of our tender years than even the carnival freaks had done, but Granny took it all very seriously. We couldn't understand why an intelligent person like her would want to be party to such weird goings-on. But that was only because we didn't appreciate, until years later, that she genuinely hoped – no matter how forlornly – that by taking us along to these meetings we might act as some sort of link between her and her fourth daughter Gertie, who, when our age, had died of scarlet fever back in Orkney many years earlier. She never did receive such a message from Gertie, yet attending these meetings and hoping that she might seemed to give her some comfort, and that was probably all she ever truly expected of the experience. 'Good night, Mrs Smith, and thank you,' she'd whisper to the medium on leaving, shaking the woman's hand as a means of discreetly slipping her a few modest coins for her trouble. 'Maybe you'll have something for me another time.'

Quite what Granny thought of our uncle Jim's attitude towards the disposal of hard-earned money only she knew. It was a subject never broached. Jim never failed to do what was required of him on the farm, she saw him most days, and as long as he was happy and the business was prospering, her attitude would have been to count her blessings and to live and let live. It was clear, in any case, that in her eyes Jim could do no wrong, and if he chose to lead a life that differed from the frugal one that she'd been obliged to live, then so be it. Her and Grandfather's years of work and self-sacrifice had been for his potential advantage, anyway. That was the way of things in farming.

Such heady financial matters couldn't have been farther from my mind at the time. I was too busy rummaging about in the Haddington rubbish tip, when school homework and weekend pipe band parades around the town permitted. It was the only way that I – and several of my pals – could sustain our participation in a new craze which had swept the country in the post-war years: motorbike speedway. There was scarcely a city the length and breadth of Britain that didn't have a professional dirt-track outfit competing in the new national league, the teams made up, to a greater or lesser extent, of young daredevil dispatch-rider survivors of the war, many of them Australians and New Zealanders, as crazy as they were fearless. You had to be a bit nuts to go broadsiding round a 400 yard fenced-in track at 60mph on a 500cc, methanol-burning, two-wheeled rocket with no brakes.

Edinburgh's speedway team were the Monarchs, their home track a red shale oval strip cut round the football pitch at Old Meadowbank, where the Commonwealth Sports Stadium now stands. A busload of us travelled from Haddington every Saturday night to cheer on our heroes in the company of perhaps twenty thousand other fanatical supporters. There was something about the death-defying, desperado atmosphere of these race meetings that attracted huge crowds to speedway in those years when rationing was still in force. People were looking for a source of excitement denied them during the ongoing austerity resulting from a war that had left the country and too many of its inhabitants all but broke.

But for some of us kids, just watching from the terraces of Old Meadowbank wasn't enough. We wanted a slice of the action, and were determined to be part of the thrilling spectacle. There were only a couple of snags, though: as eleven and twelve-year-olds, none of us were old enough to handle the awesome power of a speedway motorbike, even if we could have afforded the cost, which we most certainly could not. The next best thing, then, was to try and emulate our champions by copying their on-track motorised heroics on our pushbikes, stripped of mudguards for action, brakeless for authenticity.

Hence the reason for scouring the local rubbish tip. Within half an hour of the first race on the little track we had lovingly prepared in a disused quarry on the outskirts of town, not one bike belonging to the ten or so participants was fit for anything but that selfsame garbage heap. The staccato chime of wheel spokes doing battle with protruding pedals when dashing four abreast for that vital first corner would have been our anthem and potential swansong – *if* anything approaching common sense had prevailed. But to scrap our wrecked bikes would have been to succumb to the negative. When broke, positive thinking is called for, and all of us *were* well and truly skint. Everything for our racing bikes, from wheels, front forks, drive chains and pedal cranks to whole frames was gleaned from the tip, hauled out from among heaps of ashes, bits of woodwormy floorboards, garden refuse and all the usual household flotsam and jetsam to be found in a municipal dump. We soon learned the skills of spoking and re-aligning buckled wheels, fitting replacement spindles and ball bearings into hubs, adding or subtracting links to and from mangled chains, and all the other improvisational things that had to be done to keep an ever-battered cycle speedway bike in running order for the minimum of outlay. If your bike was still fit to be ridden home after one of our race evenings, you counted yourself lucky. Slowing down or stopping without brakes on the public roads involved mastering the knack of ramming the sole of your boot between the front tyre and forks, a hazardous technique which, if not executed with extreme delicacy, could and did result in a headlong trip over the handlebars. More often than not, it would be a matter of walking across town with your head stuck through the frame and the remains of your totalled bike draped over your shoulders. And that would be the end of your racing until another trip to the tip had been made.

Here was a sport which called for the utmost dedication, as well as a generous helping of bravery verging on total stupidity. There were, of course, occasions when the garbage heap didn't yield up the required spare parts, which meant a visit to the cycle shop was inevitable, as was the need to have money to pay for whatever you happened to need. And that's when living in the country proved to be a distinct advantage. There was always casual farm work to be had at weekends – a few shillings to be earned from picking raspberries and strawberries in the summer, or lifting potatoes in the autumn. So, by hook or by crook, we managed to support our involvement in cycle speedway, with, miraculously, only one broken arm, several permanently bruised goolies and a plethora of skinned elbows, knees and backsides to blight our fun. Naturally, every one of us without exception was determined to graduate to the full motorised version of our chosen sport whenever we were old enough. We'd be roaring round Old Meadowbank with those madcap Anzacs before long. None of us ever did, of course, and in time our enthusiasm for having the seats of our pants ripped out when hitting the deck at speed, or having our ribs raked by the jutting ends of cowhorn handlebars waned, and we moved on to other less suicidal pastimes.

The rubbish tip was returned to its rightful rummagers,

the rats and seagulls which, unlike us wannabe speedway racers, would forever leave discarded bicycle parts to rust in peace. But the experience gained of building, stripping down, rebuilding, repairing, repainting and making something workable out of worthless bits and pieces was to stand me in good stead for coping with more important necessities later in life. For the moment, however, it was time to start secondary school and to knuckle down to all the extra studying necessary to get the 'good education' that Granny, since my first miserable day in infant class, had insisted was so essential. In respect for her, if for no other reason, I'd apply myself as best I could. She was fated, though, not to see the results of her well-intentioned urgings.

*****

'Granny's sleepin' now,' was how our grandfather quietly ushered Minnie and me into the drawing room at Hopefield just four years later. Like her belief in the value of education, Grandfather's insistence that we youngsters pay our personal homage to our grandmother was an illustration of simple but cherished values that were rooted deep in his Orkney heritage. Her battle against cancer had been long and filled with suffering, both for her physically, and for the rest of the family emotionally. Unlike his sisters, who had been able to help relieve their anguish by nursing their mother during her illness, Big Jim seemed to find it hard to accept the inevitability of her passing. As can be the way with some Scotsmen, Jim had an inherent reluctance to expose certain emotions. Humour and annoyance weren't a problem – he could show those feelings freely without a second thought, but openly displaying affection, especially towards his mother, was a different matter. And yet he clearly cherished her as much as any devoted son ever could. But as her illness progressed and it became obvious that she wouldn't survive more than a week or two more, Jim's frustration and pent-up feelings of grief had turned into anger. Anger at the inability of the medical profession to cure his mother, an impossible anger that had him demanding the implementation of untried treatments, anything that might rid her of her pain and prevent her from being taken from him. It was a futile anger, of course, but the only way in which Jim found it possible to express the hopeless desperation of his own hurt.

'Remember to stick in at school,' was the last thing she had whispered to Minnie and me on the day before she died. I had always taken her advice in that regard very much to heart, and being fifteen now, with sixth year at secondary school and all-important final exams just round the corner, her deathbed words struck home with even more cogency. She was extremely frail, yet she managed a smile and a reassuring pat on the hand with fingers that had once been strong enough to milk cows, to help deliver calves, and stook sheaves from sunrise to sunset, but had become withered and weak beyond recognition. Now, in death, the lines which age and her illness had etched on her face had all but disappeared, and her skin looked almost as smooth and youthful as it appeared in her graduation photograph which hung on the wall above her coffin. It was as if all those years had been rolled miraculously back, and she was a beautiful young woman again, looking forward to a life full of promise.

'Come now and let Granny sleep,' Grandfather said, his voice unusually gentle as he shepherded us out of the room. There wasn't a trace of a tear in his eyes (he would never have let us see such a betrayal of his emotions, anyway), but there was a look of isolation in his face that not even his brave attempt at giving us a heartening smile could disguise.

We buried Granny in the quaintly named Cockpen Churchyard in a peaceful wooded glen just beyond the farthest field of the farm, a tall headstone of the finest Italian white marble expensively marking the grave of a woman who, in life, would neither have wished for nor would have been afforded such a show of extravagance. But she was worth it, had clearly always been worth it in Grandfather's undemonstrative view, his undoubted esteem for her now being shown, in his own way, for all to see. He and his Mary Pottinger had come a long way from the silver sands of Backaskaill Bay on the Orkney island of Sanday, had worked hard and prospered, had weathered many a storm and had committed their lives to bringing up a family that they were proud of. Now, though, Grandfather would have to face his twilight years without the wife who had been the wind beneath his wings, the selfless partner in a life that had seldom been easy, but had been a good and long life together, nonetheless.

How he would cope with the inevitable loneliness that would follow was our immediate concern. He would show us, however, that the indomitable Orkney spirit that had carried him through a full and testing life was still running strong in his old veins. Indeed, he had a surprise or two in store for us yet.

## CHAPTER TWELVE

## TYING KNOTS AND CUTTING TIES

Housekeepers – they became Grandfather's new torment, as big a scourge as even the 'ill-trickit' trespassers from the town who polluted his fields with their 'clarty' greyhound shite. We visited him without fail on Sundays, and it seemed for a while that there was a different housekeeper for every week that passed. We soon lost count of the number of unfortunate live-in domestics who had thrown in the towel after tellingly short spells of trying to cope with Grandfather's idiosyncracies. Some had made the mistake of bringing their offspring with them, but Grandfather was too old and set in his ways to be bothered with 'peedie scunners o' bairns' getting under his feet in his own house now. Others, particularly the more mature variety who had previous experience of the job, simply knew too many tricks of the trade for their own good. Grandfather wasn't to be easily fooled by any of their workshy 'sweep it under the carpet' capers, so, after his first tongue-lashing, they'd be heading for the bus stop as well. Then there were the younger ones, possessing various degrees of physical attraction, who no doubt thought they'd be perfectly safe living under the same roof as an ageing Mr Hayseeds figure in straw-lined wellies. How wrong they were. There was life in the old rascal yet. More than once did our mother receive an irate phone call from some shocked young woman who had bolted the Hopefield course, hastily packed clothes spilling from her suitcase as she made a dash for freedom after being chased round the kitchen table by her frisky old employer.

This bizarre state of affairs went on for several years – not an ideal atmosphere for Grandfather to be living under, we feared. But he took it all in his stride. Hiring, firing, berating, teasing and grumping at a seemingly endless succession of housekeepers had become a way of life he'd grown to accept. Or so he would have had us believe. Then came his telephone call to tell Mother that, in answer to his latest announcement in the 'Domestic Situations Vacant' columns of the *Farmers' Weekly* (we suspected that he probably had a bulk-discount arrangement with the magazine's classified ads department), a 'fine, posh-like lady' had successfully applied for the job. This one was different from all her predecessors, he enthused – a *really* grand-like lady, who had fairly taken his fancy. She was also a really sharp-like lady, as it turned out. Within a few weeks of taking up her humble housekeeping duties at Hopefield, she and Grandfather had jumped the broomstick.

Alexandra, or 'Lady Bonnyrigg', as she soon became sardonically referred to within the confidential confines of the family, had already seen off a couple of husbands. Still only in her early sixties, she had travelled north to Scotland from the heart of England, where, we were led to believe, she had been married in close sequence to two cavalry officers – first riding out nuptially with a galloping major, then promoting herself to the rank of colonel's 'memsahib'. And she certainly had the old colonial manner and plummy accent befitting a 'jolly good gal' of that ilk. Tall, slim and tweedy, with the erect bearing of the serious horsewoman, she cut an almost regal dash alongside our raggle-taggle scruff of a grandparent. Naturally, the first question to enter our minds was why such a 'grand-like lady', apparently accustomed to much better things (including servants of her own), would want to stoop to keeping house for an unsophisticated and crotchety old working farmer, far from the huntin', shootin' and fishin' gentility of the English Shires? She answered that question by marrying him, and it was generally assumed that she hadn't done so because of his captivating good looks or irresistible charm.

In fairness, though, she applied herself diligently to the unequal task of looking after Grandfather, and her arrival into his life had certainly given him a new sparkle. She even managed to cajole him not only into buying but also *wearing* a smart grey suit and black leather boots for going on drives round the surrounding countryside at weekends, a pastime he'd previously scorned as 'a damn waste o' time an' petrol'. She had also succeeded in coaxing him into purchasing a big new Humber Supersnipe, an unashamedly eye-catching example of British automotive luxury, of which she also quickly assumed driving duties. She may only have been old Tam Muir's jumped-up and stuck-up ex-housekeeper in the eyes of the more cynical of the locals, but she was determined that they'd see her playing the part in maximum style.

It couldn't have been easy for our mother to welcome her father's new wife into the bosom of the family, but she did, despite the fact that Alexandra would never have been able to hold a candle to Granny Muir in any of our eyes. Although trying to hide behind a veil of gushing bonhomie whenever we visited, the new Mrs Muir was unable to disguise her condescending manner and patently ambitious nature. Yet Grandfather was completely sold on her, proud in some obtuse way to be seen in the company of his grand-like lady. He even took her all the way to Orkney (the first time he'd been there since leaving over thirty years earlier) to show her off to his former cronies. 'There's no fool like an owld-like fool,' at least one was reported as having muttered after meeting the unlikely couple.

Oblivious of such criticism, however, our grandfather wore his new wife on his sleeve like a living status symbol, blissfully unaware that this was regarded by most down-to-earth folk who knew him well as amounting to virtually all symbol and very little status. But he couldn't have cared less for such opinions, even if anyone had dared offer him them. He had stumbled upon a hitherto undreamed-of escape from the lacklustre, disruptive domestic life of recent years, he was enjoying himself once more, and that was all that mattered to him. He was his own boss, could do whatever the 'bliddy hell' he wanted, and anybody who had a problem with that could bugger right off! And fair enough, too, it could be said. But then, totally out of character with his principle of jealously guarding the confidentiality of his financial affairs (even his bank manager didn't know what he was worth), he acceded to Alexandra's patiently persuasive demands to allow her to assume responsibility for keeping the farm's accounts.

'OK, I want to be bought out of my share of the business!' was Big Jim's response when his father delivered that bombshell of news to him. His reaction may well have been too knee-jerk for his own long-term good, and it was privately regarded as such by the rest of the family. But, when all was said and done, he *had* done all the farm's book-keeping work since the days of his accountancy apprenticeship, he was a full partner in the business (as his late mother had been), and, understandably, he took it ill that this key role had been wrested from him without as much as a 'by your leave'. Like everyone else, he had done his best to make Alexandra feel part of the family, whether he actually felt she deserved it or not. But a slap in the face like this only served to fan a fuse of resentment that had probably smouldered within him since what had been, in his eyes, his father's foolhardy marriage to someone who may have been little more than a cool and calculating gold-digger. Jim's partnership with his father was duly dissolved, and the continuation of a generations-old history of his family's farming activities was thrown into doubt in one fell clash of hurt pride and ingrained intransigence. Alexandra, if she had so wished, could not have planned or laid the foundations of her own future more artfully.

I was twenty-four by now – more than old enough to recognise the poignancy of this rift in family solidarity. In the four years following Grandfather's surprise wedding to Alexandra, I had seen a gradual cooling in Big Jim's attitude towards his father, a deterioration in a relationship which, on reflection, I suppose had never appeared particularly warm in any case. But now, the final parting of the ways really had come. If Granny had indeed had a secret hunch that the move to Hopefield might not turn out to have the positive connotations that the farm's name suggested, then her powers of intuition had now been substantiated beyond doubt. As things stood, her husband and her only son, on whom she had doted and for whom she had sacrificed so much, would never exchange another word.

So, what would become of Big Jim now? He had received a substantial amount of money in compensation from his father – not enough to buy another farm of viable size cash-down, but certainly sufficient to make a decent down payment on one. But it soon became apparent that a commitment to farming on any scale larger than Cuddy Neuk's fifty acres was not an option that Jim was interested in considering. Perhaps, then, his sharp financial brain would guide him towards making shrewd investments with his new-found capital, investments that would ensure his future security within the enviable freedom of a comfortable lifestyle. However, still smarting from the trauma of the split with his father, the 'live for today' side of Jim's nature took over, and he set about going direct for the 'comfortable lifestyle' part of the equation, and with immediate effect at that. He was still only in his mid-forties, and there were good times aplenty yet to be had. Shrewd investments and future security would have to get in line!

Perhaps this seemingly reckless throwing of financial caution to the wind was prompted by a belief that he'd be on the receiving end of a nice windfall when his father eventually died. Certainly, I'd often been told by Jim that Hopefield should have been *all* his anyway, as his grandfather had actually bequeathed Backaskaill, the family's original six-hundred-acre farm in Orkney, to him and not to Grandfather. He was absolutely adamant that this was the case, and only the fact that he'd been a minor at the time had allowed his father to 'massage' the legalities of the situation for his own ends. Why Jim hadn't used this claim to his advantage at the time of his ultimate showdown with his father, only Jim knew. In any case, the eventual outcome of such legal intrigue was still a few years away. One thing was already certain, though – *if* his stepmother succeeded in outliving his father, without first having gone the way of all previous Hopefield housekeepers, Jim would have a formidable adversary to face when the time finally did come for him to assert his alleged birthright. Time, once again, would tell.

★★★★★

The effect of all this high drama on my own future was accepted by now as being totally inconsequential. I'd long since known that, if I wanted to fulfil my childhood dreams of following in the farming footsteps of my mother's side of the family, I'd have to find a way of doing it off my own bat. Over the years, Grandfather had made his views increasingly clear to me – farming was too hard a life and I should put all thoughts of being involved in it out of my mind. It could be a 'fine-enough-like' life at times, he admitted, but a hard life, nevertheless, and one I'd be best advised to avoid. Quite how he could be a qualified judge of such matters, when he'd never known anything outwith farming himself, always puzzled me. But that apart, I'd taken it as a foregone conclusion from an early age that Jim would rightfully inherit the family farming business, and as he would eventually have, in all probability, a son of his own to pass everything on to, I had long recognised that I was one generation removed from entitlement of participation of any kind. That was a simple fact of life, and I had not the slightest complaint. I'd find my own way … somehow. But – and it was a big but – just how does a young lad with neither money nor material assets set about accumulating the sort of capital required to become a farmer? Arriving at an even faintly plausible answer to that one would take some doing. Not surprisingly, the more realistic influences of my parents were bound to prevail – at least initially.

Having dutifully heeded Granny Muir's entreaties to 'stick in at school', I'd left at seventeen with more than enough qualifications to go to university. Unfortunately, having had a natural flair for drawing, I'd been cajoled into specialising in art, which meant that to comply with the abstruse rules of Scottish education, I'd had to give up science studies at the end of third year in secondary school. Consequently, the opportunity of studying agriculture at university was denied me. By the time I'd realised the choice-limiting consequences of complying with the head teacher's erroneous but unbending assumptions that I'd take up a career in art, it was already too late. Oh, the folly of 'we know what's good for you' educationalists expecting kids of thirteen or fourteen to make decisions which can dictate the course of their entire lives – whether for better or for worse. So, what now? Well, I could always just go and work on a farm, I reasoned, but then that would fly in the face of family expectations and render the years and effort spent in higher education at school a complete waste. Art college? I'd already been accepted, after all. No, I wasn't the bohemian type, didn't fancy embarking on a career designing wallpaper, and the prospect of eventually having to take a teaching job appealed even less.

'Why not apply for the civil service?' my father suggested one day. 'You could carve out a good future in the Ministry of Agriculture, you know. OK, it wouldn't actually be *farming* as such. But, well – you know ...'

No, I didn't know.

'Your father's got something there,' my mother keenly concurred. 'Yes, the civil service. Good idea. Ministry of Agriculture ... keeping in touch with farming. You might even be working outdoors – sometimes – well, eventually.'

'And there's the security,' my father added, looking at me sagely. 'Rock-solid pension to look forward to. Plenty perks too. Hmm, and with your school qualifications ...'

It was beyond me why two intelligent people would want to encourage their own kid to embark upon a career in the very organ of government that they had both worked for and had duly escaped from without a backwards glance. Yet, the more they talked to me about it, the more I thought there might just be something in what they were saying. I'd start off with a really good salary, with automatic annual increments, and there'd be even more attractive hikes in my earnings once I got onto the promotion ladder, which probably wouldn't take that long ... with my school qualifications. Oh, and I'd have plenty of time to keep up my keen musical interests, my parents added, smiles of eager expectation on their faces.

The musical carrot did it for me. Put that way, the civil service could indeed provide me with the best of both worlds – a secure career combining good financial prospects with *some* sort of connection with agriculture, and with no threat to my passionate involvement in music. *Jazz* music, which I'd thrown myself into with unrestrained gusto since gradually abandoning my bagpipes in favour of the clarinet after seeing *The Benny Goodman Story* at Haddington picture house. Five other lads in the town also shared my enthusiasm for jazz, took up the other instruments needed to make up a band, and before long we'd formed The Hidden Town Dixielanders – the 'Hidden Town' being popularly regarded as perhaps the original name of Haddington. It probably wasn't, but we reckoned 'Hidden Town' had a good jazzy ring about it, so we hijacked it for the name of the band anyway.

Local popularity in our keener-than-accomplished efforts had grown almost as quickly as our ambition, but there was a limit to how many engagements we could obtain in a rural county like East Lothian. We could blast our sketchy repertoire of jazz standards round the same handful of village halls only so often before reaching saturation point and generating total public apathy. The time had come to launch our nascent jazz musicianship on the unsuspecting citizens of Edinburgh, and if I was actually going to be *working* in the city, just think of all the valuable contacts I'd be able to make. Band agents, jazz club proprietors, ballroom managers, tour promoters, record and radio producers … Yeah, just think!

Without further ado, I filled in the application forms for the Direct Entrant Executive Officer Scheme which the civil service had only just introduced. This was a revolutionary shortcut to an executive 'grade' that had previously taken people a few years of exam-passing and ladder-climbing even to reach the bottom rung. As long as you had university-entrance qualifications, all you had to do was submit your application, get all the required references, make a good impression in front of a panel of grey-suited old establishment fuddy-duddies, and you were in. Easy. All good and well in theory, perhaps, but when it came to the actual interview, the Grey Suits didn't take things quite so lightly, as I immediately found out. This was a very serious matter, Mr Kerr, they stressed – a requirement on their part to select, from many hundreds of applicants throughout Britain, the few young people who possessed the rare qualities of maturity, leadership, unquestioning deference to the rules of the establishment, conservatism of appearance, and sobriety of habit so essential for persons who were to be groomed for the upper echelons of, uhm, government.

I should have run a mile right there and then! But then again, I told myself when exiting on shaky legs the funereal marble foyer of the interview venue in Edinburgh's prestigious Drumsheugh Gardens, the Suits seemed to have taken careful note of my desired involvement in the practical aspects of farming. A couple of them had even asked me some surprisingly knowledgeable questions on the subject. No, on balance, it hadn't been too negative an ordeal. And even if I did become one of the chosen few (which I probably wouldn't) I'd most likely find that life in the Ministry of Agriculture would be all right. Hmm, maybe. But anyway, I'd always be able to look forward to playing in the band at weekends ... maybe some weekday evenings too, once I'd made those crucial Edinburgh connections. Still, no point in worrying about all of that for the moment. I'd just enjoy my freedom from school and forget about the future uncertainties of life while I could. I'd get some really serious clarinet-practising done – spend some time listening to those old jazz 78s that Dad had picked up from the wee record shop at the bottom of Market Street. Yes, I might even be able to buy a few more, if I could pick up a bit of farm work to earn a bob or two occasionally.

Life could hardly have been better for the next few

weeks. Then a brown envelope dropped through the letterbox, and inside was a formal notification from the Civil Service Recruitment Selection Board. I could hardly believe my eyes. My application had been successful. I was to become one of the first of the chosen few, starting my introductory training at a place and time to be notified in due course. However, the actual date of commencement wouldn't be before my next birthday, eighteen being the minimum age permitted for taking up a post as an Executive Officer in Her Majesty's Government Service. My parents were thrilled. With Minnie already established and happy in her first job at one of the local banks, they were probably also as much relieved as thrilled that I'd landed on the threshold of a 'good, solid career' as well. For myself, all I could be sure of was that I'd now have about half a year to work on the farm along the road. That, I was most certainly looking forward to.

I'd done odd jobs at Lennoxlaw at weekends and during school holidays often enough before, so I knew that farmer John, although a young man with a modern outlook, still had great respect for traditional ways and the men who had spent their lives following them. His recognition of the inevitability of progress was expressed in the form of one little grey Ferguson tractor, which Dod and Watty, his two trusty old farmhands, were quietly encouraged to drive for specific tasks. Nothing too complicated, just pulling trailers, doing a bit of harrowing, rolling pastures, simple jobs like that. The rest of the time they were left to work with their respective pairs of Clydesdale horses, following the same routines in the same way that they had done since boys. This was one farm on which gradual change was the preferred policy, unlike so many others where the old ways had been abandoned almost overnight. I greatly valued having an opportunity to work, for even those few months, with one foot in the farming past and the other in the future – no doubt for the very last time.

It was their pipes that fascinated me, and the look of sheer contentment on their faces as they lit up and released those first urgently sucked puffs of smoke out of the corners of their mouths. Dod and Watty claimed they'd been smoking pipes since they were entrusted with their first pair of horses by the farmer when they were 'just wee laddies fresh oot o' school – thirteen, maybe fourteen year-auld at maist'. And there was certainly something right, something at one about the look of the stubby little briars gripped firmly between the teeth of those wiry old boys while they went about their daily chores. Whether sitting on a horse cart bringing home 'neeps', forking muck from a midden, or building a stack of sheaves, the pipe was always protruding from their faces like a second nose. And it looked every bit as natural.

I should have known better after the nasty experience I'd had when trying to smoke a cigarette butt in the mini-pipe that Big Jim had given me all those years ago, but the spell spun by Dod's and Watty's easy execution of the art blew my common sense away like a swarm of midgies caught in their tobacco reek. I bought a pipe with my first week's wages at Lennoxlaw. It wasn't the short type with a tin lid to the bowl traditionally favoured by the old horsemen, but a more elegant model, long of stem and sleek of line, more in keeping with a trail-blazer for the new wave of youthful pipe smokers that I fancied I was about to launch. Watty and Dod were delighted – or so it appeared to me as they chortled quietly on inspecting my new purchase.

'Better fire it up then, son,' said Watty, a little man so slight of physique that you wondered how he had the strength to walk in the huge, upturned, hobnailed boots that were an essential part of the ploughman's working garb. 'Here, have a slice o' this.'

His friend Dod was about half as tall again as Wattie, as laid-back and laconic as his wee friend was perky and garrulous. But, like Wattie and all of their hard-working brotherhood, there wasn't an ounce of spare flesh to his sinewy frame, honed to a permanent fitness fundamental to the nature of their lives of labour shared with heavy horses.

'Warhorse,' Dod said, nodding his head sideways at the black, tarry-looking plug of tobacco from which Wattie was cutting a slice. 'Ye get it frae the Copie store doon the street.'

'Cannae get the flavour o' this Warhorse stuff frae nothin' else, son,' Watty declared, depositing the little piece of condensed tobacco in the palm of my hand.

I'd watched them going through this routine often enough, so I didn't need any instruction – rub the plug with your thumb until the strands separate, tease them out, then pack the wad carefully into the bowl of the pipe. The two old boys watched closely as I struck a match and took the first drag. The result was totally predictable. To my untrained palate, the Warhorse plug did have an equine quality to it, a taste more in keeping with what might have been shovelled off a stable floor than something derived from a plant, however.

'Aye, ye'd better start off wi' some laddies' baccy, son,' Watty laughed after I'd retched and coughed fit to tear my lungs out. 'Get yersel' some Condor sliced. No as cool on the tongue as the Warhorse, mind, but no just as strong either, if ye see what Ah mean.'

I didn't, but I took his word for it anyway, and gave up pipe smoking for good there and then.

'Ye can always use it for blowin' bubbles,' Dod grunted, raising a mordant eyebrow at the sight of me stuffing the pipe into my haversack.

I said a silent 'Amen' to that.

We were sitting on the ground with our backs against a five bar gate, drinking tea from our flasks and watching the day. It was a bright summer morning and we were taking a short break from loading newly baled hay onto trailers and carting it to the stack yard back at the farm. The hay field overlooked the river, its water clear and almost motionless save for the occasional plop and splash of a trout rising to take one of the tiny insects hovering and flitting over the surface. Through the lush canopy of chestnut and oak leaves whose shade dappled the wide grassy haughs beyond the river, we could see the ancient parish church of St Mary's standing solid, steadfast and buttressed, half of its great sandstone bulk showing evidence of the ruinous attentions paid to it during a long seige of the town back in the sixteenth century – the Scots and the 'Auld Alliance' of the French versus, as ever, the frequently-invading armies of the 'Auld Enemy', the English. From our vantage point on rising ground, Haddington could truly be described as a 'hidden town', nestling in its secret valley straddling a crook in the Tyne's slowly winding path to the sea.

In those latter years of the 1950s, the sounds drifting over the river from the town were the same familiar sounds of a country town going about its daily business that had prevailed for as long as anyone could remember. The metallic song of the sawmill still operating in the very heart of the town, the urgent clang of the school bell beckoning reluctant pupils to class, the creaking of the water wheel at the old Poldrate grain mill, the steady chiming of the town hall clock marking the quarter hours from daybreak carillon till evening curfew, the forlorn lowing of cattle in the slaughterhouse field, the piping whistle of a train leaving the little station on the far side of town. Soon, all but the sound of the town clock would be as obsolete as Dod's and Watty's Clydesdale horses standing patiently between the shafts of their carts, ears twitching at flies, soft mouths chewing at the bit. It was a time to be savoured … if only we'd known how short-lived those precious, unhurried days were destined to be.

From haymaking, through harvest to autumn '*tattie howkin*' time, I worked away happily with the two old chums, glad to be delegated tractor driving duties by them while they opted at every opportunity to yoke up their horses for each job as it came along. And the work of the seasons got done just the same, albeit at a slower pace than the fully tractor-powered farms round about. But there was always time to stop for a breather and a chat, a *blether* about everything and nothing, milestones of rest in the passing day's work, marked by the vital need to clean out, refill and relight those ever-present little pipes. The seasoned old pipe-smoker didn't need a watch to tell him when it was time to take a break. I could easily have swapped their simple, satisfying way of life for all the security and so-called prestige of my looming civil service career.

It was on a frosty October morning that my father came into the Lennoxlaw steading, a look of anticipation on his face. I was mucking out a cattle shed with a fork, hard pushed to keep two horse carts loaded as Dod and Watty ran a shuttle of dung deliveries between yard and midden.

'The postie just brought this for you,' Dad said, handing me the ominous brown envelope.

Ten minutes later I was in the Accident and Emergency Unit of Roodlands Hospital on the other side of the valley. I'd been so flabbergasted by the contents of the letter that I'd made to thrust the fork into the deep bed of dung I was standing on, only to misjudge the angle and stab one muck-smeared prong straight through the big toe of my right foot. The nurse's application of strong disinfectant to the wound, a quick anti-tetanus jab and a course of antibiotics would see to my toe's immediate welfare, but it was the long-term prospects for my entire life that concerned me more just then. The letter from the Civil Service Appointments Board had informed me that I'd been assigned, not to the Ministry of Agriculture, but to the Ministry of Labour – or the Department of Employment as it's called these days. Instead of keeping in touch with farming, no matter how tenuously, I'd be spending the rest of my working days submerged in the dull, airless mysteries of unemployment trends and statistics, sitting in some charmless government office building or other hatching a pension and going quietly doolally. God, the most exciting thing I'd have to do would be to sign the Official Secrets Act.

*****

The Ministry of Labour's Scottish headquarters was located in a multi-storey concrete block with windows in Edinburgh's Fountainbridge area, a nondescript back street not a stone's throw from the drab tenement underbelly of Scotland's capital that Sean Connery had just recently swapped for the bright lights of London. From the window of my fourth floor office I had panoramic views over the roof of Alexander's sprawling garage and coach works to the municipal meat market, and beyond to McEwan's Brewery and the North British Rubber Works. On a clear day, I could almost make out the smoke rising through the intervening jungle of chimney stacks from the steam trains leaving Haymarket Station only half a mile to the west.

That awful first day in infant class at Haddington school had been a breeze compared to this. Both experiences were dominated by the feeling of imprisonment, of freedom forfeited, first for the sake of education, now for the carving of a 'secure' career, a life of promised boredom in exchange for the guarantee of rock-solid superannuation after forty years of dedication to the Ministry. If I lived that long! At least I'd been able to smell the countryside through the classroom window. Whether it was the sweet June aroma of new-mown hay or the dry-hot smell of straw at harvest time, you were always just a sniff away from things fresh, wholesome and familiar. Somehow, the whiff of traffic fumes mingled with the sickly fug of fermenting malt and the viscid hum of molten rubber just didn't compare very favourably at all.

I stuck it for eighteen months – eighteen months that afforded me plenty of time during the dreary daily bus journey to reflect on the rashness of allowing your head to rule your heart in matters as important as choosing what to do with the rest of your life. It wouldn't happen again, of that I was certain. One positive thing to come of my flirtation with the city, though, had been connections made to further the progress of the band. A trip to London to make our broadcasting debut on BBC Radio led to a recording contract, and the resultant brace of 45s generated the offer of a two-month engagement in Germany – a month in Cologne, a month in Mannheim. I can now imagine that my parents' dismay could only have been outdone by the sheer disbelief of my civil service chiefs when I announced that I was resigning my post, with all its associated prestige, security and promise. Those civil service superiors didn't hide their astonishment. My parents did, although it isn't hard to envisage the misgivings that must have been bombarding them when I drove off for the Dover ferry 450 miles away one dark and rainy November night in 1959. Piled into my battered old Bedford van was a newly formed band, re-named Pete Kerr's Dixielanders, and comprising a line-up of seasoned Edinburgh jazz musicians – only one other of the original six 'Hidden Town' band members sharing my optimism enough to turn pro as well. I was still only nineteen years old, my future prospects, so recently assured for life, now stretching no farther than sixty-one days ahead, and the likelihood of somehow becoming involved in farming again seeming more remote than ever.

## CHAPTER THIRTEEN

## FROM BAGPIPES TO
## THE BEATLES AND BACK AGAIN

If I'd thought it was hard work loading cattle muck onto two horse carts all day with only one pair of hands, a fork and muscle power, I was about to be taught a lesson in the jazz clubs of Germany. Playing to hundreds of gyrating dancers in the stifling heat of intimate cellar clubs from 8 p.m. till 3 a.m. seven nights a week, with four-hour matinées every Saturday and Sunday afternoon, would have tested the stamina of even a Clydesdale horse – *if* you could have found a musical one crazy enough to take on the task. Looking back, I suppose that we, and the other British jazz bands that were taking up those offers to play in Germany round about 1959/60, were paving the way for what became known as 'beat groups', four-piece guitar-based bands like the Beatles, who would serve their rock 'n' roll apprenticeships in such clubs soon after. But for the present, jazz reigned supreme, and we delighted in the chance to play our chosen music as full-time professional musicians.

But any ideas we may have had about seeing much of Germany while we were there were soon knocked on the head by sheer exhaustion. With only two twenty-minute breaks in each nightly seven-hour session, all we were fit for when the last dancing night owls had stumbled out of the club was the short walk to our humble lodgings and a few hours' sleep, before surfacing for a bite to eat prior to a band rehearsal most afternoons. We were nothing if not keen, especially considering the modest amounts we were being paid for our sweat and dedication.

The concentrated nature of the work did much to hone our musicianship, however, and two months of being a bandleader, paymaster, counsellor, bossman and whipping boy to a bunch of obstreperous 'groovers' of jazz musicians, most of them much older than myself, taught me more about human nature and man-management than several years studying psychology (or psychiatry!) would ever have done. For each of us in our own way, the German experience was both an adventure and an education, and an opportunity to sample another country's way of life. None of us would have missed it. But, despite the success which we enjoyed in Cologne and Mannheim, no further work was forthcoming at the end of our two month stint, either in Germany or the UK. That, as we found out the hard way, is just the way it is for up-and-coming bands in a highly competitive business.

And so we arrived back in Scotland, tails firmly between our legs, with absolutely no prospects of being able to continue playing our chosen music for a living. The band duly broke up, and we all went our separate ways. My bold attempt at being my own man and starting an odyssey in search of the wherewithal to become a farmer in my own right had lasted precisely sixty-one days. Suddenly, memories of that imprisoning Ministry of Labour office in Fountainbridge and thoughts of a secure, pensionable career began to look a whole lot more attractive. But it was too late for that. Those bridges had been burned, never to be rebuilt. The civil service has a way of ensuring that those disloyal to the sacrosanct system are given forever to ponder the folly of their ways. I was still only twenty, so I was going to have plenty of time to do my own particular pondering.

I was also going to have plenty of time on my hands to make up for those two months spent away from Ellie. We had known each other since schooldays, and I suppose we'd been sort of childhood sweethearts for years without even realising it. Or maybe that was just the naivety of youth – at least on my part. The first time I saw her she'd have been about thirteen or fourteen, clambering over a wall to catch and knock six bells out of a much-feared school bullyboy who'd dared pull her hair. She had the prettiest face I'd ever seen, and a right hook to match. Just how an angelic-looking little creature like that could stand up for herself in such a determined and fearless way must have created some kind of prophetic genetic attraction for me. The very next day, I gave her a hundred 'lines' as a punishment for running in the school corridor. As a prefect, that was one way of introducing yourself to a member of the opposite sex without having to resort to some awkward teenage chat-up line. But Ellie couldn't have been less impressed even if I had, and it took several more penalties of having to write *I must not run inside the school'* a hundred times before she even deigned to look at me as if I wasn't some kind of ill-intentioned perv. Being sixteen, a couple of years older than her *and* a prefect, my attentions had painted me in Ellie's eyes as not only a candidate for a 'dirty old man' tag, but an objectionably authoritarian dirty old man at that. So, it took some time to convince her that I was actually a fairly decent bloke, despite my advanced years and position of power in the corridors of school. But my persistence was eventually rewarded by her 'allowing' me to walk her home after school one Friday evening. Yes, such girlie magazine starts to innocent teenage romances really did happen in the mid-fifties. A boy chases a girl until she catches him? Well, that's certainly how a contemporary pop song described such things, and lyric writers are usually on the ball, aren't they? Whatever, although we could never have anticipated it at the time, those very qualities of self-preservation and latent pugnacity that Ellie had displayed in seeing off the school bully were ultimately to contribute invaluably to our future lives.

I'd asked Ellie's mother, herself a native of Cologne, to translate the band's publicity material into German for me just before setting out on what had turned out to be my embarrassingly short-lived journey to fame and fortune. But in any case, Ellie and I had promised to keep in touch by letter while I was away, and she had been nothing but encouraging and supportive throughout, even when it had become apparent that my best-laid plans, like those of Rabbie Burns' famous mouse, were destined to 'gang a-gley'.

'Never mind,' she said when I eventually swallowed my pride and walked over to visit her at her mum's house on the other side of Haddington after a couple of days of wound-licking, 'something will turn up. You'll see.'

Little did I know then that those very words would be

repeated by Ellie more times than I care to remember in years to come – usually in reponse to my question: 'What the hell am I gonna do next?' But she meant what she said that first time just as much as she has since. And she's usually been right. She certainly was on that fateful winter's day in 1960 when I believed my future to be as bleak as the February weather.

'Pack your case,' my father said when I returned home a little later, 'you're going on the road with the Clyde Valley Stompers in the morning. I mean, I'm assuming you'll accept their offer, right?'

The Clyde Valley Stompers? Me? I thought he was kidding, giving my leg an uncharacteristically cruel pull. Why would Scotland's top jazz band and a national showbiz institution want me to join them? I wasn't even in their league. But Dad wasn't kidding. Once again, those two little 45rpm records that I'd made earlier with my own band had turned out to be door-openers for me. Unknown to me, hearing them, and apparently liking what they'd heard, had prompted the Clydes' leader to sound me out as a last-minute replacement for their clarinet player, who had decided not to accompany them on their impending move from their Glasgow 'home' to a new base in London. He didn't have to sound me out twice!

*****

I'd long known how hugely popular the Clyde Valley Stompers were north of the Border, filling concert halls, theatres, dancehalls and clubs to overflowing all over the country, even playing for the Queen on a recent Royal Variety Show, but the scale of their popularity in England took me totally by surprise. They were regarded as one of the top handful of jazzbands in the land, and had a date sheet of bookings as full as my own band's had been empty. Admittedly, their stature as a leading 'name' meant that they played on live engagements for an absolute maximum of only two hours per night, compared to the seven-plus hours that we'd been accustomed to doing in Germany, but when you added the volume of engagements to the travelling involved on what was a permanent round of one-night stands, the familiar exhaustion element soon crept back in. Playing the music wasn't regarded as work – getting to where you were playing it most certainly was, particularly taking into account that there was still only one motorway in England, the original eighty-mile stretch of M1 from London northward to Rugby.

Days and nights of staring up the exhaust pipes of diesel-belching trucks while wending our nose-to-tail way through Britain's hopelessly outdated and inadequate tangle of trunk roads was the price we paid for popularity. Three months on the road without a single night off was the norm. Added to that were recording sessions, radio broadcasts and television appearances, all squeezed into an already over-full diary of one-nighters. Not too surprisingly, the leader of the Clydes packed it in after the band's first year based in England, retiring, burned out, to a quiet family life on the island of Jersey. At the age of twenty-one, and only twelve short months since staring musical oblivion in the face, I found myself leading a band once more, but this one with a whole new heap of responsibilities and commercial commitments attached. At that level, there's no room for mistakes. Agents, managers, promoters, producers and the public alike have expectations which have to be met, the bottom line being that good money is involved, and they all want value for it.

It was generally suspected that, without the Stompers' long-established bandleader at the helm, we would soon land flat on our faces. But with the injection of some fresh talent and musical style in a shaking-up of the band's personnel, we not only maintained the status quo of success, but quickly built on it. Things were going so well, in fact, that on my first fleeting visit back to Haddington, I drove Ellie in my brand new Ford Zephyr car to Edinburgh Zoo, there, in the romantic setting of the penguin enclosure, to pop the question. To Ellie that is, not to a penguin. We were married on the following New Year's Day, the only day off the band had on our annual two-week winter tour of Scotland. With my new wife beside me, I hit the road back south for London again immediately after the reception. Life was rushed, but good.

Our first record under a new contract with EMI, a jazzed-up version of Prokofiev's *Peter And The Wolf*, became not only the Clyde Valley Stompers' first entry into the pop charts, but also one of the earliest chart successes for our producer George Martin, who would shortly lend the benefit of his skills to an unknown quartet of Liverpool lads in the same Abbey Road recording studio in London. But just then we knew no more about the Beatles than we did about any other of several similar Liverpool groups who played the interval spots for touring jazzbands like ourselves when booked to appear in the sweat-oozing confines of the city's now-hallowed Cavern Club. How quickly and spectacularly billings and fortunes would change.

The success of *Peter And The Wolf* opened new doors of

opportunity for the Clydes – invitations, for instance, to play guest spots in movies starring Norman Wisdom and Tommy Steele, plus a flood of network television engagements on shows like *Thank Your Lucky Stars*. It was on one of those that I first recall encountering the Beatles – a weary-looking bunch of fellows who'd arrived at London's Teddington Lock Studios in a little Ford Thames van with no side windows, lugging their own equipment, and looking as if they'd been travelling all night and needed a good sleep. Nobody gave them a second glance. They did their spot on the show, a live performance of their first EMI single, 'Love Me Do', to a reception from the audience of teenage girls that was more polite than even mildly excited. The girls were no more interested in the Beatles than they were in a plethora of other hopeful new groups that were around in the UK then. It was a current pop superstar called Billy Fury they'd come to see, scream at and – according to the blasé television floor manager – to wet their knickers about. Later, when we were leaving the studio car park in the relative comfort of our Commer minibus, we waved goodbye to the Beatles, who still looked jaded and totally fed up as they lugged their instruments back into their little van, unnoticed by the crowd of young female fans wildly mobbing Billy Fury just a few paces away.

But almost before anyone could yell *Help!*, the Beatles had graduated from their cramped Ford van to stretch limos and private jets, had overtaken Billy Fury and his like as the knicker-wetters' delights, and every type of popular music that didn't conform to what had been swiftly dubbed the Merseybeat Sound was starting to feel the effect of change in the public's fickle taste. Yet the Clyde Valley Stompers, in their own field (which was a world apart from the Fab Four and the whole pop music genre anyway), looked in good shape to weather any approaching storm. Our records were selling well, our engagement diary was as full as ever, and we were still pulling in full houses all over the country. Then Dame Fortune decided to wet her own knickers – right on top of us!

A dispute with the all-powerful management people who were the de facto owners of the band resulted in their stripping us of the very name that we'd done so much to widen the popularity of during the previous few years of incessant work and commitment. And Grandfather thought that *farming* was too hard a business to get involved in!

We resolved to keep going under a different name, but the speed at which the work ceased to come in was an education in the volatility of human loyalties and the shallowness of public acclamation. A few weeks previously we'd been appearing at the Royal Albert Hall in London, now we were struggling to get bookings in the back rooms of provincial pubs. Same band, same music, but no longer flying the Clyde Valley Stompers banner. We struggled on for a year, glad to travel any distances to fulfil whatever engagements did come in. On one occasion we even made the epic journey from a university hop in Southampton to Lerwick in the Shetland Isles – almost 600 miles by land and sea, and just about as far between gigs as it's possible to travel in Britain. But the whole music scene had changed, and the stark reality of just what we were up against was thrust home with bitter irony one miserable, rainy night in north London.

The whole band was living under the same roof in Finchley, existing on luxury food like sausages and beans when we were flush, but more often on a staple diet of bread, milk and curried cornflakes. Feeling more down in the dumps than usual this particular night, we decided to buy ourselves a little cheer by pooling what little money we had and nipping round the corner to the pub for a drink. There wasn't even enough change left over to buy a packet of peanuts, so we just sat there in a huddle, sipping our half pints of beer as slowly as we could, and watching the news on the TV set above the bar. You can imagine the po-faced silence that greeted the headline, which went something along the lines of: 'The Beatles take America by storm! Unprecedented scenes of fan hysteria welcome them as they touch down at New York Airport!'

And the newsreel pictures were right there on the screen to prove it. The Beatles had come a long, long way from the car park at Teddington Lock TV Studios. And so had we – but, unfortunately for us, we'd headed in totally the opposite direction.

*****

Ellie had gone back to Scotland with our infant son Sandy shortly after the demise of the Clyde Valley Stompers. It wouldn't have been a life for either of them having to struggle by in some miserable bedsit in London while I was on the road with the band trying to scrape a living. So she'd moved in with my parents in Haddington, my mother looking after Sandy while Ellie picked up her career as a nurse, cycling six miles to the hospital and back every day to earn, not just enough for her and the baby's needs, but also to send me the occasional survival donation with which to buy the vital cornflakes and curry powder. The sacrifices that jazzers *and* their long-suffering wives make to keep the precious music alive!

Broke, all the money that I'd saved during the good times having been spent in trying to keep the band going during the past year, I was faced yet again with zero prospects, and now with three mouths to feed instead of one. But then Dame Fortune decided to show a bit of compassion for a change. The Edinburgh record company chief who'd helped launch my career as a professional jazz musician by releasing those two 45s of my first band threw me a lifeline just when I needed one most. I'd had experience of working under the top record producer in London, he said, so how would I like to give his Edinburgh-based label the benefit of that experience by helping produce records for it? The fact that I was an ex-piper myself would be a great advantage too, he reasoned, as his company specialised in recording purveyors of Scottish music, *including* the World Pipe Band Champions.

Little had I imagined when that old fiddle teacher died all those years ago how my resultant learning of the bagpipes would one day save my bacon. And even less did I imagine now how a future bagpipe connection would give such a fortuitous boost to my aspirations in a totally different sphere.

# CHAPTER FOURTEEN

## GOING HOME

It was going to take a long time to stop missing the thrill of playing jazz for a living, of that I was certain. You don't spend your time travelling, eating, drinking, living, laughing, arguing, celebrating triumphs, sharing disappointments and, best of all, playing that magic music in the company of the same bunch of guys for so long without being consumed by a feeling of emptiness when it's all suddenly taken away. But I was a family man now, with the headache of having to start off from scratch financially once again, but with a cosy little rented cottage back in the heart of the East Lothian countryside, and a new career to carve out in record production. Yet, although this fresh involvement in another aspect of the music business would soon help diminish my pining for the one I'd left behind, that same old longing for the land was still lurking at the back of my mind, a longing as deep as ever, no matter how remote the likelihood of ever being able to satisfy it now.

Meanwhile, Big Jim had settled with unbridled enthusiasm into his chosen life of financial and personal independence at Cuddy Neuk – his financial independence having been created by his business separation from his father, his personal independence the result of the breakdown of his marriage of several happy years. Whether the latter separation had been a result of the former, albeit indirectly, is not beyond the realms of possibility. Could it have been proof of the old adage that says, 'When pleasure becomes a habit, it ceases to be a pleasure'? Perhaps, for not everyone had Jim's capacity for living life to the limit when the mood took him. And the mood to do just that appeared to be taking him ever more frequently these days. On his own again, and with no offspring to provide a future for, Jim had opted for a lifestyle that saw him dividing his time between visiting his favourite watering holes and working at Cuddy Neuk. The more he visited the watering holes, of course, the less time he had for work, but the more his circle of like-minded 'friends' increased. And although he did have some genuine friends, their ranks were now becoming swollen with an increasing number of people who were as much attracted to Jim's free-spending ways as to his infectious, convivial personality. Everybody liked Big Jim, and Jim loved that. He enjoyed nothing more than to sit on his favourite bar stools in the Fly Half lounge in North Berwick, Haddington's Tyne House Hotel, or the Goblin Ha' in the village of Gifford, holding court and distributing his geniality to his social subjects in equal measures with his generosity. Loneliness would surely never be a problem for someone as popular as Jim, not when the living room at Cuddy Neuk was seldom without impromptu gatherings of so many merrymaking mates – particularly when the pubs were closed!

By comparison, the atmosphere in the farmhouse at

Hopefield was almost sepulchral. I used to make a point of dropping by there to visit Grandfather on my way home from the studios on the few occasions when a recording session had finished reasonably early in the evening. The sparkle in his demeanour that the novelty of being married to his new wife had injected was now much less evident, if indeed it had survived at all. Alexandra always put on a show of affability when I turned up, of course, but her performance was less convincing these days, her underlying mood one of creeping boredom, combined with a reluctant acceptance of her present lot – which was evidently lasting a lot longer than she'd anticipated. After exchanging the usual pleasantries, Grandfather would now lead me through to his favoured 'peedie' sitting room for a chat, leaving Alexandra in the kitchen. The 'grand-like lady' appeared to have slipped in status perilously close to that of her original position of housekeeper. But appearances can be dangerously deceptive.

Grandfather's fitness, meanwhile, was visibly on the wane. He was still strong-willed enough to get up as early as ever in the morning to give the day's instructions to his farmhands, still able to get about the fields nearest the house to check on his cattle, albeit with the aid of a walking stick, but his health was beginning to fail, his thoughts returning ever more frequently to the past. During those little conversational lulls when more is often conveyed through intuition than actual words can express, I would watch Grandfather's gaze wander up to where Granny's old graduation photograph now hung above the fireside next to his easy chair. How he must have missed her. In those few quiet moments, all the bluster and bravado that had been his lifelong armour was stripped away, and he was a lonely, vulnerable old man, longing to speak to the only person to whom he could ever confide his true feelings.

'What news o' Cheem?' he said to me on one such occasion, still staring at the photograph. 'Does thoo see much o' Cheem this weather, boy?'

He himself hadn't seen Big Jim for years – not since the dissolution of their business partnership, in fact. I admitted that I did see Jim quite regularly, but avoided telling him that this was in part because Jim had recently lost his driving licence for being drunk in charge, and I was taking my turn, with a few chosen others, to ferry him between Cuddy Neuk and those favourite watering holes of his.

'And what news o' the peedie ferm? Is Cheem still doin' away fine-like at Cuddy Neuk?'

Oh yes, I replied, Jim was doing well at Cuddy Neuk – the land in good nick, all the crops looking grand. I hadn't the heart to tell him the truth, that the place was falling steadily into a state of neglect, with Jim relying more and more on paying contractors to do essential field work for him, as what little equipment he had of his own became increasingly dilapidated. Yields were decreasing, while infestations of expensive-to-combat weeds like wild oats and couch grass were on the rise – both conditions symptomatic of the 'easy' regime of continuous cereal-growing that Jim had followed in the years since going it alone. His father would have been more saddened than annoyed to hear about that, so I thought it best to leave him with the impression that all was well.

Grandfather's sigh and the downcast look in his eyes spoke volumes as he drew his gaze away from Granny's picture. I sensed that he would have given anything just then to have Jim back in the fold, yet his stubborn pride still held him back from even phoning him to ask how he was. Perhaps he still secretly hoped that Jim would one day drive into the yard at Hopefield, bygones would be bygones, and things would be all right between them once more. If only Granny were still alive, I thought to myself, she would have brought Grandfather and Jim together again, a gift for pouring oil on troubled waters being one of her many virtues, one that she'd had ample opportunity to perfect during her lifetime of being married to Tam Muir. But then if Granny hadn't died, the present sorry state of affairs would never have arisen. It was one of those 'if only' situations to which there seemed no solution. All that I and the rest of the family could do was stand helplessly by and watch our two best-loved relations sinking towards unhappiness in their own obstinately contrary ways.

Grandfather died without having exchanged another word with Jim. The old man had been in hospital following a spell of feeling generally unwell. The doctors had been unable to find anything in particular wrong with him, however. It was probably just his age, they'd told my mother – just the old machine running down, showing the effects of a long life of hard work. There was no real cause for concern, though, no need for us to worry, they'd said. But they were going to keep him in hospital for a week or so all the same, just for observation, maybe run a few tests. Never having been hospitalised in his entire life before this, Grandfather hated the feeling of confinement with a passion. Without a shadow of a doubt, he'd have stomped out without even taking time to pull on his wellies ... *if* he'd had the strength. But he was already too weak even to get out of bed without help. It was awful to see someone who'd always been so active and self-sufficient going downhill so rapidly.

'Can thoo no get me oot o' this bliddy place?' he'd pleaded in a faint voice to Mother during one of her visits. 'Mercy me, lass, I'd do anything, *anything*, tae get away hame noo.'

Mother knew that Grandfather, if he insisted, could just sign himself out. But he didn't know that, and as she genuinely believed that his own best interests would be served by following the doctors' advice and staying put, she elected not to enlighten him. For all it hurt her to see her father so distressed, it was simply a case of being cruel to be kind. One person saw the situation in an entirely different light, however. And that person was Grandfather's wife. Here was an opportunity for Alexandra to put into motion the wheels of the agenda which she'd kept hidden (no matter how flimsily) for so long. Mother was told the unsavoury details of it all by a worried and remorse-filled nursing sister when she walked into Grandfather's ward at the start of the next visiting hour, only to find his bed empty.

Almost in tears, the sister related how Grandfather had been particularly upset when his wife visited earlier in the day, dispirited in a way that she'd never seen him before – confused, distraught and begging to be allowed to go home. After some whispered words to him from a purposeful-looking Alexandra, Grandfather had perked up noticeably, pulling himself up into a sitting position in his bed and beckoning two young duty nurses to come over from their desk by the ward door. It was then that Alexandra produced a document and a pen from her handbag, showing Grandfather where to put his signature, then instructing the nurses to sign as a witnesses. Mrs Muir had then returned the document to her handbag, walked out to the sister's office off the corridor, and told her that Mr Muir wished to sign himself out of hospital – immediately. It was only after Grandfather, looking frail and bewildered, had been taken away in a wheelchair that the young nurses told the sister the full story of what had led to his unexpected and ill-advised departure. Apologising profusely to my mother, the sister was at pains to stress that the young nurses had done, in all innocence, what they thought was right. It was only to be hoped, the sister went on, that Mr Muir's condition wouldn't be allowed to suffer now that he'd be without the close nursing care which he clearly needed. Almost as an afterthought, and with little conviction, she added that she trusted the document that had been signed and witnessed in the ward would not have been of any real importance.

At least Alexandra's perfidious actions had granted Grandfather his wish to return 'home', where he died just a few days later. He was laid to rest beside his longed-for Mary in Cockpen Churchyard on a still, misty morning when, just as we were lowering his coffin into the ground, a stiff breeze rose for just a few seconds, causing the little huddle of us who were holding the cords at the graveside to lean momentarily into the wind. Though we were miles from the coast, I could practically catch the tangy whiff of the sea wafting through the valley, could almost hear a familiar wheezy chuckle mingle with the sough of the breeze as it rustled through the branches of the watching trees. It was comforting to imagine that the spirits of Granny and Grandfather had re-found happiness, that they were together again with their peedie daughter Gertie, back on their beloved Orkney island of Sanday at the end of a lifelong journey, gazing out side by side over the wide sweep of

Backaskaill Bay. Home. The thought of it brought a tear to my eye and a sad smile to my lips.

But it was Alexandra who had the last laugh. When Grandfather's will was read, it came as no great surprise to learn that everything of any value, including the farm, had been left to her. The new document which she'd produced from her handbag in the hospital had made certain of that. If indeed Big Jim had been clinging to a hope that he would yet, in some way, benefit from his father's estate, he had been holding onto an unlikely dream. He wasn't even mentioned in the will, and for reasons known only to himself, didn't bother to assert his claim that *all* of the family's farm business had been rightfully his from the time of his own grandfather's death. Maybe, deep down, he'd known all along that such thoughts amounted to no more than rainbow chasing. Or perhaps it was merely that dogged Muir pride that prevented him from contesting the will, in what he would have seen as a demeaning squabble – an undignified legal brawl, which he might very well lose. Alexandra would have done her homework meticulously. She'd had years to do it in, after all. Yet, instead of showing any animosity towards the woman whose scheming had driven a permanent wedge between him and his own father, Jim, in a bizarre show of his often to-a-fault chivalry, invited her out to the local pub for a drink after the will-reading. His invitation was accepted with pop-eyed surprise and patent delight. Paradoxically, Grandfather would never have allowed her even to go near such a place. That would have been totally unacceptable social behaviour for 'decent-like' womenfolk where he came from. Accordingly, Alexandra had allowed herself not even the smell of a gin and tonic since accepting the post of his housekeeper so many rigidly temperant years ago, so there was plenty of lost time to be made up for now, and she couldn't have chosen better company in which to do it. Big Jim, remember, was a seasoned master of the art. He'd been diligently practising it since the day he'd been bought out of the farm following Alexandra's assumption of his long-time responsibilities for looking after the accounts. Maybe there's a touch of irony in there somewhere, but I've never quite been able to figure it out. Had Jim merely been trying to show Alexandra up for what she'd purported not to be by taking her to the pub, or was he genuinely just attempting to bury a hatchet that he'd never really wanted to brandish in the first place? Whatever the truth of the matter, his buying her a few drinks was to make no difference to Alexandra's plans.

Within a matter of weeks Hopefield Farm was on the market. 'Lady Bonnyrigg' couldn't wait to cash in her chips and abdicate. The 'dominion' that her marriage to old Tam Muir had provided had never been one that she either felt or appeared comfortable in, but her perseverance had finally paid off, and she was all set to head back to where she came from as quickly as possible, flaunting the spoils of her … well, of her *perseverance*. Third time for the oft-married Alexandra had proven extremely lucky indeed, as she was at last about to become a very well-off woman. Grandfather's inherent pecuniary prudence and the local council's ongoing purchasing of slices of his land for house building had ensured that all he owned was paid for, his bank balance healthily black and obesely bulging. And just how much folding money was stashed in countless pairs of worn-out wellies safe from the taxman's prying eyes had always been anyone's guess. The patient Alexandra would know precisely how much now, though.

For our mother and her two sisters – one still living in Holland, the other now in Canada – Grandfather's death was mourned in the quiet, undemonstrative way of their island kinfolk. But their grief was none the less painful for that. They felt a terrible sense of loss at the passing of another cherished parent, and since thoughts of ever gaining materially from that loss had never entered their minds, the machinations of the will hadn't really concerned them directly. They'd always assumed that Jim, as the only son, would be the ultimate beneficiary, and while they were deeply saddened by the way things had turned out for him, it was ultimately his business and his business alone. He'd had his chance – a better chance than most could ever dream of – had been master of his own destiny, and would now have to make the best of things. The sisters had all had to do just that, right from the days when they'd been obliged to leave home on Sanday for a whole school term at a time. As always, however, their 'peedie brother' would get all the affection and moral support he might need. With their own individual family responsibilities and commitments, that's all they could offer. And that was probably more than Big Jim, in his stubbornly independent way, would ever have wanted from them anyway.

But it was soon going to take more than an independent nature for Jim to be able to maintain the lifestyle that he'd become accustomed to. If he'd been walking a financial tightrope, the safety net had now been crudely removed.

'Still daft enough to want to be a farmer, Wee Pete?' he asked me when I was visiting him at Cuddy Neuk soon after Hopefield had been put up for sale. He didn't even wait for me to catch my breath. 'Well,' he continued, 'you're big enough and old enough to know better, but if you're determined to give it a bash, fire ahead.'

'How d'you mean?'

'I'm getting the hell out of this bloody farming caper once and for all, so the tenancy of Cuddy Neuk's all yours. Just make your own arrangements with the landlords.'

I was almost stuck for words. 'But – but what about you? I mean, what are you going to do?'

'Never mind about me. You'll have enough problems of your own trying to make ends meet on this place. I think you're off your head if you take it on, but I'll give you one piece of advice now, and that'll be the last.' He looked me sqaurely in the eye. '*Don't* give up your day job, or you'll be following me out of here within a year. Now then – don't just stand there with your mouth hanging open.' Grinning broadly, he brushed his hands together as if ridding them of a lifetime of unwanted dust. 'Fetch a couple o' glasses and let's have a bloody drink!'

Big Jim's decision to quit farming and give me the chance that I'd believed to be less and less likely to happen took me totally by surprise. I was going on thirty, with two young sons now – seven-year-old Sandy's brother Muir having been born just three years earlier – and with only fifteen hundred pounds to my name, I wasn't exactly well set up financially to equip and resurrect the fortunes of what was now a fairly run-down farm. Although I wanted to grab the opportunity more than anything, with a wife and two children to support and a ludicrously inadequate amount of capital available, hitherto unfamiliar doubts and fears suddenly began to take hold of me. Maybe Big Jim was right. Maybe I'd be off my head to take such a risk.

'Don't be silly,' said Ellie when I poured out my thoughts to her that evening. 'You'll never get the chance again, so grab it with both hands.'

'But the money. Let's face it, what we've got in the bank isn't going to see us far. OK, I can keep the freelance record production work going, but if that takes a downwards turn, and if we have a disastrous first harvest because of the weather or whatever, we could be in the deep stuff before we –'

Ellie held up a calming finger. 'Listen, we'll be fine. Fair enough, it won't be easy – nothing ever seems to be. But don't worry about the money side of it, and forget all the negative things that might happen or you'll never get out of the bit. We'll do it, *and* we'll make a go of it. Something will turn up – you'll see.'

Once again, Ellie's unflagging optimism won the day. We decided to take the plunge, knowing full well that we'd have to survive *and* embark on a lengthy improvement programme at Cuddy Neuk with what little funds we had available to us. Going to the bank for a loan was not an option. The last thing we needed when setting out on such a precarious venture was to put ourselves immediately into debt. Not that it was likely the bank would have entertained such an approach anyway. What would we have put up as collateral? We had no assets. We'd only be small tenant farmers, and rookie ones at that, with more high hopes than solid business prospects to trade. And even being granted the tenancy of Cuddy Neuk turned out to be no foregone conclusion. The landlords, quite understandably, wanted to see that we would be worthy custodians of their property before formally transferring the lease to us. They'd make their decision at the end of the first year. Until then we'd be walking our own tightrope without a safety net. A daunting thought.

'So it's shit or bust, is it, Wee Pete?' Jim laughed when I told him. 'Well, you can always jump off that wee cliff up on the hill field if things go tits up. Grand place for a suicide that.'

He was referring, though quite inadvertently, to that same little bluff where I'd tried, unsuccessfully, to emulate my grandfather's ability to lean against the wind all those years ago. The significance of Jim's unwitting analogy was not lost on me, however. If I failed in this challenge, I'd have more than just a smearing of cow dung down the front of my clothes to bother about. And this time Grandfather wouldn't be around to scrape me down at the midden.

\*\*\*\*\*

Alexandra didn't have long to wait for a buyer for Hopefield to come forward. In fact, she only had a couple of brief months in which to act the gentlewoman farmer before the legal missives and dipositions transferring ownership of the property were exchanged and signed. The auction sale of the farm equipment – the *roup* as it's called in Scotland – took place a couple of weeks before the new owners moved in. Everything had been set out in neat rows in the open yard at the side of the steading. When Ellie and I arrived, the place was already milling with people, farmers from near and far wandering along the lines of items for sale, inspecting them carefully, then muttering among themselves about what they thought of the condition of this and that, and what prices might be fetched. There was something a bit ghoulish about the aspect of so many strangers picking over what had been the implements and tools of Grandfather's trade, but Alexandra was obviously enjoying every moment of it. She was moving gracefully among the crowds of dungaree-clad and flat-capped farmers, resplendent in her expensive tweeds, nodding condescendingly hither and thither in distinctly queenly fashion. The aloof and majestic image was dented somewhat, however, when on commencement of the sale she took up position at the auctioneer's elbow, produced a notepad and proceeded to write down the price that every item sold for, right down to the last rusty claw hammer and biscuit tin of used fence staples. The fact that the auctioneer's attendant clerk was already doing that as a matter of course seemed not to matter a jot to the untrusting Alexandra.

'Penny-pinchin' auld hoor,' one unimpressed worthy was heard to mumble to his crony. 'Feart in case she gets done oot o' the price o' a bent fuckin' nail, is she?'

The answer to that rhetorical question would clearly have been 'yes'.

More as a token of maintaining contact with my grandfather's farming past than to further swell the bulging coffers of the rapacious Alexandra with a donation from my meagre resources, I'd resolved to buy a few implements which I knew I was going to need anyway. The autioneer 'knocked down' to me a plough, a fertilizer spinner and, most significantly, an old grass seeder which I remembered Grandfather saying was the sole survivor of all the implements he'd brought down from Orkney with him on the Leith steamer thirty-odd years earlier. That same rickety old grass seed 'barrow' had also been the last implement to which young Fanny, Grandfather's favourite Clydesdale mare, had been yoked before her untimely death at Cuddy Neuk when my sister Minnie and I were young children. It meant much, much more to me than the few quid I paid for it.

'Ah, there you are,' Alexandra beamed on seeing me emerge, cheque book in hand, from the auctioneer's temporary office in one of the sheds after the sale. 'And Ellie too. How sweet. Come round to the house, do. I have something for you.'

Well, well. Surprise, surprise. At least the old tightwad was going to part on a sociable note. And why not, too? Hadn't Ellie and I, like every other member of the family, always gone out of our way to show good will and courtesy towards her, no matter how much her insincerity had made it stick in the craw at times? She could have no beef with us. Perhaps she was about to offer a bit of reciprocation for Jim having treated her to those drinks in the pub. Even if it did just turn out to be a cup of tea and a rock cake in the kitchen, it would be good to have one last look at the old place. Consolidate the memories before the final ties were severed.

'Quite a good turn out for the sale,' I said to Alexandra by way of small talk on the way across the yard to the back of the house. 'Nice day for it too. Quite happy with the prices, were you?'

She didn't answer, so we walked the final few yards in an awkward silence. I opened the door and stood aside to let Alexandra and Ellie through.

'Just wait here,' Alexandra said, sweeping past me. 'Shan't keep you both a moment.'

I was so taken aback that I hardly noticed the small

procession of strangers who then followed Alexandra unannounced into the house. I hadn't a clue who they were – new 'county' acquaintances of Alexandra, obviously, and each one exuding that over-familiar air of the natural upstart that Grandfather wouldn't have suffered within spitting distance of the outside of the farm gate, never mind inside his house. So this was what had finally become of the enterprise of generations of feet-on-the-ground Orcadians, clawing their way up through sheer hard work and personal frugality from their humble origins.

'I thought you might be interested in having these,' Alexandra said, reappearing at the door amid the sound of clinking glasses and unfamiliar laughter from within. 'I certainly shan't have any use for them.' She handed me a large paper bag, then said through a stiff smile, 'I don't suppose we'll meet again. Goodbye.' With that, she closed the door in our faces, and was gone.

Inside the bag were the two old sepia photographs, hand-tinted enlargements of posed studio portraits of my great grandparents, the trail-blazers who had made that first courageous step from the tiny croft of Lealand to the large farm of Backaskaill back on the island of Sanday so long ago. Grandfather had always given these pictures pride of place on the fireplace wall in the 'best' front room. Now Alexandra, in a final show of pent-up disrespect, had even removed the ornate gilt frames before passing on the fragile old prints to the person destined to make some sort of attempt at continuing the family's farming traditions, albeit from the bottom rung of what was now the most insecure of ladders. But Alexandra's revelation of her underlying disrespect for everything and everyone I held dear only made me more determined than ever to succeed, or at least to go down fighting.

'Come on,' I said to Ellie, gritting my teeth. 'Let's go back home – home to Cuddy Neuk. We've got work to do!'

## CHAPTER FIFTEEN

## DAME FORTUNE IS A TRANSVESTITE

'Never trust a grain merchant.' That had been one of
Grandfather's favourite dictums. And he'd had every reason
to be suspicious of that most influential and, indeed, most
powerful of farmers' 'friends'. For not only does the grain
merchant sell the farmer his seed in the springtime, but in
all probability will also buy the resultant grain after it's been
harvested in the autumn. Add to this the possibility that
the same merchant may well have sold the farmer the
fertilizer required to grow the crop – maybe even the
chemicals to control the weeds as well – and you have a
person who holds the potential ability to make the
difference between profit or loss for his trusting clients.
It's all a question of prices. And that's where the all-
important matter of trust comes in, because all the prices
involved – whether selling the seed or buying the grain –
are controlled by the merchant. 'Oh,' he will promptly add,
'strictly according to market conditions prevailing at the
time, of course.' Of course. And this was the root of the

sting by which Grandfather was once almost very painfully stung.

His main arable enterprise at Hopefield was growing barley, a commodity for which there has traditionally been a ready market in Scotland, either for livestock feed or for malting purposes. Cue the sting. The best quality barley is sold to the maltsters, the brewers of beer and the distillers of whisky, whose very existence depends on a reliable supply of the carefully husbanded, low-nitrogen-content grain. Naturally, barley which complies with those customers' strict criteria commands a premium over the price of the lower-quality stuff which goes to the stock-feed market. If that premium is, say, £10 per ton, and you have, as Grandfather had on this particular occasion, maybe five hundred tons or so to sell, the difference to your pocket, depending on which of the two markets you're able to sell to, is going to be quite considerable. It follows, of course, that the same difference applies to the pocket of the merchant who is buying the grain from you, and in those days in particular, you only had his word for which side of the line the essential lab analysis of your barley came down on. This time, the harvest-time sample of Grandfather's barley had analysed favourably as usual, a price had been agreed, and the thousands of sacks of grain were uplifted in due course and transported by road to a distillery in Fife. Then came the lethal phone call from the merchant:

'Sorry, Mr Muir, but spot samples of the barley taken on its arrival at the distillery show that the nitrogen content is too high for malting purposes after all.'

Silence.

'But don't you worry – I've managed to get a reasonable price for your barley from one of the feed mills. A lot less than the malting price, of course, but the good news is that the mill's gonna take delivery right away, straight off the same trucks. Really good news that, 'cos otherwise it'd all have been dumped back at Hopefield, with you having to pay the extra haulage costs. I mean, I really bent over backwards to make sure that wouldn't happen to you, Mr Muir.'

Silence.

'Ehm, Mr Muir … you still there, Mr Muir?' (Nervous laugh.) 'Can't win 'em all, eh? But don't you worry, we always do our best for our most valued customers. The delivery slips and so on are in the post to you, so I'll, ehm … I'll pop in with the cheque the next time I'm –'

'Fuck right off, ye bliddy thievin' bastard!'

Disconnected tone.

At that, Grandfather had jumped into his Ford V8 Pilot and hadn't taken his welly off the 'go' pedal till he reached the distant distillery in question.

'Barley from Muir o' Hopefield at Bonnyrigg?' he barked at the startled weighbridge clerk.

The clerk fumbled nervously through his pile of papers. 'Aye, it's – it's all here, sir,' he stammered. 'All arrived OK.'

'And whar the hell is it now, boy?'

Looking bemused, the clerk shrugged his shoulders. 'Well, up in the big bulk storage silos on the other side o' the yard there. Went straight in off the lorries.' His face fell. 'Here, hope ye're no wantin' it back, are ye?'

Grandfather gave him a rare flash of his gap-toothed grin. 'Nah, nah, thoo's a' right, boy. Just thoo mak me a copy o' yon paper work. That'll do me just fine-like.'

His subsequent threat of taking the sneaky merchant to court for fraudulent dealing resulted in Grandfather receiving an even bigger premium than originally agreed for his barley that year, and his future financial transactions with the same man tended to be notably one-sided – and not, it goes without saying, in the merchant's favour either.

That experience of Grandfather's had served as a valuable lesson in the need to be vigilant in business, and it was one that I hadn't forgotten. That said, it amounted to yet another nerve-fraying item to add to those I'd already accumulated since deciding to take the farming plunge. But I needn't have worried. Compared to some of the shysters I'd encountered in the music world, the folk I now found myself doing business with were the very epitome of openness and straight dealing. Admittedly, the basic principles of looking after your own corner applied just as much as they do in any area of commerce, but the pervading atmosphere in farming circles seemed to be one of fairness and support. In fact, within a couple of days of taking over at Cuddy Neuk, no fewer than four local grain merchants had called, offering us the benefit of their long-established experience and good standing in the business. They knew we were only just starting off, *might* be a bit stretched financially for a while, and would be more than pleased to discuss – if we should ever see the need – trading terms that would help us get on our feet.

So that was one source of worry ostensibly eliminated, and without even trying at that. We knew, however, that equipping the place to a reasonably self-sufficient level wasn't going to be so easy. For starters, we'd bought what little gear Jim had ended up working with. This consisted of a set of five-leaf harrows that badly needing re-toothing, a three-barrel land roller with one barrel cracked and the bearings worn out, a flatbed trailer that was falling to bits, and an old Nuffield Tractor so neglected and exhausted that it had to be parked on a hillside to have any chance of starting the engine again once stopped. Even with the few other implements we'd bought at the Hopefield *roup*, we were still a long way from having enough equipment to get by. We simply had to face the fact that, if we were to avoid the crippling cost of having to hire contractors to do certain essential work for us, we'd have to get our hands on some decent tackle – fast. But that was going to take money, and money was a commodity of which we were already dangerously short. Still, at least my record production work would cover our living expenses, so things could have been worse. With that in mind, I'd even thought of trying to drum up additional recording projects in an effort to earn more disposable capital, but even if that had been possible, it would only have resulted in me having less time to work on the farm. We were heading for the classic catch-22 cul-de-sac.

And the look on the face of our landlords' factor when he paid us his first visit did little to cheer us up. He had a cursory look at the neglected state of the farm equipment and buildings, threw a sidelong glance at the bloom of couch grass showing green above the ploughed furrows in the near field, shook his head, then said through a knowing smirk, 'See you in a year's time then.' He hadn't added the expected '*If* you're still here,' but it was plain he was thinking it all the same.

Then our occasional visitor Dame Fortune decided to call on us again, this time in benevolent mood and dressed in a green, grease-smudged boiler suit. She had adopted the cheery form of Tommy, an old neighbour, the son of a small farmer himself, and for long regarded as one of the county's most skilful agricultural engineers. I hadn't seen Tommy for years. He told me he'd been heading back to his Haddington base after doing an on-farm repair job down the coast near Aberlady, and thought he'd just nip in on the way past to see how I was. Not to disturb me, like – just to see how we were doing.

'Oh, fine thanks, Tommy. Just doing a bit of maintenance here before bashing on with the spring work, you know. Yeah, we're doing OK, thanks.'

I was in the old stack yard overlooking the Aberlady/Haddington road, the open space behind the steading that had once fairly buzzed with the magical activity of the travelling threshing mill when I was a kid. Now the yard stood forlorn and empty, save for our old banger of a tractor and the few hard-up implements I was gamely trying to make a tad more serviceable with what tools I had. I watched Tommy cast an appraising eye over the contents of my miserable little junk yard. Were we going to rely on contractors to do most of the work, just as Jim had done latterly, he asked.

'Nope. Can't afford that luxury, Tom. No, 'fraid we'll just have to make do and mend.'

'So how're ye gonny grub all that chokin' couch grass out o' the land without the right kind o' cultivator? How're ye gonny sow yer barley and stuff without a grain drill? How're ye gonny spray yer weeds without a sprayer? Come to that, how're ye gonny do *any* field work with *that*?' He gestured towards the Nuffield tractor, standing of necessity at the top of the little slope leading down to the farm gate.

There was no answer to his questions. He'd just drawn a word picture of the tip of the iceberg of my equipment nightmare.

Tommy slapped my shoulder and climbed back into his van. 'Free Sunday mornin', are ye?'

'Yeah, nothing much doing on Sunday, Tom.'

'Right, I'll pick ye up at seven in the mornin' – sharp!'

Tommy's work took him to farms all over the county, and, in addition to those much-in-demand expert hands of his, he also had a pair of very good eyes, which he employed to useful effect. As a boy, he'd known his own father to be in a similar position to the one I'd found myself in now, struggling to be self-reliant with little or no money to buy the implements required. His father's way of solving the problem had been to go round the larger farms, picking up for a few bob any suitable items of redundant tackle that the farmers were disposing of for scrap, then he'd patiently restore them to working order for use on his own little place. Tommy had been brought up to keep his eyes open for such likely articles, and the habit had never left him. So even today there was scarcely a farm in the area with *some*thing salvageable lying half hidden in a clump of weeds behind some shed or other that Tommy didn't know about. It struck me that it was a commendable mentality, born of necessity, and not unlike the one that had once prompted my speedway-freak mates and me to go rummaging in the municipal rubbish tip for sundry bits of pushbikes to recycle. By the end of that Sunday, Tom had led me to the various items of equipment that I most urgently needed, including a serviceable starting motor for the tractor, and I'd bought them all for less than fifty quid. It was now up to me to revive the renovation skills learned in those same cycle speedway days twenty years earlier. So, in a bizarre way that I'd never have dreamed of back then, it suddenly appeared that the hassles and headaches of replacing all those ripped wheel spokes and bent pedal cranks were going to prove worth it in the end.

*****

The price paid for the wonderful views that can be enjoyed from Cuddy Neuk is the buffeting of the winds that the farm's elevated position exposes it to from time to time. And seldom more so than when bone-chilling northerlies sweep down from the Arctic Circle in March, the crucial month for the sowing of spring grain in this part of the country. The March winds that poetically doth blow seldom bring snow to East Lothian, though, so the local robins don't have that to worry about. And fidgeting farmers, anxious to get onto the land at the earliest opportunity, positively welcome the drying blasts that will render workable their soil that has lain wet and cold during the long, dark months of winter. Accordingly, as soon as the surface of our own land started to show the right signs on that first spring, the freshly painted and painstakingly refurbished old grain drill that Tommy had found for me was yoked to the tractor and made ready to work without a moment's delay. No thought of following Grandfather's principle of first checking that the moon was in waxing phase even entered my head. People round about were already out in their fields, clouds of dust billowing from the rapidly drying land as they pressed on with their sowing operations, and that was all I was bothered about. I was gripped by the same dread of being left behind that strikes panic into farmers the world over at the impatiently awaited onset of each and every seasonal task throughout the year. Yesterday wouldn't have been too soon to get going, and a minute from now will be too late!

Ellie had married a professional clarinet player, and now found that she'd become a farmer's wife. Earlier in the decade, she'd unselfishly accepted the life of a jazz widow in the loneliness of London during a period that others were calling the Swinging Sixties, while I toured the clubs and concert halls of England for months on end. Then she'd been marooned with two young children in a cottage in deepest East Lothian, while I worked the antisocial hours required of a record producer week after week. I needed the car to get to the studios in Edinburgh, the cottage wasn't on a bus route, so when Ellie needed to escape, even to do a bit of essential shopping in Haddington, she'd had to walk the four miles in each direction, and with two little kids in tow at that. She hadn't had it easy, but to her eternal credit, had never once complained. Grain-sowing time on the north-facing slopes of the Garleton Hills would turn out to provide the ultimate test of her long-suffering nature, however.

Hitched behind the tractor, the old seed drill certainly looked the part, newly painted in its original livery of red, yellow and grey. But having completely stripped it down myself to replace broken and worn components, I felt that I knew too much about its working innards to trust the competence of the reborn machine entirely. What worried me most was the trip lever that lowered the wide row of seed-delivery spouts into the ground at the start of each pass across the field. This was intended to be operated from the tractor seat by me giving a tug on a rope – easy enough to do, but the trouble was that it wasn't really possible for me to see if *all* of the spouts had been brought into play. Better, I reasoned, to get Ellie to stand on the long step at the back of the drill and lean forward to trip the mechanism up or down by hand at each end of the field. Riding on the machine, she'd also be able to see if everything was functioning properly as we went along. It made sense to me, and Ellie accepted my invitation without a word of protest, although she must have been looking forward to the task about as much as she'd have relished having her teeth pulled without an anaesthetic. There was a bitterly cold wind scudding over the field, and she'd be standing out there, totally unprotected from its cruel bite, while I sat in the comparative comfort of the tractor's cab. She deserved a medal for self-sacrifice beyond the call of duty. What she actually got, however, was something notably less rewarding.

'Jesus Christ, woman, can't you bloody well do a simple thing like tripping the machine properly! Hell, a monkey could be trained to do that in five bloody minutes flat!'

'It *is* tripped,' she yelled back. 'See – all the spouts in the ground!'

'Bollocks! Half of them are still raised! Look – just trip the left side of the machine again, for Christ's sake!'

I could see her muttering to herself, her words unintelligible amid the diesel growl of the tractor and the howl of the wind as she crouched down to check that all the drill's moving parts were behaving as they should.

'And stop mumbling! Nothing more annoying than somebody mumbling! If you've got anything to say, bloody well speak up, OK!'

Looking back now, I can't believe how insufferable my bad-tempered outbursts must have seemed to Ellie, nor can I praise her enough for putting up with such inconsiderate tantrums. If I'd spoken to hard-bitten musicians like that, I'd have had a thick lip to go with my big mouth, maybe even a few teeth to play with too. Certainly, any woman with less dedicated patience than Ellie would justifiably have told me to get on with being Mr Perfect by myself, before immediately swapping imposed discomfort in a windswept field for a nice cosy seat by the fireside. Unless said woman happened to be a farmer's wife, that is. For fortunate indeed is the spouse of a grumpy peasant who hasn't had to endure at regular intervals the rantings and ravings of her purple-faced husband when something, *any*thing, has gone wrong – or even when he simply just doesn't actually know what the hell he's doing. If you haven't got a dog handy for kicking on such occasions, take it out on the wife – that's the age-old male peasant's maxim.

Ellie bought a dog the very next day. Jen was her name, a year-old Border collie bitch, being 'reluctantly' sold by an old shepherd holed up deep in the Lammermuir Hills above Gifford village. The reason for parting with such a 'braw wee dug' was that she wasn't taking to working the sheep quickly enough for his liking. He was a very busy man, after all. But she'd make a grand farm dog, he'd promised Ellie – a fine guard beast to have about the place. Oh, and really good-natured too – very good wi' bairns, like. Perfect, thought Ellie. We didn't have sheep anyway, so no problem there. But we did have kids. Jen was duly bundled into the back of the car and transported to Cuddy Neuk. My heart skipped a beat when I first saw her. She was the very image of Nellie, my grandparents' enigmatic collie. It was as if the clock had been turned magically back when Jen came sidling over the yard to greet me in her pseudo-subservient collie way. And her appearance and personality weren't the only things she shared with old Nellie, as time and bitter experience would teach us. But for the moment she was everything the old shepherd had promised, playing football with the boys for as long as they had the energy to keep up with her, living contentedly in an old henhouse in the corner of the yard, and dutifully barking if any stranger drove into her 'territory'. In fact, her only vice appeared to be a weakness for trying to round up the postie's van when he was leaving the farm. Curiously, she ignored him completely on his arrival, but her herding instinct kicked in the moment he headed for the gate. Maybe she thought his van was actually an errant red metal sheep.

But who can fathom the convoluted workings of a collie's brain? I certainly couldn't, nor was I particularly concerned. All that really mattered was that everything seemed to be falling nicely into place. Admittedly, there was still a heap of hard work to do if we were going to avoid being turfed out by the landlords at the end of our first year. It was a bit like being on probation, truly feeling as if the sword of Damocles was suspended above our heads on its fragile strand of hair. But Ellie was rising to the challenge and positively thriving on it, the boys couldn't have been happier, I was doing what I'd always wanted to do, and now we even had a collie that reminded me of Nellie. Also, I'd managed to organise the schedules of my record production work so that I was only away from home for an average of a couple of days most weeks, so although there was precious little time to relax, we were settling into a workable routine and making progress. Things were looking pretty good.

★★★★★

There was no likelihood of our ever reviving dairy farming at Cuddy Neuk. Too much had changed in the business since the days my grandparents and Big Jim had hand-milked their herd of Ayrshires in the byre every morning and evening. Milk production had now become a big operator's game, like so many farming enterprises that were destined to follow the same route soon enough. But we did need a source of farmyard manure to help restore the depleted fertility of the land, so we'd have to find a way of procuring some dung-makers within the limited budget available to us. Bucket-rearing calves – that was the answer, I reckoned. If we bought week-old animals judiciously, we'd be able to build up a small herd to raise for selling on as yearling 'stirks'. A system like that would keep feed requirements and, therefore, costs to a minimum. By the same token, it would be a slow process to create a decent-sized muck heap in this way, but we had to start somewhere, and there was no time like the present. The rows of two-cow stalls in the same byre where I'd first seen a calf born were duly demolished and calf pens built in their place. We were all set, with enough easily manageable accommodation for housing up to thirty calves, and it had cost us nothing but a few buckets full of our own sweat and a load of second-hand timber from a demolition yard.

Wednesday was calf-selling day at Gorgie Livestock Market in Edinburgh, so that became our required port of call every Wednesday from then on. We soon learned the ropes of checking the look and general condition of the dozens of calves huddled in their holding pens before making their individual appearances in the sale ring, confused at the sight of the surrounding sea of human faces, and bawling for their mothers. And there was the rub for prospective buyers. The dairy-cow dams of these little mites could have been over 400 miles away in the south-west of England, and their calves may already have been put through several such market rings by their new dealer-owners in search of the quickest profit possible on the long route north. Edinburgh's Gorgie Mart provided the calf dealers with one last chance to turn their young charges into cash, or be faced with the unthinkable prospect of having to transport them all the way back south again. So there was always the possibility of picking up bargains at Gorgie. Big, strong, lively calves always attracted keen interest and top prices, but the smaller and dejected-looking sorts tended to be shunned by farmers who had more money than the time or inclination required to nurse them into a thriving condition. Those were the ones Ellie and I bid for. And we seldom returned home without at least four lying in the back of our station wagon, each one tied into a sack with only its head sticking out – probably their first rest, enforced though it was, since starting their long road journey several days earlier, when probably only a week old at most.

This factor contributes more than anything else to the gamble you take when buying this poorer class of calf. There might be nothing wrong with it that a feed of warm milk, a cosy bed of fresh straw and a good sleep wouldn't cure. Conversely, the traumas endured during the disruptive first week of such a calf's life may have put it at death's door by now. There was no way of telling, for instance, if it had been denied an essential drink of its mother's first milk, thus leaving it with no natural protection against the very real risk of picking up a life-threatening infection on its travels. Then again, the bewildered and exhausted little creature may simply have had the will to live drained from it. Ellie and I soon learned that there is no such thing as a bargain calf.

Many were the nights we'd have to take turns at getting out of bed at two or three-hourly intervals to go out to the byre and try to coax a sick calf to drink a little life-prolonging milk from a lemonade bottle with a rubber teat. Often enough, these calves had developed 'the scours', a contagious form of diarrhoea which, if not successfully treated, quickly renders the young animal too weak to even stand, with death usually following within a day or two. It's a heart-breaking experience to witness the abject misery that such calves suffer, lying there in their own foul-smelling faeces, their eyes sunken and sorrowful, the bloom faded from the coat, the skin stiff and unyielding. Keeping such a calf alive when it has reached that stage of debility is an almost full-time task, requiring a bottomless well of dedicated compassion on the owner's part, born more of concern for the animal's welfare and survival than any thought of the loss of investment. Yet the latter aspect can't be ignored either. One dead calf, the saying goes, carries the profit of ten live ones to the knackery with it. So the realties of hand-rearing batches of young calves as a commercial enterprise quickly became apparent to us. The job could be, and usually was, a much harder and time-consuming one than the childhood memories I had of Granny happily bucket-feeding the occasional home-born calf while my sister and I raided the feed bin for scraps of cows' chocolate. This really was a matter of life and death – not only for the calves, but for our budding business too. We couldn't afford to lose *one* calf in a byreful of thirty, never mind one in ten. Enter another incarnation of Dame Fortune.

Big Al was a partner in the local veterinary practice, about the same age as me, and with a small collection of young farm animals of his own, which he and his wife kept for the love of it in a little paddock beside their house in the countryside on the other side of Haddington. What Al hadn't learned about the problems and wellbeing of bucket-fed calves and other four-legged orphans wasn't worth knowing. We'd had to call on his services more often than was financially prudent for us (house calls by the vet don't come cheap), and Al, being an extremely aware and sensitive bloke, knew that this was a situation that couldn't continue indefinitely. He would have been perfectly entitled, of course, to adopt the attitude that our parlous financial state wasn't his problem; if we couldn't afford to continue paying for the benefit of his expertise, then tough. But Al was of a different cut from any such mercenary members of his profession – given that any do actually exist, as the occasional malicious rumour would tend to suggest. Al spent his own valuable time teaching Ellie and me the basic skills of administering the vital sulpha drugs and multivitamin injections ourselves. He gave us invaluable tips on self-treating all manner of calf health problems, even going on to show us how to surgically castrate bull calves, and how to painlessly remove, for the future safety of both man and beast, the tiny, emergent horns from the calves' heads using a red-hot gouging iron specially designed for the job. For me, this was all a long way from playing jazz clarinet on the same TV bill as the Beatles, though not such a metamorphosis for Ellie with her previous nursing experience. Suffice it to say that I never risked shouting abuse at her on the grain drill again once she'd mastered the technique of cutting the testicles off calves. But all that aside, in Big Al we'd not merely found a new friend, but an extremely generous one who had arrived at yet another crucial time in our lives.

It seemed that somebody 'up there' really did like us – that is until we saw just how severe was the infestation of wild oats on our land when the dreaded weed began to raise its multiple heads above our young barley crop. Before we took over from him at Cuddy Neuk, Big Jim had elected to grow oats continuously for many years, simply because oats could thrive better than other cereal types on land that was becoming progressively poorer in heart. That suited his low-input policy perfectly well, but the snag was that the cultivated oats had concealed the true extent to which their invasive weedy cousins were contaminating the soil. Only now could their dark green flag leaves be identified above the shorter, lighter-hued foliage of the barley – barley that we were banking on being of suitable quality to be sold at a premium for malting purposes. Polluted by such a quantity of wild oat grains, however, the barley would be rejected without even needing to have its malting qualities analysed. And the infestation was beyond the stage where the wild oats could be 'rogued'; in other words, removed by hand while still growing, and before their seeds had been shed to contaminate the soil still more. Spraying with a selective weedkiller was an option, but a very expensive one, and a remedy which we simply couldn't afford to pay for. Yet we couldn't afford to risk not making the malting grade with our barley crop either. We desperately needed to earn that premium price and, even more crucially for the sake of securing the tenancy of the farm, to rid the crop of its unsightly blight before the landlords' fastidious factor set eyes on it. We were spiked once more on the horns of a dilemma.

'King and Queen Canute, I presume?'

It was the voice of Ian, son of the local newsagent, a recent graduate from agriculture college, and a good friend who liked nothing better than to lend us a hand whenever he had a bit of spare time. He was making his way along the rows of barley towards where Ellie, young Sandy and I were wading through the crop, gamely pulling wild oat plants from the ground and stuffing them into plastic fertilizer bags. So desperate were we to make at least a small reduction in the wild oat population that we'd have roped wee Muir in to do his share of roguing too, but at barely four years old his legs were still a tad too short. We'd left him playing with Jen where we could keep an eye on them at the headland of the field.

'Aye, farting against thunder would be another way of putting it,' I admitted to Ian when he'd caught up with us, 'but getting rid of *some* of the buggers is better than nothing.'

Ian took a look at the patches of the dark green invader smudged all over the field. 'You'd be just as well to go to church on Sunday and pray for a bloody miracle.'

'Thanks for the encouragement, mate,' I said. 'But if you really want to be of some use, grab yourself a plastic bag and get pulling.'

'No can do, I'm afraid. Nothing I'd like better, mind you.'

'Yeah, yeah, yeah – I meant pull wild oats, not my leg.'

'Seriously – just don't have the time. Too busy. Just started a new job, you see.'

'Well done!' beamed Ellie. 'Good for you!'

'Yeah, congrats,' I said. 'But shouldn't you be getting on with it instead of standing in the middle of a field taking the mickey out of us poor sods?'

'I am getting on with it, and it's good for you too.'

'No offence, Ian,' I grunted, 'but if I was in the mood for playing guessing games, I'd settle for something simple like I Spy. What the hell are you on about, good for us too?'

'Just that the new job's for a big chemical company, that's what.' Ian stood grinning from ear to ear, delighting in my look of puzzlement.

'And you're getting on with the job by standing there doing bugger all? Sorry, Ian – I don't get it.'

Ian tried to keep the suspense going for as long as he could, but the threat of having his head tied inside a fertilizer bag quickly inspired him to blurt out the good news. His appointment with the chemical company was as local area manager of their agricultural division, and his first task was to run field trials of some newly developed sprays for killing wild oats. He needed a farm with a significant infestation of the weed on which they could test the chemical in a range of control plots covering several fields.

'I don't suppose you'd be interested in letting us loose on this place, would you?' he joshed.

I didn't even bother answering that one. The whoops of joy from Ellie and Sandy said it all. Detrimental commercial considerations of wild oats apart, roguing them is one of the most thankless and boring drudgeries imaginable in farm work, even when there's a faint hope of winning the battle. We hadn't had a hope in hell, so Dame Fortune had come good for us yet again, in the third of her male-impersonating personas – first as Tommy with his secret sources of refurbishable implements, then as Big Al the benevolent vet, and now in the form of our friend Ian, who just in the nick of time had mutated into our caped chemical crusader, had galloped in as our personal US Cavalry reinforcement in our hitherto unequal struggle against the scourge of wild oats.

And our good luck held through harvest, when our weed-free barley crop yielded much better than we could previously have hoped for, and was accepted for malting at a very favourable price indeed. The cheque arrived from the grain merchant on the same day the postie popped through our letter box a bank statement which noted our credit balance as being just fifty-three pence. Yet another eleventh-hour delivery had been made by our transvestite taliswoman, and at last we had some cash available to crack on with much-needed repair work to the the farm buildings before the landlords' man came to make the crucial decision that would see us emerging as fully-fledged tenants of Cuddy Neuk, or calling up the removal company to transport us and our worldly belongings to an unknown destination in Shit Street.

'Well, Mr Kerr', droned the factor after he'd given everything the required once-over, 'I can see you've done a bit of work about the place since the last time I was here. But ...'

Ellie and I were standing with him in the middle of the yard on what was already a dismal November afternoon, a cold mist hanging ominously from the brow of Byres Hill like a shroud waiting to be draped over our death-throe aspirations. The factor's dramatic pause in the pronouncement of his sentence had our hearts in our mouths. His suspending in mid air of the 'but' word had us convinced that all our struggles of the past year had been in vain. Dame Fortune, according to the law of averages, had to dump on us sooner or later, and I could already visualise her adopting the required squatting position above our heads right there and then.

'But,' the po-faced factor intoned again, 'I have to tell you that the improvement work you've done is not sufficient.'

He paused again. We held our breath. I could hear a faint

pinging noise as the strand of hair supporting the Sword of Damocles began to fray. A humourless little smile began to tug at the corner of the factor's mouth.

'I'll be looking to you to continue the good work with equal enthusiasm for the duration of your tenure of this holding.' The humourless smile spread into a grin as the factor reached out and shook our hands heartily. 'I'll bring the tenancy agreement for you to sign within the week.'

If our sighs of relief didn't blow the mist away from Byres Hill, they certainly should have done. Our gamble had paid off after all. Ellie and I could at last start to enjoy our life with the boys at Cuddy Neuk, free from the fear of impending eviction. After twelve harrowing months for us both (and a lifetime of wishing for me), we could finally allow ourselves to feel securely 'at home', could really look forward to building a permanent future for our little family in a place that each one of us truly loved. We could hardly wait for tomorrow to come.

## CHAPTER SIXTEEN

## BALANCING THE SCALES OF FATE

Although Big Jim, on giving up at Cuddy Neuk, had told me that he wouldn't offer me any advice other than telling me not to give up my 'day job', he *had* stayed on in the area, dropping by from time to time 'just to see if ye've committed suicide yet', and mucking in to help us when he knew we were really pushed. To him, I was still Wee Pete, and liable to piss my metaphorical breeks again at any time. To me, Jim was still the big brother figure I'd looked up to since childhood, a never-far-away cushion that I knew I could always fall back on. He'd been living in a little house in North Berwick during our first year at Cuddy Neuk, just a stone's throw from the town's quietly spectacular West Bay, with its captivating views to the old harbour and the imposing bulk of the Bass Rock rising from the waters of the Firth of Forth beyond. It's a scene whose beauty has been described by many a seasoned traveller as one that is totally unique in the world, not because it boasts any qualities of grandeur, for understated could best describe its particular charms, but rather because the serenity endowed upon the bay by its northerly aspect and the resultant reflected light from the sea lends it a certain magic that is truly beyond compare. It's even claimed that Robert Louis Stevenson, a devotee of this beguiling stretch of coastline in his youth, said that Fidra, one of the little islands that pepper the waters thereabouts, was his inspiration for *Treasure Island*, and a precursor of North Berwick's Old Ship pub the model for his Admiral Benbow Inn. But while I'm sure Jim appreciated the aesthetic qualities of his adopted environs, I suspect that it was the little house's handiness for a few of his favourite carousing haunts in the town that had most attracted him to the place. Having already been 'banished to the infantry' once, drinking and driving wasn't a risk he was prepared to take again, it seemed.

Be that as it may, no sooner had I signed the tenancy agreement for Cuddy Neuk than Jim announced that he was heading for pastures new. He had friends in the south of England that he was going to visit – a North Berwick couple who'd lived in the West Country for years – a really nice part, with good country pubs and plenty of cheery local folk for company. Aye, he might even settle down there for a while. A change of scenery would do him good. That's what he said his reasons for going away were, anyway. But I had a feeling that maybe there was more to it than that. While I knew nothing of the jealously-guarded details of Jim's financial affairs, it didn't take a brilliant mathematician to calculate that, however healthy his bank balance had been on splitting with his father, his spending habits during the ensuing years must have taken their toll on his solvency. I'd noticed for some time that he hadn't been quite his old philanthropic self in the bars where he'd once been surrounded by so many 'friends', and the fewer rounds of drinks he bought his erstwhile disciples, the more depleted became their ranks. Knowing Jim and his doggedly proud nature, I was tempted to think that, if the dash of his public image was about to be tempered by financial restraint, he would probably rather it happen far away from his established stamping grounds. Also, it's very possible that he had been delaying a long-contemplated move from the area for just long enough to see the tenancy of Cuddy Neuk safely transferred to me. Having successfully passed me what was left of the baton of the family's farming heritage, it was now up to me to carry it forward as best I could. In his own oft-spoken words, I was big enough, old enough and daft enough to get on with it now. And, when all's said and done, he was absolutely right. He'd spent the best years of his life working at something his heart wasn't in, and he was entitled to ring the changes now, if that's what he really wanted.

I'd miss him, though. We all would. He'd taken to our own children the way he'd taken to Minnie and me when we were nippers, and it would be strange not having him around any more, making us laugh, leading us harmlessly (sometimes) astray, encouraging us to get up to mischief. And I don't mean just the kids in those latter respects, for I'd had countless fun-filled experiences in Big Jim's company since becoming an adult myself. There had been wild parties during his 'single' years at Cuddy Neuk, when the beat drummed up by jazz musicians jamming in the living room shook the wee house to its very foundations; there had been laughter-laden nights locked inside the bar of Haddington's Tyne House Hotel with other after-hours imbibing stalwarts (including the police!); and there had been pre-breathalyser nocturnal drives from country watering hole to country watering hole that would have risked, not just a driving ban, but deportation to the barren wilds of South Georgia, had today's less lenient traffic cops been on the prowl at the time. So, although it would be strange not having him around, maybe it would turn out to be for the best as far as our getting on with the job was concerned, even if Jim *had* now drawn his social horns in a bit.

★★★★★

Just when we thought we'd got our still-shaky finances for the next year worked out satisfactorily, the government decided to do away with an agricultural subsidy which, up until then, had provided Jim with a cheque large enough to pay his annual fertilizer bill. Its withdrawal denied us one source of income on which we were very much depending. 'The Lord giveth and the Lord taketh away,' I remembered Granny telling me often enough. Although not a regular church-goer, she did have strong spiritual beliefs, and an almost secular faith in the inevitable power of fate, which was, perhaps, a legacy of her Norse descent. In any case, I'd never really regarded such sayings of hers as anything more than that – just old sayings that she came out with from time to time, probably without even thinking. That particular saying got *me* thinking this time, though, because before we could tear out too much hair over the loss of the vital subsidy, the American recording giant RCA got in touch to say they'd decided to set up their own UK operation, and would I be interesting in assembling and recording a new 'stable' of Scottish artists for them? *Would* I? They'd have to lock me up to stop me!

Once my initial euphoria subsided, however, it became clear that this new venture of RCA's wasn't going to make us rich overnight. In fact, it would never come close to doing that, for the simple reason that all they really wanted from me was a handful of low-budget albums covering the most popular forms of Scottish traditional music. It seemed a fairly odd request from the company that boasted Elvis Presley among its galaxy of world-famous stars, but there would be enough money in it for me to cover our fertilizer bill for the year, so I wasn't about to query their motives. I don't know if the Lord, the Fates or Lady Luck had any particular influence over the decision makers at RCA Records, but we *were* being given back the equivalent of what had just been taken away, so I gave them all the benefit of the doubt and offered up my silent thanks just in case.

It eventually emerged that putting together a small catalogue of Scottish records was just one aspect of RCA's broader policy of 'filling in the cracks' of their established list of mainstream popular and classical output. Now that they were going to have their own British set-up, fully geared to compete on level terms with existing major UK record labels, their strategy was to become players in every area of the field. In this way they'd be in a position to fight for their share of whatever demand existed in every sphere of the market, whether mass or niche, and including Scottish music. 'Carpet bombing' it's called in military circles, I think. Yet, from this most unlikely source emerged a musical phenomenon that was to change our financial fortunes at a stroke. And, once again, the old bagpipes connection was behind it.

'Amazing Grace' by the Royal Scots Dragoon Guards was extracted as a single from an album which I recorded with the regiment's military and pipe bands in just two three-hour sessions in an Army barracks in Edinburgh. The budget for the entire LP would hardly have kept Elvis in hamburgers for a week, yet on its release in the spring of 1972, 'Amazing Grace' hit the No 1 spot in the UK charts, repeated the feat in several countries throughout the world, and went on to become the biggest-selling instrumental record of all time. In keeping with the production budget, however, my producer's royalties had been set at a correspondingly modest rate, so I knew I wasn't about to be rolling in money, despite the record selling many millions of copies. But I couldn't complain. It had been a totally unforeseen success (or 'a complete bloody fluke', as some of the more cynical music business types put it), and I did earn enough to buy a better tractor and to build a new cattle shed to accommodate the increased number of young cattle that we now planned to invest in as well. Why, Ellie and I were even invited to a cocktail party at our bank manager's house one fine Sunday afternoon. It's absolutely amazing what a few far-fetched rumours of impending wealth can do for a chap's social standing – no matter how temporarily. The invitations ceased with the non-arrival in our bank account of the expected millions, needless to say!

Such comically predictable incidents aside, though, the success of 'Amazing Grace' helped generate more record production work for me, most notably recording military bands, many of which were stationed overseas. More work meant more welcome income, but the down side was the travelling involved and the consequent increased time I had to spend away from Cuddy Neuk. But Ellie coped. She always had, and I knew she always would, even now that we had rented some more land in order to increase our cattle-grazing acreage. 'Amazing Grace' and subsequent spin-offs had given us the wherewithal to buy some really good calves – Hereford-cross females that were to be the nucleus of our own beef-breeding herd. We certainly weren't rich, but we were on a more sound financial footing at last, our topsy-turvy lifestyle finally taking a settled form that we could enjoy while we worked. The boys, too, were in their element – Sandy, by that time nine, helping his Mum and me like a grown-up, and even young Muir, who was going on five and preparing to start school, doing his bit with bucket-feeding the calves and other little chores that he could manage. Fate, Dame Fortune, or whoever, had given us more than we could have hoped for just a couple of years earlier. Life was wonderful, and there couldn't have been a happier little family than ours.

Then came a knock at our door one Thursday morning in November, only six months after the unexpected success of 'Amazing Grace' had done so much to change our lives for the better. Ellie and I had just seen the boys off to catch the school bus, a short walk for them of only a few hundred yards to the junction of the Athelstaneford and Haddington roads. It was a routine which we followed every morning without giving it a second thought. On hearing the knock, we opened the door to one of our neighbours who lived near that very junction. He'd obviously been running, and the look on his face told us that something dreadful had happened. Sandy and Muir, he told us, had been knocked down by a car. Their two young friends from the neighbouring farm had been hurt too. He didn't know how badly injured any of them were, but an ambulance had been called and was already on site. The boys were being looked after. It would be all right, he said, the tears in his eyes immediately contradicting his well-intentioned words.

The kids were lying in a field, strewn like rags at various distances from the car that had mowed into them, the wire fence that they'd been hurled through torn up and smashed by the ferocity of the impact. Sandy's legs had been cruelly slashed by the wires, but at least he was still alive, though in shock, semi-conscious and moaning, as were our neighbours' two boys. Muir, being the smallest of the four, had been flung the farthest ... and had been injured the worst. It didn't take the medics to tell us that. Not a word was spoken as they gently lifted him and carried him to the ambulance. Everyone knew that his chances of survival were slim, and there was nothing that Ellie and I could do but stand and look helplessly on. Fate had swung the balance back. The giving had been mercilessly squared by the taking away.

'Just believe that Sandy's going to pull through, work away as hard as you can, and devote whatever you create here at Cuddy Neuk to the wee fellow's memory,' my father said to me a few hours after Muir's funeral.

I was in the field in front of the house, cutting kale and loading it onto a trailer for the cattle's evening feed, thinking of the happy times I'd had there since my earliest childhood, bittersweet recollections of the good times that Ellie and I had shared with our own two boys mingling with the terrible feeling of loss. All our struggles and sacrifices now seemed to have been in vain. All the chances taken trying to raise enough money to get involved in farming now appearing to have been so futile. All the hardships of the months and years spent touring as a professional musician now counting for nothing. All of that had been merely in pursuit of a dream – a dream which had finally come true, yet had now turned into a nightmare. Whatever we had managed to achieve materially, both Ellie and I would have given up willingly for the return of our little son and the lifting of the threat to the life of his older brother, who was still gravely ill in hospital. But what my father had said to me was profound in its apparent simplicity. Life would have to go on, and we were fortunate in that we still had the challenge of continuing to improve the lot of the little farm. Sandy would indeed survive, despite having suffered horrendous injuries. We were fortunate in that as well, and we had a future with him to look forward to.

But Granny's prophetic words still echo in my head to this day. The Lord, as she chose to call whatever power she believed in, does seek at least his pound of flesh at times. Not always is the gift of good fortune bestowed without a price having to be paid – a price sometimes far in excess of the value of what has been received.

*****

A year after the accident that both broke our hearts and almost shattered a dream, Charlie was born, a new little brother for Sandy and another new life that Ellie had been granted the priceless gift of bringing into the world. Whatever contorted ways fate had been working in mattered little to us now. While the birth of one child will never compensate for the loss of another (for the two lives are equally precious to the members of a caring family), Charlie's arrival was a blessing that helped soothe the hurt that we had all been feeling for so long, and in a way that's hard to explain gave us a renewed sense of purpose and optimism. The balance of the scales had swung again. The creation of this new life had imbued a feeling in us that we could all now start our lives afresh as well, and we threw ourselves into doing just that with renewed vigour and enthusiasm.

And the fun in our lives that had been shrouded under a cloud of grief for that dark year soon began to return too. I had been worried about just how Ellie would cope running the place on the occasions I'd be away producing records now that she had a baby to look after as well. And I did have a particularly busy production schedule coming up, much of it involving journeys to Germany and the Middle East. I was going to be away a lot. Enter Dame Fortune yet again, this time posing as a hen, with certain delusions of peacock and pheasant. It was Bruce, a local chum of ours who had an unusual way of making a living: by escorting and tending to pedigree bulls that were being shipped from Britain to buyers all over the world. On one trip he might go to America and Canada, on another to Australia or New Zealand, and on occasions perhaps to Argentina and Brazil. Usually, Bruce would try to find work on the ranches and cattle stations to which he'd delivered the animals – maybe just a month or so, maybe a year or more – whatever work happened to be available to him at the time. In this way he not only travelled the world, but gained the experience of actually living in many different countries also. He led a nomadic existence, but one of freedom that he loved.

It was a warm summer evening, and I'd been checking on a new batch of young calves out in the byre. I walked back over the yard towards the house, too busy admiring the ever-breathtaking Cuddy Neuk sunset to notice Bruce's car parked over by the old stable. Inside the house, I found

Ellie and Sandy standing looking out of the big west-facing picture window, little Charlie gurgling away happily in his baby chair beside them.

'Hmm, it's a fantastic sunset again tonight, isn't it?' I said, joining them. 'Just look at all the colours in those high clouds – all reflected on the water of the Firth too. Magic scene.'

'Not as magic as the scene you're about to see,' Ellie remarked deadpan, a mischievous twinkle lighting her eyes.

'Yeah, just wait till you see this,' giggled Sandy, pointing out of the window to where a humanoid figure was appearing at speed from out of the shrubbery.

The figure was naked, except for a rubber chicken mask over its head and a spray of pheasant and peacock feathers sticking out of its rear end. To hoots of eye-watering laughter, the likes of which hadn't been heard in our wee house for too long, the figure proceeded to do a series of 'fly-pasts' on the lawn, elbows flapping like wings, feathers plucked one-by-one from its backside by the slipstream.

'Bruce,' I spluttered through a fit of sniggers. 'It's Bruce back again from somewhere, isn't it? There's only one bugger loopy enough to act like that.'

Indeed it was Bruce, doing things as only he knew how to lift whatever gloom he felt might still be pervading the place. And it had worked, courtesy of the arrangement of large feathers which Ellie had recently given pride of place to in a vase on the mantelpiece above the fire. After his performance, Bruce feigned offence at Ellie's polite refusal to have the feathers back, and pretended to be hurt at her declining his offer to allow her to smell their quill ends, 'Just to prove,' as he indignantly put it, 'that I keep a clean arsehole'. However, a spirit of fun had returned with Bruce, and we knew that his acting the fool in the way he had was the mark of a true friend – or a complete nutcase. Maybe a generous mix of both. But in any event, there were plenty more laughs to enjoy on what turned out to be a very long night. Many a dram of whisky was shared over recollections of happy times past, and many a glass clinked toasting even happier ones in the future, as through the window the lights of Edinburgh and Fife blinked cheerily in the distance. And the best news was that Bruce had several months free before his next bull-transporting mission, and could think of nothing he'd like better than to take on all the Cuddy Neuk work whenever I had to be away. The fickle finger of fate was making kindly gestures to us yet again, and all that Ellie and I could do was to think ourselves very lucky indeed.

## CHAPTER SEVENTEEN

## OF GOBLINS, GHOSTS AND GOODBYES

And so our lives progressed, usually with too much work to do and seldom enough time to do it in. But isn't it true that work doesn't really seem like work when you enjoy doing it? And, by the same token, doesn't time fly when you're enjoying yourself? The years were fairly rolling past, and thankfully with everything heading in a very positive direction at last. Improvements to the farm and its land were being made continually, and we could really take a pride in how it was all shaping up, as well as welcoming the added income that the long striven-for increase in crop yields was generating. Also, our herd of hand-reared Hereford-cross heifers had grown in size to some forty head, all fully mature suckler cows now, with their own home-bred calves at foot. For Ellie and me, what pleasure could compare to wandering up to the hill field with the boys on a long summer's evening, to stand at the gate and watch the cattle contentedly grazing against the backdrop of that stunning East Lothian view? Each of us – Charlie included, though still just five years old – had made our particular contribution to building up this little enterprise, and such moments of quiet joy that we were now being rewarded with were priceless indeed.

Having said that, farming being farming, there had been and still were plenty of moments when the word joy didn't figure in the vocabulary at all. Moments like the one when our two young German Simmental-cross bulls, Herman and Shultz, escaped from their pen into a paddock full of adolescent heifers. The heifers weren't yet at a stage of maturity that would have made a 'romantic dalliance' with the opposite sex even remotely desirable. Herman and Shultz were only just at the age of bovine puberty themselves, but as we'd noticed that a couple of the heifers were on their first 'heat', we couldn't risk having the young ladies' maidenhood terminated by our two aspiring studs. Any chance, no matter how slight, of the heifers being put in calf at such a young age had to be avoided at all costs. But as all the beasts had been hand reared and were, therefore, relatively tame, I was sure that Ellie and I could sort things out without too much trouble.

For 'trouble', substitute the name of Jen, our Border collie bitch. We'd long known that she had a penchant for rounding up the postman's van, and a bit later we found out that, whenever cattle were being moved, some ancient pack instinct that her breeding should have rid her of, rendered her unable to do anything but single-mindedly try to chase them back in the direction that they were being driven from. 'A to B' wasn't a notion that existed in Jen's brain – only 'A'. And the fact that she chose to go completely deaf when in that mental state only added to the chaos that she inevitably caused. Having learned the hard way about this trait, we then always made a point of shutting her in her old henhouse whenever beasts had to be moved. But in this instance, any chance of taking such precautionary measures had been obviated by the swift escape move that Herman and Shultz had cunningly pulled off.

Jen entered the heifer-paddock arena with the speed and keenness of a champion sheepdog – a canine blur of black and white, crouched low, barking wildly as she went, scattering heifers in all directions. Instant and utter bloody pandemonium. I knew of old that yelling instructions, curses and threats of instant death at Jen did nothing but give me a sore throat and hypertension, but I did it anyway, surprising even myself at the range of foul language that I had at my command. No trooper could have bettered it. All that this shouting did, of course, was to add to the confusion. The shambolic situation was already deteriorating into potential disaster by Herman and Shultz trying to mount every heifer that hadn't already jumped the paddock fence, with the real risk of leaving their developing (and commercially essential) little tits hanging on the top strand of barbed wire.

I'd never shot a dog let alone a bull before, but I swear that if I'd had a twelve-bore gun handy that day I'd have had a bash at it. It took Ellie and me hours to catch the impassioned Herman and Shultz and get them back into their pen, and it was two days before we retrieved the last of the dozen or so escapee heifers from a field of young wheat a good three miles distant, the imagined laughter of the old shepherd who'd sold us Jen ringing loudly in my ears. Come to think of it, if he'd still been around, I'd probably have shot the old shepherd too.

Then there was the moment I woke up on a June morning expecting to see the sun shining, eager as I was to get on with baling a particularly heavy crop of hay that I'd cut a few days earlier. But there were no neat rows of cured grass lying out there on the face of the hill where I'd left them only the previous evening – just a thick blanket of white, and it wasn't manna from heaven either. Snow! Midsummer snow in Lowland Scotland? Who'd ever heard of such a freaky happening? I certainly hadn't, but it was there for all to see, as bright and crisp and even as on an olde-worlde Christmas card. Now, haymaking, as we know, can be a tricky enough operation at the best of times, the quick drying of the grass and ensuing good quality dependent almost entirely on the kindness of the weather. An occasional light shower may not do all that much harm, as long as the sun reappears soon, but heavy soakings of rain over a prolonged period can render the crop virtually worthless – nothing but a field of rotting, mouldy vegetation. And there seemed every likelihood that this is precisely what we'd be left with when the thick covering of snow thawed and permeated the almost-made hay. It would soak the wetness up like a sponge, and the bulk of our winter cattle-fodder supply would be ruined.

I'd grabbed a couple of bread rolls and a half-full carton of milk as an on-the-hoof breakfast before rushing from the house to inspect the damage close up, and had just finished eating the first of the rolls when I reached the hay field. My hitherto keen appetite rapidly left me. Just as I'd expected, the hay was going to be totally wasted when it eventually emerged from beneath the snow. OK, I now had up-to-date machinery to turn and ted the stuff, but even at that, I didn't stand any more chance of saving this vital ten acres of hay than they would have had doing the job with pitchforks back in Grandfather's early days on the place. I leaned against the gate, head in hands, staring blankly over into the hill field beyond, the same field in which I'd watched Grandfather miraculously leaning against the wind when I was only four years old. Grandfather, I thought to myself – I wonder what he'd have done in a hopeless situation like this if he'd been alive. More than likely there would have been nothing that he could have done either, but it would have been a comfort to have had a chat with him about the problem all the same.

And then it struck me like a flash of Orkney lightning: the *peedie hogboon* – the benevolent little spirit fellow that Grandfather claimed had followed him down from Sanday. God, it was so long ago since he told Minnie and me about the hogboon that I'd almost forgotten all about it. And what had he said? Yes, that was it – 'Dinna thoo ever forget tae give him a sup o' milk when things are goin' weel, and the peedie hogboon will never let thee doon.' But, I wondered, what would be the hogboon's attitude to helping us when things weren't going *quite* so weel? Only one way to find out. Nothing to lose. The knoll that he was supposed to live under was only a few paces away on the other side of the fence, and there were still a couple of mouthfuls of milk left in my carton. I know it sounds silly, but I did actually say a few pleading words to the top of the wee mound as I poured the milk over it as Grandfather had once instructed. And I admit to feeling a little shiver running down my spine as a strangely warm breeze suddenly licked across my face, and a shaft of bright sunlight cut through the leaden cloud cover above. 'A change in the weather comin' right enough, boy,' is what Grandfather would have said, I'm sure. And he wouldn't have been wrong. By the time I got back to the house, a good drying wind was blowing in from the west, the clouds breaking up to reveal great swaths of clear, blue, sunny sky. Maybe things weren't going to be so bad after all. The weather that was setting in would be perfect for salvaging a soaked crop of hay. So, if these conditions would only hold for a few days …

'Remind me to take a full carton of nice creamy milk up to the hill field tomorrow,' I said to Ellie over a proper breakfast.

'What on earth for?'

'There's a wee elf sort of Orkney man who lives under a knowe up there, and I think he might just have done us a good turn.'

'You haven't been eating funny mushrooms, by any chance, have you?'

'Scoff if you like,' I said with a self-satisfied smirk, 'but if we get that hay crop safely in, it'll be all down to my Grandfather's hogboon.'

'What the *blazes* is your Grandfather's hogboon, if you don't mind me asking?'

I tapped the side of my nose. 'Ah well, that's a wee secret I just *might* let you in on … *if* we get that hay crop safely in, that is.'

'Hmm, don't count your chickens. I heard the weather forecast on the radio while you were out, and it isn't too good.'

But, strange though it may seem, the good weather did hold, the snow soon melted, and the wind, sun and our hay tedder did the rest – with more than a little help from the hogboon, I like to think. When I told Ellie the Orkney fable of these little folk after we'd stacked the last hay bale safely in the shed, all she did was give me an old-fashioned look and offer to introduce me to a psychiatric nursing sister she once worked with.

'She's dealt with a lot of cases like yours, I'm sure. Won't be one type of nutter that she hasn't had to deal with over the years, actually. Have a word with her at least.'

'Well, thanks for the offer, Ellie,' I smiled, 'but if I'm going to talk over problems, mental or otherwise, with anybody from now on, it'll be with my peedie goblin chum up in the hill field.'

\*\*\*\*\*

A year or so later, Bruce arrived back from a bull-delivering trip to Australia to announce that he'd just visited an area of New South Wales that so impressed him that he'd decided to accept an offer of a permanent job there. Wallace Munro, a cattle breeder of Scots descent and the owner of one of the most renowned herds of pedigree Beef Shorthorns in the world, had asked Bruce to work for him on his huge Weebollabolla spread near the town of Moree in the north-east of the state. A new house would be provided for him, and as Wallace planned to extend his already diverse agricultural activities into a big increase in the production of cotton and wheat, he felt that Bruce's experience of all kinds of farming in so many countries would be invaluable to him. For Bruce, it amounted to an opportunity too good to be missed. Once he'd helped us with our barley harvest, he'd be packing his bags yet again – except that this time he'd be leaving East Lothian for good.

He'd have to have a farewell party, of course. That went without saying. Any excuse for a party was good enough for ultra-gregarious Bruce, and he did have a wide local circle of friends, so a big bash would have to be laid on to say goodbye to them all in style. Never one to spare expense, Bruce asked if he could *borrow* our byre for the occasion. It would be a sort of disco version of the old 'kirn' barn dances, he said, but with a touch of the flavour of the outback shearing shed parties he'd been to in Australia a few times. And, uhm, there'd be plenty of booze, naturally. Australian stuff, of course. His mate Douglas at the Goblin Ha' Hotel up in Gifford had promised him a good deal on 'tubes' of Foster's and Castlemaine XXXX beer and all that bonzer Oz grog. 'Oh, yeah,' he added after a moment, 'and I know a bloke who'll fix me up with a bunch of two-litre bottles of wine – Egyptian or Libyan stuff, I think he said, but with French labels – really cheap and dead strong.'

How could I refuse? The byre and all its five-star facilities would be his for the night.

'How about food?' Ellie asked him. 'You'll have to provide something for your guests to eat, you know. Booze isn't the be-all and end-all for everyone at a party, after all.'

Bruce shot her a puzzled glance, then conceded, 'Yeah, well … OK then, I'll lay on a few packets of crisps and peanuts for the sheilas. That should be fair dinkum tucker for them, I reckon.'

If the purpose wasn't to buy drink with it, Ellie muttered, there was about as much chance of getting a pound out of Bruce's pocket as there would be of finding a tenner in a kangaroo's pouch. 'Don't worry,' she said, patting the wallet-bulge in his jacket, 'I'll cook up some decent grub for the night. Regard it as my goodbye present.'

Bruce's farewell knees-up turned out to be a big success, and one that his cobbers in the outback would have felt at home at, Spartan conditions inside the old cow shed and all. We'd made a bar from three upended oil drums with an old door laid over the top, Bruce's prudently purchased stock being served up by sixteen-year-old Sandy. No point, Bruce had determined when appointing our son to the task, in having a barman old enough to have a taste for the grog himself. And, as with all good parties, the more the evening drew on, the louder became the music and laughter, and the more freely flowed the conversation and drink. Everyone was having a great time giving Bruce a sendoff to remember – even if most of them wouldn't. By the time the clock struck two or three (or was it four?), the last of the woozy ravers had bid their emigrating pal their final bleary-eyed, slurred-speeched farewells, and Ellie and I were busy sweeping up the debris of a long night. Bruce appeared at the byre door, looking nicely wobbly and smilingly content, having been outside to relieve himself of another litre or two of part-digested 'Four-X' at whatever convenient spot he'd chosen. That's one thing about farm steading parties – everywhere is free game for use as a gents' latrine.

Bruce pulled a five pound note from his pocket. 'Thish – thish for the boy,' he grinned, articulating with some difficulty. 'For – for Sandy, you know – did well, I'm sayin' – runnin' the (*burp*!) bar, you know. Devers – zervs – desrevs the (*hick*!) pive founds.'

'I'm sure he'll be delighted, Bruce,' Ellie yawned. 'You can give it to him in the morning. He went off to bed ages ago. Which is what I'm going to do. I'm dead beat.'

'Me too,' I said, my head singing with an elephant's sufficiency of Bruce's bargain wine. 'You'll find your way to your room when you're ready, Bruce, eh?'

We left him in the byre, happily slumped on a straw bale, savouring the memory of his big night, while slurping a final tube of Foster's in the glow of a solitary storm lantern.

'Sandy's left his bedroom light on,' Ellie remarked as we approached the house. 'Must've fallen asleep without switching it off.'

'Yeah, he'd have been bushed. Not to worry – I'll turn it off before I turn in.'

But there was no Sandy to be seen in his bedroom. His bed hadn't been slept in, and there was no sign of him anywhere else in the house either. Ellie was naturally worried when I told her, her motherly instincts clicking into overdrive and speeding towards panic. Under the calming influence of the wine, my own concerns were much more tempered. She should just relax and go to sleep, I told her. I'd find Sandy. No problem. He'd probably just have gone to check the calves in their shed after he'd left the party. Maybe just sat down on some bales while he looked them over. Fell asleep there and then, no doubt. No problem.

Back outside, the rosy finger of dawn was already tracing a thin smear of light along the eastern horizon, though it was still too dim to see properly without my flashlight. I made my way to the calf shed and looked inside. All that greeted me were pairs of sleepily blinking calf eyes, but no sixteen-year-old slumbering on the straw. What now? I checked every other building in turn, even looking inside the cabs of the tractors. Still no Sandy. I should have been getting worried by now myself, but the effect of the cool morning air on my wine-numbed brain was having the predictable effect. Sandy? No problem. More than likely back safely in his bed by now. Or with

Bruce in the byre. Forgot to look in there. Whatever – everything'll be fine.

As I ambled aimlessly down towards the main road, I forgot what I was supposed be doing out there anyway, suddenly more interested in enjoying the sound of the dawn chorus drifting over from the woods on Byres Hill. Then I heard a faint 'clunk' coming from somewhere down by the farm gate. Or could it have been a 'clink'? Then a muffled groaning sound. Strange. Maybe my ears were just playing tricks on me. Should've gone easy on that cheap plonk. Still, better investigate all the same. The nearer I got to the gate, the more I got the impression that the sounds might have been emanating from the other side of the road, by the old stone wall that was said to be a remnant of the ancient Cuddy Neuk carters' inn. I crossed the road, rummaging with my feet in the long grass, directing the beam of my flashlight along the bottom of the wall, then over it. Not even a mouse stirred. Nothing there at all. Must've been imagining things right enough.

I was just about to turn and head back to the house for some long-overdue sleep, when I felt wet, deathly-cold fingers close round my ankle from behind. Then a ghastly moan drifted up from the same direction. An icy shiver ran through my body as my befuddled senses were hit by the sudden realisation of what this was.

'Jesus Christ!' I yelled, dropping my flashlight as I tried to struggle free. 'The ghost! The Bogle o' Cuddy Neuk!'

The memory of Jimmy Walker the roadman's scary tale from my infancy had long since drifted from my memory. Or I thought it had – until then. The drunken innkeeper who'd drowned himself in the ditch, that very ditch right there behind me, the ditch from which the gripping fingers and spooky groan had just risen. The clinking of his bottles – could that have been what I'd been hearing all along? Time stood still as my eyes were drawn instinctively upwards. There, just as Jimmy said it would be, was the moon, ghostly pale itself in the dawn light.

'Geeza hand, pal,' a voice croaked from the ditch. A drunk voice. Then that weird clinking sound again!

The chill fingers tightened their grip on my ankle. My blood running cold, I spun round to see a face staring up at me, it's distorted, dripping-wet features eerily uplit by the beam of my dropped flashlight.

'The Bogle!' I hollered again, trying to pull away, panic-stricken now. 'Hands offa me, ya horrible bastard!'

'Aw, z'you,' the voice slurred, sounding somehow a mite less menacing now – oddly familiar, even. 'Whaa … whaaw you doin' here?'

'Sa-Sandy?'

'Yeah, z'me, Dad. Geez … geeza hand outta here, eh?'

I looked at the distinctive shape of a Gordon's gin bottle tightly clenched in Sandy's free hand, the frame of his bike draped crookedly over his shoulders. Squinting into the gloom of the ditch, I could see that the bottle was empty.

'You're drunk!' I gasped, suddenly sober. 'Pissed as a fart!'

'Juz had – had a wee sip – coupla sips – at the party 'n'everthing. S'nize stuff, eh – thiz gin? S'nize'n … s'nize'n (*belch*!) tasty.'

In his plastered state, it didn't take much persuasion to get Sandy to divulge that he'd secreted the almost-full bottle on his person when purportedly abandoning his barman's duties for bed. Already tiddly, he'd then decided to 'go for a wee cycle ride somewhere'. He couldn't remember how he'd ended up in the ditch, but he did remember waking up down there.

'Zum filsy swine waz peein' on me, Dad. Whiss – whizlin' 'Waltzin' Matilda' an' peein'. Honest! See – thaz how'm all wet 'n'everysing.'

'Yeah, well don't worry about that right now,' I said, hauling him out of the ditch. 'You'll feel a lot better about it when you're paid a fiver by the culprit in the morning. Now then, let's get you home and into the shower.'

'G'day there, boyzzz!' came Bruce's warbled greeting from over by the gate. He was standing swaying like a sailor and grinning like a slice of melon, cans of beer in both hands, more sticking out of all his pockets. 'Fanzy a – fanzy a wee nightcap?'

I didn't bother answering, but left him bonding with the gatepost and trying to feed it sips of beer. I lugged rubber-legged Sandy, still wrapped in his bike, back towards the house. Glancing over my shoulder, I saw the first rays of the sun creep over Byres Hill and gingerly touch Bruce on his hunched, soon-to-be-Australian shoulders. I hoped that fair country would be ready for him, yet somehow doubted it. And we'd miss him, just as we missed Big Jim and others who had passed through our lives at Cuddy Neuk, pausing on their way to help us over the stile. Thanks in no small measure to them, we were established now, still with much to do on our way up the ladder, but well off the bottom rung and climbing. And tomorrow – or today as it now was – would be another day.

'Time for bed,' I said to Sandy.

'Yez, Dad … time for bed, said Zebedee … *"Oh-h-h, who'll come a-waltzin' Matilda wiz (hic!) me?"*'

EPILOGUE

## ANOTHER STORY

'No pain, no gain' was the slogan of a mushrooming army of keep-fit fanatics in the early 1980s. It also appeared to sum up the British government's attitude towards the recession into which the country had been plunged. The effect of the hard times would shake out all the dead wood from inefficient industry, they deemed, leaving big business leaner and fitter. Oh yeah? Well, maybe so, but this scything political policy cut the feet from many already efficient small businesses as well. But who cares about 'small' in a commercial world in which 'big' is becoming increasingly more beautiful? How many millions, after all, are received in political parties' coffer-filling 'donations' from the guy who owns the village shop?

For some obscure reason, the farming industry bucked the recessional trend of those years, and prospered as never before. So confident were Ellie and I, in fact, that we took the plunge and bought Cuddy Neuk from the landlords – with more than a little help from the bank, admittedly. But our farm income had never been healthier, and with record production work continuing to roll in, we felt that this was a gamble we had to take now, or in all probability never would. It was an opportunity to own our own farm that, even in our wildest dreams, we would never have thought possible when nervously taking on the tenancy of the place. Now, if things kept going the way they were, we could be looking at the very real possibility of being in a position to pay off the bank loan in just a few short years, and Cuddy Neuk truly would be *ours* at last.

Now seventeen (and never another drop of gin having passed his lips!), Sandy was preparing to go to agricultural college, with eleven-year-old Charlie already well accustomed to tractor driving and doing all of the other tasks required of him to help on the farm. Our family farming moon, as my grandfather might have said, was most certainly in the waxing phase. I even indulged in ambitious thoughts of soon being able to buy a bigger spread – one that would be large enough, not just to support Ellie and me, but to provide work and a living for the boys too. Another rainbow was there to be chased, and I already had my feet firmly in the starting blocks.

When the recession hit the recording industry in Britain, it hit it like a hurricane – at least as far as I was concerned. At a stroke, my freelance production work for the major companies fell from upwards of a dozen albums a year to none. Overnight and without warning, we were facing a situation in which, instead of looking towards the possibility of taking on a larger farm, the ability even to make ends meet where we were had been taken away. Without the record-production income, servicing the bank loan was no longer remotely feasible in the longer term either. Hard decisions had to be made, and urgently at that. Even in the teeth of the recession's fiercest bite, agricultural land prices were at an all-time high. So, the tormenting reality of our position was now staring us squarely in the face – sit tight and try to hold on somehow to Cuddy Neuk while awaiting a financial miracle, or sell up while the land market was on our side. Painful though it was, the fact had to be faced – we'd have to try not to look upon the little farm as a cherished place that had been 'home' to three generations of the family, but as a material asset whose value we had added greatly to through years of determination and sheer hard work.

Just how much we had progressed since the day we paid Big Jim a few hundred pounds for his worn-out old tractor, trailer, harrows and roller was there for all to see – and to bid for – on the day of the Cuddy Neuk farm sale. The array of tractors, implements and equipment lined up in rows in the paddock behind the new cattle shed made even the contents of the Hopefield *roup* fourteen years earlier seem fairly sparse by comparison. The hordes of potential bidders and time-passing busybodies outnumbered the Hopefield attendance twofold as well, their cars, trucks, tractors and Land Rovers parked on the road verges all the way from the farm gate to the Athelstaneford road end. But unlike 'Lady Bonnyrigg' and her gloating attention to every extra pound that the auctioneer coaxed from the bidders on her farm-sale day, we could only stand and look sadly on from a distance. Each and every item coming under the hammer represented much more than just money to us. This was the relinquishment of the stuff of a dream, the disposal of the bricks on which Ellie and I had been building the foundations of the family's future for so long. And only when the throngs of buyers had departed with their purchases, and the paddock stood empty and forlorn in the half light of evening, did I fully realise the heart-rending significance of our now-irreversible, though inevitable, decision to sell Cuddy Neuk. For a family farm is more than just a business, the farmhouse more than just a home. Both are as much part of the family as the family itself, for reasons that only those fortunate enough to have experienced the highs and lows, the losses and rewards, the sowing of the seeds and the harvesting of the crops (both actual and metaphorical) can ever fully appreciate. Parting with such a place can be as painful as losing any other member of the family, of which we were becoming ever more aware as our time to leave approached.

The morning after the *roup*, I walked up to the hill field for what I knew would be the last time. I could see the whole farm from up there – every field, all the way down to the old road, and back towards the farmhouse and steading, sitting neat and snug in the lee of Byres Hill, with the stone finger of Hopetoun monument rising majestically above. The stark finality of the card that fate had now dealt us struck like an arrow to the heart, and I smiled a wistful smile as I glanced at the little mound beneath my feet and pondered that even the peedie hogboon could do nothing to help now. The die was cast, and no amount of sadness and remorse would alter that.

I wandered along the crest of the hill to the little bluff, where as a child I'd stood by Grandfather's side and watched him lean against the wind. I stopped and stood again on that very same spot, my gaze directed northward to the distant hills of Fife, looking back at me over the wide expanse of the Firth of Forth. It seemed only yesterday that battleships patrolled those same waters, on which great oil tankers now lay peacefully at anchor, awaiting their turn to fill their vast bellies with North Sea oil from pipeline terminals further up river. The skies above were quiet now too, those same boundless East Lothian skies that once buzzed with Spitfires and Mosquitos, but where now only birds lazily congregate, just as they have always done, above the lost hamlet of Caldera and its spectral Clinky Mill. So many memories came flooding back just then. Memories of endless summer days among the oat stooks, the metal chattering of a hay mower in a nearby field, the steady thud of heavy hooves, the jangle of gleaming harness. Memories of melodeon music by the fireside, of clootie dumplings for breakfast, of threshing mills and an old roadman's yarns. Memories of a lifetime. Memories of Cuddy Neuk.

I couldn't help feeling pangs of guilt as I thought back to the generations of the family who had preceded me; Orkney forebears I never knew, but whose labours and canniness had finally led to me being given a chance to work the land and raise livestock just as they had done. And now I had relinquished that heritage. And what of my father's soothing words after young Muir's tragic death twelve years before? … 'Devote whatever you create here at Cuddy Neuk to the wee fellow's memory.' I had followed that advice as best I could, but now that we were leaving, we would surely also be turning our backs on that very part of the fabric of Cuddy Neuk that Muir's memory was still so much part of. My heart was heavy with a growing sense of failure.

And then that magical west wind began to rise again, whispering through the branches of the high hawthorn hedge at the top side of the field, and blowing away the cobwebs of self-reproach that had been gathering in my mind since the day the decision was made to sell up. As the wind tugged at my clothes, I could almost feel Grandfather's strong fingers at the scruff of my neck, pulling me out of my dark mood just as he'd pulled me up from the dung pat on this knowe so many years ago. 'Dinna thoo fret, peedie boy,' his voice seemed to say in the wind. 'Thoo's done weel. Thoo's done as weel-like as a body could, so just thoo roll up thee sleeves and shak thee feathers again!'

True enough! What was I getting so morose about? We *had* done well. With the willing help of family and friends we had turned a neglected holding into as trim and productive a little farm as you'd find anywhere – well equipped and stocked and in better heart than it had ever been. And we had built it up from nothing. Would Grandfather or his father have allowed themselves to become downhearted at having realised an asset that they had created, if faced with the dilemma that we'd been faced with? No, of course they wouldn't. They had moved on themselves when circumstances dictated it, after all, and that's precisely what I was doing. There was no denying the cherished memories that would forever centre on Cuddy Neuk, but they were in the past, and we had a future full of new memories to create for our family now. We'd get our sleeves rolled up and 'shak' our feathers, just as the echo of Grandfather's voice had told me to do.

Buoyed up by the thought, I stood and inhaled deeply, filling my lungs and lifting my spirits with the fresh breeze that carried on its breath the distant tang of the sea that had reminded Grandfather so much of his true home. I wondered if I would find such a spot from where to transport my own memories back to Cuddy Neuk, *my* true home. For tomorrow we would be in another place, in another land, having travelled much farther than even Grandfather had done to follow his dream. But the thread of the family's farming line would still be intact, though tied to a type of farming that I knew dangerously little about.

But that, as I've said before, is another story.

### THE END

## ALSO BY PETER KERR:

'THIS SHOULD DO FOR SPAIN WHAT
A YEAR IN PROVENCE DID FOR FRANCE.'
THE SUNDAY POST MAGAZINE

# SNOWBALL
# ORANGES

ONE MALLORCAN WINTER

PETER KERR

summersdale *travel*

## SNOWBALL ORANGES
### ONE MALLORCAN WINTER

AVAILABLE FROM ALL GOOD HIGH STREET AND INTERNET BOOKSHOPS

SHORTLISTED FOR THE WHSMITH TRAVEL WRITING AWARD

# PETER KERR

## Mañana Mañana

### ONE MALLORCAN SUMMER

summersdale *travel*

## MAÑANA MAÑANA
### ONE MALLORCAN SUMMER

For a current catalogue and a full listing of
Summersdale books, visit our website:

**www.summersdale.com**